Britain and the European Community

Made Simple

The Made Simple series
has been created
especially for self-education
but can equally well
be used as
an aid to group study.
However complex the subject,
the reader is taken
step by step,
clearly and methodically,
through the course. Each volume
has been prepared by experts,
taking account of
modern educational requirements,
to ensure the most
effective way of
acquiring knowledge.

In the same series

Britain and the
European Community

Made Simple

Keith Perry, BA, MA, ARHistS

Made Simple Books
HEINEMANN : London

Printed and bound in Great Britain
by Richard Clay (The Chaucer Press) Ltd, Bungay, Suffolk,
for the publishers William Heinemann Ltd,
10 Upper Grosvenor Street, London W1X 9PA

British Library Cataloguing in Publication Data

Perry, K
    Britain and the European Community.—
    (Made simple books, ISSN 0265–0541)
    1. European Economic Community—Great Britain
    2. Great Britain—Economic conditions—1945–
    I. Title   II. Series
    330.941′0857   HC256.6

ISBN 0–434–98593–7 hbk
ISBN 0–434–98594–5 pbk

Editorial: Robert Postema, F. G. Thomas
Production: Martin Corteel
Cover illustration: Derek Hazeldine Associates Ltd. Euro symbol by courtesy of the EEC Commission
Text diagrams: Reproduction Drawings Ltd

Foreword

January 1983 marked the tenth anniversary of Britain's entry into the EEC but it was an event celebrated with little enthusiasm in the United Kingdom. To many British people the economic losses of membership had seemed greater than the gains. In one sense, such an assessment was and is impossible to make because we cannot know for certain what the state of affairs would have been if Britain had remained outside the EEC. To the present writer the evidence seems to show that the British economy would have done no better and possibly even worse outside than inside the EEC but readers must come to their own conclusions on a subject that is still controversial and often misunderstood. However, it may be salutary at this point to record the majority view in industry on which the future of Britain depends. In January 1983 John Raisman, chairman of the CBI's Europe Committee, stressed that Britain's industrial success in the Community had been under-estimated and he urged that Britain should not only continue to sell to Europeans but should also collaborate with them in making goods to sell to the world. In this statement he was merely reinforcing the opinion of the 1981 CBI document 'The Will to Win' that to leave the EEC would be an act of the greatest folly.

Two factors bedevil a proper understanding of the European Community—the poor press that it has received in Britain and the very complexity of Community affairs. To take but one example, the EEC is often caricatured as an army of bureaucrats bent on trying to abolish the British way of life and turn Britain into a province of the Continent. In 1981 the *Daily Mirror* commented: 'The abiding obsession of the Common Market bureaucrats is the creation of an Identikit European. If they had their way, we would be alike, and do alike and talk alike. They would build a Community whose ideal citizen wore a beret and lederhosen, smelt of garlic, spoke Esperanto and played cricket.' In fact the bureaucracy of the EEC is not huge as many British people assume; it is about 10,000 strong and about the same size as the London borough of Barnet.

What adds to the Community's complexity is its position as a kind of shifting target. It is a constantly evolving creation and no book on it, however recent, can hope to be completely up-to-date on all developments. The writer would therefore advise those who wish to stay completely abreast with Community affairs to peruse the quality newspapers and journals such as *The Economist*.

It is hoped that this book will make some contribution at least towards helping the reader to identify and clarify the main issues in an organisation which for better or for worse will probably exercise increasing influence on the lives of the British people. It should prove of value to schools, colleges and universities for a wide number of courses as its central theme impinges on history, economics and politics syllabuses at A level and beyond, as well as various Business Studies courses.

I gladly express my thanks to the director of the Made Simple Series, Mr Robert Postema, for his habitual guidance and also to the library staff of the Dorset Institute of High Education for their unfailing patience and the volleys of valuable reports and other publications which they pointed in my direction.

My over-riding debt is to my daughters and especially my wife who typed the manuscript. They patiently endured a bear with a more than usually sore head while this book was being written.

KEITH PERRY

Contents

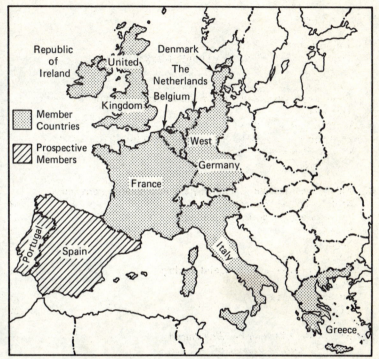

Fig. 1. The Countries of the European Community 1984

1
Origins and Development of the European Community

Early Concepts of European Unity

The idea of a united Europe is many centuries old; indeed such an aim cannot be much less old than the practice of war. The interest shown in this aim has been most intense after periods of especially destructive war.

In the history of modern Europe it was only rarely before the eighteenth century that such ideas were mooted. Usually commentators were inspired by the great days of the Roman Empire, a period in which there was a single European government with Rome as its capital. The idea of Rome was not lost in subsequent centuries. The Roman Catholic Church in its area of control, character and forms of administration reflected the Roman Empire and the empire of Charlemagne in the early ninth century was allegedly a Holy Roman Empire. Dante in *Monarchia* written in 1310 was concerned to revive the Roman Empire as a solution to Europe's warfare.

Others rejected this as impracticable, Pierre Dubois asserting in 1306 that it was impossible for one individual to rule over the diverse populations of Europe. As an alternative to a revived Empire, he suggested that the sovereigns of Catholic Europe should form a Common Council which would appoint arbitrators to settle all disputes between them. The Pope would be, in the words of F. H. Hinsley, 'the court of moral appeal against the Council's awards within Europe'. This solution would in fact have suited French interests as the French controlled the Papacy at that point in time.

In the early seventeenth century Emerii Crucé advocated an association of European states with a standing assembly of ambassadors at Venice, decisions by majority vote and mutual collaboration in dealing with refractory states, if necessary by armed force. He envisaged a World Council as his association including all the nations of the known world. Better known than Crucé's work is the 'Grand Design' of Maximilien de Béthune, duc de Sully, who was chief minister to Henry IV of France. Sully proposed an association of Christian monarchs but as he also suggested a reduction in the power of Austria as one of the objectives of the association, we must again suspect that, as in the case of Dubois, an ulterior motive was the aggrandisement of France. Yet Sully did point to the need for a general council representing all states with the power to settle all disputes referred to it.

With the advent of the wars of Louis XIV in the later seventeenth century, it is not surprising that internationalist ideas were again discussed, chiefly by the Quaker William Penn and Abbé de Saint-Pierre. Penn published his 'Essay towards the present and Future Peace of Europe' in 1693 and Saint-Pierre his *Perpetual Peace* in 1712. There was nothing essentially new in their work. Both advocated an international organisation confined to Europe. In Penn's European Diet member states would be allotted representatives in proportion to their wealth, whereas Saint-Pierre gave all member states one deputy and one vote, regardless of size or power. Later in the eighteenth century Rousseau turned to a federal solution for uniting Europe. His League was to have the power of intervening in the internal affairs of member states, an odd proposal from the writer who was the apostle of modern nationalism!

Following the French Wars of 1792–1815, Henri de Saint-Simon brought out impressively far-reaching ideas in his *De la Réorganisation de la Société Européenne*, written in 1814. Europe was to have a single parliament and a single king and they would regulate not only foreign policy but the economic and social affairs of the component states. He justified his ambitious ideas by an appeal to the continent's history of earlier medieval unity. Saint-Simon was not alone in making such proposals. Even Napoleon, in exile on St Helena, claimed that he had been attempting to create a European Federation and only England's refusal to co-operate had forced him to use war as the means of attaining this objective. Victor Hugo at the third Universal Peace Congress in 1849 looked forward to a United States of Europe similar to the United States of America and the 1867 Geneva Peace Congress resulted in the creation of a journal called *The United States of Europe*.

The First World War with its totally new scale of senseless slaughter led to renewed consideration of the European idea. The outstanding figure in the interwar years was Count Coudenhove-Kalergi. His international outlook is understandable when it is recalled that his father who was of Greek and Dutch extraction was an Austro-Hungarian diplomat and that his mother was Japanese. The Count started a Pan-European Union which had the support of several famous politicians, notably Aristide Briand. Briand who was the first to coin the phrase 'Common Market' was French foreign minister in the 1920s and in 1929 he put forward a scheme for a European Union to the League of Nations. It was, however, too long and vague. It was received with considerable reservation by most countries, including England; the onset of the Great Depression, the rise of Nazism and the death of Briand himself in 1932 ensured its complete failure.

It was the impact of the Second World War which really stimulated genuine moves towards European integration. The war had impoverished Europe, destroyed Europe's political system and had seen such a collapse of all civilised standards that bold new solutions were considered essential. It was now widely believed that Europe could only be rebuilt by a cooperative effort in an age when the nation state was no longer a viable unit.

The creation of new institutions was accelerated not only by the natural fear of a future revived Germany but also by the prevalent apprehension about the intentions of Russian communism under Stalin. The West feared both the sheer military might of Russia and the kind of subversion seen in the communist takeover of Czechoslovakia in 1948. The presence of large communist parties in both Italy and France made the communist threat appear only too real. Integration was also encouraged by United States pressure in favour of a united Europe, as the Americans believed that such a Europe would be prosperous, thus providing both a barrier to Communism and a market for American exports and investment.

After 1945 solid support for European initiatives came from a group of dedicated European-minded politicians whose experience and background made them loathe the internecine warfare in Europe since 1914. Three of the men in the vanguard of the movement were devout Catholics—Konrad Adenauer, the anti-Prussian Mayor of Cologne who became Chancellor of West Germany, Alcide de Gasperi, a deputy in the Vienna Diet while Austria–Hungary was fighting Italy in the First World War, then Prime Minister of Italy after 1945, and Robert Schuman, a German national during the First World War and then Prime Minister of France after the return of Alsace-Lorraine. Special mention should also be made of Jean Monnet who died as recently as 1979 at the age of 90. He was more responsible than any other man for bringing the nations of Europe together in the Common Market and his ultimate aim was a truly united Europe. Though he was one of the most remarkable Frenchmen of his time, he was a prophet with little honour in his own country because much of his work and influence was exercised behind the scenes. He served in the Franco-British Economic Co-ordination Committees in both world wars and was responsible for the adoption of the 'dirigiste' approach in French economic planning after 1945. It was Monnet who conceived the idea of Franco-German co-operation in economic matters which finally bore fruit in the Schuman Plan and the European Coal and Steel Community of 1951. Next Monnet founded the Action Committee for the United States of Europe, a body which played an important role in the negotiations leading up to the ratification of the EEC in 1957.

The Creation of New European Institutions

The Organisation for European Economic Co-operation

With the proclamation of Marshall Aid in 1947, the Organisation for European Economic Co-operation (OEEC) was established. Its first task was the delicate one of dividing American aid among the member states. This objective was successfully achieved over a three year period. The second principal activity was the liberalisation of trade, the free flow of which had been severely limited by many restrictions in the post-war period. As tariff reductions were the concern of GATT, the OEEC concentrated on other barriers to free trade, principally quantitative restrictions. Within six years trade between European nations doubled. A third area of activity lay in finance. To improve the system of payments between member states, a European Payments Union was created in 1950 to institute a general multilateral system of payments.

Some members wished to push ahead and develop a European customs union, a move opposed by Britain because of her close ties with the Commonwealth. Despite this disappointment, the OEEC flourished. By 1959 it had 18 members including Spain and since then the United States, Canada, Japan and Australia have joined to convert the organisation into a more global institution. The word 'Europe' has been dropped and it has become the Organisation for Economic Co-operation and Development (OECD), reflecting one of the major problems of our time—the economic development of underdeveloped countries.

The Council of Europe

Economic institutions have played the most important part in the moves towards European integration after the war but they have tended to concentrate on specialised functions. A more comprehensive attempt to unite Europe has been attempted under the Council of Europe, established in 1949 by ten West European states. Again the British attitude at the time profoundly disappointed other European states. Though Britain became a founder member, Attlee's Labour government regarded the Council of Europe with the utmost reserve. The British were not attracted by the abstract idea of European unity, a concept they distrusted as a potential infringement of sovereignty. At this stage, too, it was felt that Britain's true interests lay more with the Commonwealth and the United States than with Europe.

Nevertheless the Council expanded its membership to 17 countries by 1971. With its headquarters in Strasbourg, it has two central organs, a Committee of Ministers composed of the foreign ministers of the member states and an Assembly whose members are elected by the parliaments of the member states. The Assembly is not a parliament as such, for it has no authority to legislate for the member states. If a two-thirds majority of the Assembly is in favour, it can make recommendations to the Council of Ministers which in turn can make recommendations to the member states. Real power has therefore so far eluded the Council of Europe as individual states guard their sovereignty.

The Council has failed to achieve its original aim—the political unity of Europe—but it has been useful as a policy-formulating body, sponsoring some important treaties like the European Convention for the Protection of Human Rights and Fundamental Freedom which came into force in 1953. In the first 20 years it has concluded over 70 agreements, mainly on matters relating to welfare.

The European Economic Community (EEC)

The first success for the apostles of economic union was the economic integration of the Low Countries, with Belgium, Holland and Luxembourg forming the Benelux Union in 1948. At the same time French statesmen, notably Jean Monnet and Robert Schuman, were active in promoting European integration. In 1951 the heavy industries like coal and iron came under the control of a European Coal, Iron and Steel Community which established a common market in these products and a common programme of expansion. In the 1950s supranational machinery was set up to supervise the work of this organisation. Again while many European countries expressed an interest in joining, the British preferred to stay aloof.

The evolution of a common market in coal and steel was of profound importance in preparing the way for more fundamental attempts to establish a European Community. In 1955 delegates representing Belgium, West Germany, France, Holland, Italy and Luxembourg met at Messina and agreed to form the European Economic Community. The constitution and programme were worked out in the next 18 months and in March 1957 the Treaty of Rome, setting up the EEC was ready for signature. It established a customs union of the six countries concerned, pledged to reduce and by 1969 abolish all tariffs on their mutual trade. However, this was only the initial objective of the EEC for in the preamble to the Treaty of Rome was stated the intention to establish the foundations of an ever closer union among the European peoples. Therefore from the start the political concept of European union has underlain the whole endeavour. The aim has been to end historic rivalries in a fusion of essential interests and therefore the title 'Community' is a more appropriate one than 'Common Market'. The aim of the Community is not merely the establishment of free trade in a common market but the harmonious development of all economic activities, a rising standard of living and closer relations between member states. Obstacles to the free movement of persons, services and capital were to be abolished and a common agricultural policy was to be inaugurated. Other aims were the improvement of working conditions, the use of a European Investment Bank and the expansion of trade with overseas countries.

The European treaties were negotiated in a short space of time because the Six agreed on goals and principles but did not even try to resolve most of the problems inherent in an economic community. The Treaty of Rome only established a framework within which policies were to be devised at a later date. In other words, the Six adopted the notion of 'agreeing to agree', leaving the details to be worked out later. Perhaps the British made an error in not following such tactics in their first attempt to join the Community. Instead they sought detailed arrangements, a course which gave de Gaulle an opportunity to block British membership (see pages 10–12). By 1970 the British had evidently learnt the lesson. Heath's government then made it clear that the priority was British accession to the Community rather than working out the fine details of entry.

British Attitudes to European Unity

Britain had co-operated with her West European neighbours after 1945 on matters of economic recovery and defence—for example in the distribution of Marshall Aid, the work of the OEEC and the creation of the North Atlantic Treaty Organisation (NATO). But British governments had remained convinced that co-operation in Europe must not advance to a point at which there was a risk of the loss of British independence. Therefore in 1957 Britain was unwilling to sign the Treaty of Rome which set up the EEC and her rather disdainful diplomacy seemed designed to minimise the importance of the new institution. In 1957, for example, the British suggested to the OEEC that all non-EEC countries in the OEEC should join in a free trade area. For Britain this would mean that she could keep her preferential links with the Commonwealth and her system of agricultural protection (an advantage that she would have to forfeit in the EEC with its common external tariff). The six countries of the EEC opposed the British proposal and as a result Britain's only option was to set up a small free-trade area centred on herself. In 1959 the European Free Trade Association (EFTA) was created, comprising Britain, Sweden, Norway, Denmark, Austria, Switzerland and Portugal.

Thus the idea of European unity was one from which British governments, whether Labour or Conservative, shrank. It was traditional British policy to avoid firm commitments in peace time and also the British feared that European unity might turn into unity against them. Even if this were not the case, the process of attaining unity in Europe presented Britain with an awkward choice—to join or not to join. If she chose the former course, she might endanger her position as a world power while if she chose to stand aside, she might lose much of her European influence.

An understanding of psychological factors is essential if we are to understand British attitudes in the immediate post-war years. F. N. Northedge refers to 'the notorious emotional detachment of the British people from mainland Europe', a detachment which perhaps prevented a proper appreciation of national interests. Europeans were foreigners who ran their affairs badly (like the Frenchmen of the unstable Fourth Republic) and who dragged honest Englishmen into costly or risky wars. The British survival during the Second World War heightened what has been termed 'the Channel Complex'. In her finest hour Britain had stood alone. She had been undefeated, she had escaped occupation and she emerged from the war with renewed pride in her national virtues and institutions. The countries of Western Europe, on the other hand, had just passed through the worst ordeal in their history and the common experience of Nazi occupation made it imperative for them to develop some form of European unity from the ruins.

In government circles the belief that Britain could still maintain a world role died hard. As Winston Churchill phrased it in 1950, Britain stood at the intersection of three overlapping circles—the English-speaking world, the Commonwealth and Europe. It was by her unique position within all three that she might still play a unique world role. Therefore as Uwe Kitzinger emphasises, 'none of these three bonds, and certainly not that with Europe, could afford to be tightened to the extent that they might damage the other two'.

To put it bluntly, Europe was by far the least important of the three overlapping circles to Britain in the immediate post-war years. There was still considerable belief in the idea of the Commonwealth and in the 'special relationship' with the United States of America. It should also be remembered that the British standard of living in the late 1940s and early 1950s was far superior to that of the Continent and therefore there seemed little to be gained from integration with nations suffering economic difficulties and political instability.

Nevertheless a thorough re-examination of Britain's relationship with Europe was taking place by the 1950s and it led to a considerable if reluctant change of attitudes. Again psychological factors were important. The movement of the Six towards unity, in the words of Northedge, 'left Britain stranded and increasingly cut off from one of the most notable forms of political change in the twentieth century'. As the Community progressed towards harmonised economies and political integration, Britain would be shut out of a new union of 200 million people.

Economic factors also influenced British thinking. By 1961 the EEC was proving itself in economic terms with EEC countries forging ahead while Britain stagnated. Enjoying internal tariff cuts of 30 per cent by 1960 the EEC countries succeeded in raising industrial output by more than 50 per cent between 1954 and 1960 while Britain's industrial output rose by only 20 per cent in the same period. This EEC economic performance appeared to be attracting American investment which had previously gone to Britain. Before the EEC came into existence, over half of American investment in Europe was in Britain; by 1960 this percentage had fallen to 41 per cent.

Nor was EFTA any real substitute for the EEC. It came into existence in 1960 but, as Edward Heath said, its primary purpose was to enable EFTA countries to reach agreement with the EEC. In the words of Miriam Camps, EFTA was 'a way of buying time without it prejudicing the later re-opening of negotiations'. It was merely a free trade area with little said about further co-operation. It was indeed of little value to Britain commercially. Trade between Britain and her EFTA partners was already duty free or subject to low duties and the total population of all EFTA countries was only 90 million. Nor did powerful industries exist among Britain's EFTA partners capable of giving the competitive thrust to British manufacturing. Membership of the EEC, it was argued, might give just such a salutary shock.

However, arguments over the economic merits of joining the EEC have always been evenly balanced as the 1975 debate was to demonstrate. In the late 1950s, as Miriam Camps reminds us, 'to most people the political reasons for joining were more important than the economic reasons and as time went on, the political case seemed to most people to grow stronger and the economic case rather weaker. It is clear in the British government's decision, political considerations were the controlling ones.' As Edward Heath put it, 'We now see opposite us on the mainland of Europe a large group comparable in size only to the United States and the Soviet Union, and as its economic power increases, so will its political influence.' It seemed clear that the EEC could become a third superpower and that British non-membership would lead to political insignificance.

The decline of the so-called 'special relationship' with the United States reinforced such thinking. The limitations of this relationship had been cruelly demonstrated by the Suez disaster of 1956 when Britain, in collusion with France and Israel, invaded Egypt in an attempt to retain control over the Suez Canal, only to be forced primarily by American pressure to call for a ceasefire after one day's fighting. This humiliation was one of many incidents which showed that the greatest issue in Anglo-American relations in this period was not so much similar interests (as the British had optimistically assumed before 1956) but the conflict between Britain's desire to retain a measure of global influence, and the American desire to inherit that influence, a desire which sometimes masqueraded as support for self-determination for colonial peoples.

The Americans tended to regard Britain as an aging prima donna and her stand outside Europe tended to confirm this opinion. As British power and influence plummeted, the United States became ever more the superior partner. 'All notion of equality on which the special relationship seemed to rest was visibly eroded,' remarks F. N. Northedge. The old role of Britain as a mediator between East and West no longer existed even as a theory after Russo-American detente followed the 1962 Cuba crisis. The cancellation of Blue Streak in 1960 meant that the British would in future have to accept dependence on the United States for her nuclear armoury. In the future it appeared that the United States would be more likely to forge new special relationships with the EEC. Therefore if Britain wished to retain any vestige of the old special relationship, then she should join the EEC.

The second of Churchill's overlapping circles was also declining in importance by the early 1960s. Strong forces made for a rapid disintegration of the Commonwealth and Empire after 1945. The hostility of the two superpowers towards traditional colonialism, Britain's lack of coercive power after 1945, the growing strength of colonial nationalism and the growing belief in British government circles that colonial peoples should be encouraged to seek independence—all these factors contributed to the rapid demise of Britain's imperial legacy. For a time the disintegration proceeded slowly but by the late 1950s and early 1960s it had become in D. K. Fieldhouse's phrase, 'an uncontrolled gallop'. For example Cyprus, Malta, Ghana, Malaya, Singapore, Nigeria and Uganda all received their independence between 1957 and 1962. Nor was this regretted by the British who felt as Northedge explains, 'a perceptible feeling of grievance at the anxieties and burdens of empire, a desire to be rid of the imperial mantle and to begin a quieter life at home'.

The idea of the Commonwealth forming any kind of unity around Britain was in any case a fiction. The growth of colonial nationalism excluded any scheme of political unification and strategically the Commonwealth had lost whatever unity it had with Britain's inability after 1945 to offer any protection to Commonwealth countries against external attack. Economic ties were also becoming less important. Britain was too poor herself to give much aid to the Commonwealth and her trade with the Commonwealth suffered relative decline as the new countries were too poor to buy British exports. While Britain's exports to Western Europe rose, her exports to the Commonwealth fell from 45 per cent of total exports in 1945 to 25 per cent in 1960.

The rapid pace of decolonisation forced a change in attitudes to the Commonwealth within the Conservative Party. Conservative devotion to the Commonwealth idea was reduced by the transformation of the 'Family of Nations' from a white man's club into a mainly Afro-Asian grouping of self-governing countries. The British prime minister, Harold Macmillan in his 'Wind of Change' speech in 1960 did his best to convert the old guard in the party to the idea of the new Commonwealth but it is likely that more important than his efforts was the enforced withdrawal of South Africa from the Commonwealth in 1961, a withdrawal provoked by former colonies against the wishes of Britain and the old dominions. 'From then on for many Tories,' suggests Nora Beloff, 'the Commonwealth remained an object of hope and charity but was no longer an article of faith.'

Thus by the late 1950s the Churchillian notion of Britain as the overlapping area in three international circles was plainly in need of revision. So unconvincing had the other two circles become as homes of last resort that there was nowhere else for Britain to go but into the Europe of the Six.

In addition to the broad issues outlined above, there were a number of short-term reasons which help to explain the precise moment of Britain's conversion to the idea of joining Europe. Firstly a considerable shift in public opinion had taken place in 1960 by which time the Common Market debate was well under way. Apart from the Beaverbrook press and the *Daily Worker*, the British press was united in the feeling that Britain should work for the closest possible relationship with Europe and several advocated joining the Common Market. The government's decision to abandon Blue Streak was seen by several commentators as a turning-point which proved that Britain needed to join the EEC; this was the view of *The Financial Times*, the *Guardian*, *The Economist* and the *Observer* and it was a view shared by many in the business community. Pressure on the government came from a number of members of parliament from all three major parties. Major debates took place in the Commons in the summer of 1960 with motions on the need for political and economic unity in Europe passed overwhelmingly.

Nora Beloff gives three reasons for the government's conversion. 1960 was for Macmillan a disillusioning year. After the 1959 'hat trick', when the Conservatives won their third election in a row, an autumn budget was necessary in 1960 to check a run on the pound. As Beloff puts it, 'the stop–go policy seemed to be more stop than go, and only accentuated the contrast between Britain's stagnant economy and the continuing boom across the Channel'. Even more important was the evident failure of Macmillan's visit to Moscow in 1959 to prepare the way for a new Summit meeting. In 1960 the U2 spy plane incident gave the Soviets a convenient excuse to explode the Summit meeting scheduled to take place in Paris. 'The Prime Minister was badly shaken,' asserts Beloff. 'Those who worked most closely with him believe that it was this experience which launched him on his European course.'

But Beloff adds a third factor. After nine years in office the party needed a new policy and the Conservative Central Office had come to believe that a bold bid for Europe might give the party the new look which it needed to win another election. This motive appears a valid one especially when one recalls the political capital which the Labour Party was making out of the government's European policy. In the summer of 1960, after the failure of the government to throw a bridge between the EEC and EFTA, the Labour leader Wilson declared, 'The free trade area is dead and damned. Europe is looking to Britain for leadership and the Government seems to be in a rut.' So was the Labour Party on this issue but the Conservatives were the party in office and knew that too static a policy would play into their opponents' hands.

Finally there were two hopeful developments on the international scene which seemed to augur well for the new policy. Macmillan visited the new American President, John Kennedy, in April 1961 and was left in no doubt that the United States government would welcome British entry into the

EEC. As Miriam Camps suggests, 'the reflections that the shortest and perhaps the only way to a real Atlantic partnership lay through Britain's joining the Common Market seems to have been a very important—perhaps the controlling—element in Mr Macmillan's decision that the right course for the United Kingdom was to apply for membership'. The other hopeful sign was a partial reconciliation with West Germany. The West German Chancellor, Konrad Adenauer, had no reason to like the British, who had dismissed him as Mayor of Cologne after the war; he was also on very good terms with the French President, de Gaulle. However by August 1960 when Macmillan visited him, the German Chancellor was under pressure from German business interests and appeared more favourable to the idea of British entry. In fact he still had reservations on the matter and these were to become apparent, but at the time his attitude encouraged Macmillan to seek full membership of the EEC.

In July 1960 Macmillan gave his government an overhaul which marked the advance of the pro-Europeans. Lord Home became Foreign Secretary, Edward Heath was given special responsibility for European Affairs and Christopher Soames became Minister for Agriculture. The reshuffle indicated that the European question was to be genuinely investigated not merely as a commercial problem but as a key foreign policy issue. At the same time one feels that the government as a whole was still acting out of necessity rather than conviction and three important government ministers—Butler, Maudling and Hailsham—had considerable reservations on the issue. Indeed Macmillan himself feared to give too strong a lead and did not try to sell the European idea to the public lest the question split the party. Yet though it handled the question in a low key, the Macmillan government initiated negotiations with the Six in August 1961.

The Decade of British Frustration

The French President Charles de Gaulle had been born in 1890, midway in the period between the Franco-Prussian War and the First World War. What moved de Gaulle was the fallen greatness of France and the absolute necessity of restoring it. He was sceptical of post-war developments like the EEC and believed in close ties with Adenauer's West Germany. He was profoundly opposed to any Anglo-Saxon influence in Europe and believed that Britain in the Common Market would be a kind of American Trojan horse. When in December 1962 Macmillan and Kennedy came to a rapid agreement on Polaris missiles, de Gaulle commented sourly on the contrast between Britain's 16 month haggling over the terms of her Common Market entry and her nuclear settlement with the United States in 48 hours. He saw in this yet more proof that Britain was more concerned for the American connection than for links with Europe.

His attitude to British membership was in any case inflexible. There is no doubt that British interest in the EEC was genuine as links with the Commonwealth loosened. Perhaps the British negotiators made an error in insisting on certain conditions before entry, primarily the safeguarding of agriculture, trade with the Commonwealth and the future of Britain's partners in EFTA. This led to lengthy negotiations and gave de Gaulle an opportunity to assert his will. In January 1963 he announced at a press conference that Britain was not yet ready to join the Community but his real motive was his fear that Britain would become a serious rival to France inside the Community. France's partners favoured British entry but were not consulted by the General before he applied his veto which provoked a crisis in the affairs of the Community. As A. H. Robertson explains, 'France was criticised by her partners on the grounds that once the decision to open negotiations had been taken unanimously it was contrary to the spirit if not to the letter of the Rome treaties that one member should go back on that decision contrary to the wishes of the others.' However, the alternative was an EEC without France and France's partners yielded.

When the Wilson government applied for membership in 1966 it was no more successful than the Conservatives. Again the British overtures were rejected largely because of de Gaulle's attitude. To demonstrate France's independence of the United States was the keynote of de Gaulle's foreign policy and he disliked Britain's 'special relationship' with the Americans and Anglo-American co-operation in the field of nuclear research.

However in 1967 the General used new arguments to reject British entry, asserting that Britain was not yet sufficiently strong economically to enter the Community. But his real reasons were political as Guy de Carmoy has stressed. 'Britain's presence would alter the balance of power within the enlarged Community. France would no longer have the freedom of action she enjoyed in an institution where she held the political reins and Germany was content to follow her lead.' By now three other countries were also applying for Community membership and de Gaulle was concerned to retain French dominance. In 1966 he remarked to George Brown, Deputy Leader of the Labour Party, on the impossibility of two cocks (France and Britain) living in one farmyard with ten hens. Brown records de Gaulle as saying that 'he had had a lot of trouble getting the five hens to do what France wanted, and he wasn't going to have Britain coming in and creating trouble all over again, this time with ten'.

The General's second attack on European unity was aimed at the structure of the EEC itself. The two main decision-making organs of the Community were the Council of Ministers and the Commission, the former composed of the Foreign Ministers of the Common Market countries with a voting system giving more votes to large countries than to small ones. In the Commission a more supranational approach was adopted, the Eurocrats of the Commission representing the common interests of the organisation. The national governments had already begun to view the work of the Eurocrats in Brussels with suspicion. They feared that this supranational authority, already possessing 3,000 personnel by 1962, was becoming too powerful and were apprehensive that a new technocratic elite was being created whose first loyalty was to the EEC, not to their own country.

De Gaulle was particularly hostile to the attempts of the Commission to increase its power. In 1965 he took a dislike to the Commission's proposals on agricultural policy which involved not only increases in farm prices (which France wanted) but also independent financing of the Community out of its own resources (which the Commission wanted). He threatened to withdraw France from the Community unless a solution acceptable to France was adopted. His real aim was to weaken the strength of the Commission and forestall any possibility of France being out-voted by her partners. Even the Germans were angered at the General's outrageously high-handed approach and in the end the French made some concessions on agricultural policy, but De Gaulle's real objective was achieved. All important decisions were in future to be decided by the Foreign Ministers and the Commission's authority was weakened. The General's vanity may have temporarily strengthened French prestige but it weakened Europe. The process of European unity was delayed by a decade and only after de Gaulle's retirement could it again move forward.

New Horizons—and New Problems

With the accession to the French presidency of Pompidou in 1969, the European climate changed. Politically the mood was suited to a more favourable consideration of British membership. West Germany's Chancellor Willi Brandt was a good European but his Ostpolitik (an attempt to reach better relations with East Europe) and the growing political and economic strength of West Germany made other EEC members wish to see Britain in the Community as a counter-balance to West Germany. French attitudes to British entry certainly changed but the reasons for this are still a matter of historical debate. It has been asserted that de Gaulle's attitude to Britain mellowed in the final year of his presidency. If this is the case then Pompidou merely followed a policy already laid down by his illustrious predecessor. An alternative view is that the main pressure on Pompidou was exerted by the other five Community members, anxious not to see Britain rebuffed for a third time. Pompidou himself was not hostile to Britain, though coming as he did from peasant and banking stock he had a keen eye for French interests.

The new British Prime Minister in 1970 was Edward Heath, a man with genuine and fervent European attitudes. He had in fact made his maiden parliamentary speech in 1950 attacking the failure of the then Labour government even to consider joining the Schuman Plan. His travels in Europe in his youth and his experiences as a lieutenant-colonel in the Second World War helped to form his commitment to Europe and in the 1950s he had taken a far more European line than his party leaders. Heath's European sentiments were not merely negative in the sense that he saw integration as a means of avoiding war; as Uwe Kitzinger has explained there was a more positive side. Heath believed that European countries did some things better than Britain and he anticipated that if Britain joined Europe she would gain economically and culturally. The British Prime Minister was also a most stubborn individual in pursuit of what was his major political objective—British membership.

Accordingly, the Community opened negotiations in 1970 with Britain, the Republic of Ireland, Denmark and Norway. At one point discussions with Britain seemed to be reaching an impasse but this was solved by private Anglo-French talks after six issues had caused a political row—Britain's budget contribution, her application of Community preference, New Zealand dairy produce, cane sugar, sterling and fish. Eventually the Treaty of Accession was signed and came into effect on 1st January, 1973.

Ireland and Denmark joined Britain as new members of the Community but the Norwegian people rejected membership in a referendum.

For various reasons the year 1975 proved to be crucial for the survival of the Community. The British elections of 1974 had returned to office a Labour government pledged to fundamental renegotiation of Britain's terms of entry to the Community and the putting of the results to the whole British people. This hurdle was eventually overcome in June 1975 when the Labour government, having renegotiated the terms, put the issue in the hands of the British people through a referendum. The result was a massive 'Yes' to staying in by 17 million votes to 8 millions and Wilson hailed the vote as 'the end of 14 years of national argument'. On this point he was emphatically wrong; the arguments over British membership have continued into the 1980s with considerable opposition to membership within the Labour Party especially.

1975 was also a critical year in purely economic terms. The startling rise in oil prices in 1974 pushed the Community towards recession and in 1975 the Community suffered its first negative rate of growth which resulted in a decline in living standards in some countries and dealt a brutal blow to Community confidence. By 1977 over five million people were out of work and by 1982 this figure had risen to ten million.

Community leaders put a brave face on it asserting that the unemployment and inflation would have been much worse but for the existence of the Community. As Walter Scheel, President of West Germany, emphasised in 1977, 'Individually we would not have withstood the storms of world economic development—that is, the crisis that began in 1973—at all. Each country would have been sucked into catastrophe. So we must agree that it was indeed well that 20 years ago we founded the European Community.' Yet as the 1980s arrived, the Community faced a formidable array of problems of which rising unemployment, budgetary issues and agriculture are only the most obvious. Such problems are likely to be exacerbated by the enlargement of the Community. Already Greece has raised the number of countries in the Community to ten (January 1981) and both Spain and Portugal are applying for membership.

Further Reading

Camps, M., *Britain and the European Community 1955–63*, Oxford University Press, London, 1964.

Camps, M., *European Unification in the Sixties*, Oxford University Press, London, 1967.

Cipolla, C. M., *The Fontana Economic History of Europe*, 'Contemporary Economies' chapter 3, Collins, London, 1980.

Hinsley, F. M., *Power and the Pursuit of Peace*, Cambridge University Press, London, 1963.

Kitzinger, U., *Diplomacy and Persuasion: How Britain Joined the Common Market*, Thames and Hudson, London, 1973.

Kitzinger, U., *The Second Try: Labour and the EEC*, Pergamon, London, 1968.

Northedge, F. N., *Descent from Power: British Foreign Policy 1945–73*, Allen and Unwin, London, 1974.

Vaughan, R., *Post-War Integration in Europe*, Edward Arnold, London, 1976.

Questions

(1) Why was the movement for European unity particularly strong in the years after 1945?

(2) Critically examine the reasons for British reluctance to join the EEC in 1957.

(3) Account for the Macmillan government's decision to apply for membership of the EEC in 1961.

(4) Why was British membership of the EEC delayed until 1973?

2
Objectives of the EEC and Theory of a Customs Union

The Objectives of the European Community

Political Objectives

Coverage of the European Community in the media is normally obsessed by the nuts and bolts of its operations—on farm prices, Britain's contribution to the Community budget, disputes over fishing, and so on. As a result, it is all too easy to forget that political motives were perhaps stronger than economic motives in the creation of the Community. A former President of the European Commission, Dr Walter Hallstein, once said, 'We are not in business at all; we are in politics.' The political nature of the Community is evidenced by the fact that it has several important political institutions such as the European Parliament and the Council of Ministers.

Four major political objectives of the European Community may be discerned.

Political Unity

Although since 1957 the Community has been primarily concerned with economic integration, the ultimate aim of the founding fathers of the European movement has always been that close economic ties would eventually lead to political unity. The Treaty of Rome of March 1957 pointed to a determination 'to lay the foundations of an ever closer union among the peoples of Europe'. It was believed at the time that the development of economic ties would lead naturally and inevitably towards the goal of political union but events have not borne out such optimism.

In fact, as Stanley Henig shows, there is an element of paradox in the situation because the very successes of the Community have helped to perpetuate the national attitudes it was supposed to replace. 'The achievements of the European Community have in practice strengthened rather than weakened the nation state. Certainly they have not publicly demonstrated the need for it to wither away as the central repository of popular political allegiance. This is perhaps the greatest irony in the development of European integration.' In other words, the development of the Community and its policies have gone hand in hand with a weakening rather than a strengthening of the vision of a politically united Europe. Opponents of the Community like Tony Benn often attack the Community for damaging national sovereignty but though this may be true in a purely legal sense, nation states have become politically much stronger.

It is doubtful whether any of the member governments now fully believe in the goal of European political union. This was made abundantly clear in 1975 when Leo Tindemans, the Belgian Prime Minister, produced his report on the need for a new initiative in European unification. The report tried to show the value of a united Europe and point to ways in which real political union might be achieved through a single decision-making centre. The Tindemans Report was greeted with overwhelming apathy by the member states, an apathy that demonstrated that the political will for European unity simply does not exist.

Peace

The Community was created partly as an instrument for the cementing of peace in Europe. The Treaty of Rome promised 'to strengthen the safeguards of peace and liberty by establishing this combination of resources and calling upon the other peoples of Europe who share their ideal to join in their efforts'.

Such concern for peace was only natural given the bitter enmities engendered in Europe by two world wars which had seen the breakdown of all civilised standards. It is in this context that we can appreciate the importance of the creation in 1951 of the forerunner of the Community, the European Coal and Steel Community (ECSC). Its greatest achievement and aim was to make war virtually impossible between France and Germany. The ECSC was based on the Schuman Plan, the brain-child of Jean Monnet and put forward by Robert Schuman in 1950. Fear of a reviving West Germany was the driving force of the Plan which was essentially political in character; it sought to end the bitter rivalry of France and Germany and to do this by making a war between France and West Germany virtually impossible by creating a common market in coal, iron and steel. The Plan solved the problem of the Saar as France was willing to return this important coal area to West Germany if West Germany was firmly integrated in a coal and steel community. For Germans the Plan offered a return to international respectability and a stimulus to economic expansion. The European Community was able to build on the foundations laid by the ECSC and it is too often forgotten that one of the great achievements of the Community has been its contribution towards European peace, a period of peace in marked contrast to the 30 years before 1945 in which there were two terrible world wars, both of which had their origins in Europe.

It can of course be argued that war was no longer an instrument of policy for solving differences between the states of Western Europe and that a period of peace would have ensued from the 1950s with or without the existence of the European Community. But at the very least the Community does offer a forum within which conflicts between member states may be resolved. In the past, the absence of such an appropriate forum for conciliation has allowed international disputes to escalate into war.

Democracy

The number of states in the world which are parliamentary democracies is—and always has been—small; only about 25 out of 140 member states in the United Nations may be called democracies in any meaningful sense. Of these 25, 10 are members of the European Community. An important aim of the Community is the strengthening of democracy in Europe and the founding fathers hoped that the development of the Community into a parliamentary democracy itself would strengthen democracy amongst its member states. The Treaty of Rome pointed to the pooling of resources as having as its aim 'peace and liberty'. In his memoirs, Jean Monnet emphasised that 'the essential thing is gradually to create among Europeans the broadest common interest, served by common democratic institutions to which the necessary sovereignty has been delegated'. One of the chief motives for welcoming Greece into the Community in 1981 was the belief that membership would buttress the rather frail democracy in that country. It is also a prime consideration in the current negotiations with Spain and Portugal over their membership of the Community, planned to take place in 1984.

Naturally, the Community itself has attempted to be a democratic organisation. From the start, work began on the development of a European Parliament and as a democracy implies participation, it has always been one of the guiding principles of European decision-making that there would be consultation with interest groups through a Consultative Committee which would include representatives of producers, consumers, workers and traders. In time this led to the creation of the Economic and Social Committee (ECOSOC) and other bodies representing important interest groups.

Political Co-operation (a Community Foreign Policy)

In a world of superpowers and economic blocs, individual European states since 1945 have lost the power and influence that they once exercised separately. Only a Community of 270 million people speaking with one voice has sufficient influence and authority to defend the common interests of its member states on the world scene.

The idea of a greater world role for the Community is one that has deeply interested a number of prominent political figures, including Hans Dietrich Genscher and Emilio Colombo as well as the former British Foreign Secretary, Lord Carrington. They have firmly asserted that for too long the Community has been an economic giant but a political pygmy and they have called for a more integrated Community approach to foreign affairs to give the Community more political clout in the international arena. This search by the Community for a collective identity or common foreign policy is usually given the name Political Co-operation.

Indeed in recent years there has been a shift of emphasis away from internal economic matters to international affairs as the main bond among the member states, this marking a turn-around from the 1960s when the member states agreed on economic issues and disagreed sharply on foreign policy issues. Three reasons help to explain this development. With a growing number of members and with the advent of a world recession, the member states have found progress on common economic policies much more difficult to achieve than was the case in the 1960s. Secondly, the relative decline of American world power in the 1970s has forced the member states to realise that the complexities of foreign affairs require a common approach. This feeling has been reinforced by growing concern in Western Europe that the United States is less inclined to take Community interests into account, as seen in the 1982 row over European involvement in the Soviet pipeline (see chapter 13). Thirdly there has been growing fear in the West about Soviet intentions and Soviet power as Soviet Russia has built up its SS20 medium range nuclear missiles (deployed against Western Europe) and in addition continues to enjoy a huge superiority in conventional weapons.

An important step forward in Political Co-operation came in October 1981 with agreement by the Ten's foreign ministers on what is now called the London Report. The foreign ministers stated that it was their constant concern to strengthen their political co-operation which had already demonstrated that it 'answers a real need felt by the member states of the European Community for a closer unity in this field'. In a period of world tension it was felt that the need for a coherent and united approach was greater than ever. But they noted with dissatisfaction that the Community member states were still far from playing a role in the world appropriate to their combined influence and they affirmed that the Ten 'should seek increasingly to shape events and not merely to react to them'.

The Ten made a commitment to consult their Community partners 'before adopting final positions or launching national initiatives in all important questions of foreign policy which are of concern to the Ten as a whole'. In these consultations each member state would take full account of the position of other partners and would give due weight to the desirability of achieving a common position. This was an important commitment which underlined a growing readiness of Community member states to limit voluntarily their freedom of action in areas of foreign policy in order to strengthen the process of political co-operation. As John Wyles has demonstrated, independent initiatives without prior consultations remain one of the most dangerous threats to European Political Co-operation. When the French President, Giscard d'Estaing arranged a surprise meeting with the Soviet leader, Leonid Brezhnev in the spring of 1980, it hardly helped the build up of a strong body of international opinion against the Soviet invasion of Afghanistan in the previous December.

The basic arrangements for Political Co-operation were created by the Luxembourg Report of 1970 which agreed that foreign ministers should meet at least every six months for discussions on political co-operation. The Six then agreed that they could be replaced by Heads of Government if circumstances justified it.

The Luxembourg Report also created the basic bureaucratic machinery as it set up a committee of Political Directors composed of senior officials from the member states' foreign offices. The committee meets monthly to prepare the ground for meetings of the foreign ministers so that the Community can react more rapidly and in a more united fashion in the event of crises like the Russian invasion of Afghanistan.

The country occupying the presidency of the Council of Ministers (which rotates from one member state to another every six months on the alphabetical principle) has to ensure that Political Co-operation works smoothly. In the view of Douglas Hurd, then the Conservative Minister of State for Foreign and Commonwealth Affairs, this system works well because the change of presidency leads to new ideas being presented every six months. It is also relatively cheap to run.

To strengthen the bureaucracy, it was agreed in London in October 1981 that a small team of officials should be seconded from the succeeding and preceding presidencies to preserve continuity from one presidency to the next.

Several foreign ministers, particularly Britain's Lord Carrington, had found it a bitter experience that the Ten were unable to consult until the Soviet invasion of Afghanistan was more than two weeks old. The London Report, therefore, created for the first time emergency procedures which provided for meetings of either the political directors or foreign ministers within 48 hours if three or more of the member states made such a request. In the past reactions had been very much slower. The President, for example, could only call a meeting if all the member states agreed. The new emergency procedures should make a considerable difference to the Ten's capacity to react to a crisis and in fact were proved to be effective by the Community's rapid response to the Falklands Crisis in April 1982.

At a diplomatic level the degree of co-ordination has become increasingly impressive. The Ambassadors of the Ten meet regularly in the major world capitals and in the United Nations the Community has secured a common voting record to the extent that in recent years the Ten have voted together on about 80 per cent of all resolutions. In addition the Ten have taken up a common position over several recent major international issues, for example over the Middle East, Poland and the Falklands Crisis.

A significant moment in the development of the Community's Political Co-operation came in June 1980. At the Heads of Government summit meeting at Venice a firm declaration on the Middle East was made in which for the first time the Ten asserted a common determination to play an active role in this dangerous area of conflict. The Community leaders took the view that American diplomacy through the Camp David accords was praiseworthy but in some ways inadequate because it failed to acknowledge a Middle Eastern settlement involving the Palestinians. Several member states had modified their positions to make a joint declaration possible. The Ten asserted the need for Palestinian autonomy and the need to consult the Palestine Liberation Organisation (PLO) in the peace negotiations. The declaration enraged the Israelis and disturbed the Americans but right or wrong the declaration was positive and far removed from previous anodyne Community statements on the Middle East.

The next major move by the Ten was the decision to supply troops for a peacekeeping force in the Sinai following Israeli withdrawal in April 1982, the first example of military co-operation in the Community's history.

In January 1982 the Community managed to achieve a co-ordinated response (with the exception of its newest member Greece) to the imposition of martial law in Poland. The member states condemned the violation of human rights by the Polish regime and the part played by the Soviet Union in the repression. The members refused to go along with the American line of immediate sanctions against Poland but did hold out the threat of future sanctions if the situation in Poland did not improve. When no such improvements were forthcoming, sanctions were applied against the Soviet Union in February by the banning of a small percentage of Soviet exports to the Community, notably luxury goods.

The most spectacular example of the Community's Political Co-operation came on 10th April, 1982 as a result of the Argentinian invasion of the Falkland Islands. Very speedily the Ten agreed to impose a ban on all imports from Argentina for one month and this despite the acrimonious state of Anglo–French relations over farm prices and despite the fact that such a decision was against the interests of several member states. For example West Germany exported goods worth £500 million to Argentina and Italy had 1.5 million nationals living there. Both the Irish and Italian shoe industries stood to suffer from the cutting off of their traditional purchase of hides from Argentina while the Irish government was exercised at a decision which threatened its traditional neutralist stance in international affairs. The relatively speedy Community response to the British predicament contrasted dramatically with President Reagan's remark that the United States was the friend of both Argentina and Britain, even though American attitudes later in the dispute became much more favourable to Britain.

Critics of the Community contrasted the speedy and resolute Community action against Argentina with the slower and more feeble response to the Polish crisis but the key difference was that in the former case the territory of a member state had been attacked. Support for Britain, it must be admitted, became more qualified as the Falklands Crisis led to open warfare but nevertheless the unanimity of the embargo and the speed of its imposition were testimony to the growing effectiveness of European Political Co-operation.

Nevertheless there are obstacles to the further development of Political Co-operation. For example smaller members wish to go more slowly in establishing it for while they wish to support joint endeavours they do not wish to submit to a directorate of the 'Big Three', Britain, West Germany and France. Nor should one overstate the level of agreement reached so far in this field. Many areas exist where no common Community line has been adopted, for example at the Cancun Conference over North–South relations in 1981. In the words of Douglas Hurd, close Community co-operation on international issues still only amounts to 'islands of agreement amid a sea of matters where there is still no European line'.

Economic Objectives

Negative Integration: The Development of a Customs Union and the Free Movement of Goods, Persons, Services and Capital

Article 3 of the Treaty of Rome called for 'the elimination, as between member states, of customs duties and of quantitative restrictions in regard to the import and export of goods, as well as of all other measures having equivalent effect; the establishment of a common customs tariff and of a common commercial policy towards third countries'. Such arrangements were to be accomplished within 12 years starting 1st January, 1958 with the Common External Tariff (CET) being set at the level of the average of tariffs in force on imports from the outside world.

The elimination of intra-Community tariffs and the Common External Tariff were both achieved one and a half years ahead of schedule despite some quarrels along the way, for example the temporary tariff which the French imposed on imports of Italian refrigerators. In 1973 the new members had to eliminate tariffs and quantitative restrictions on imports from the EEC with reciprocal arrangements by the Six. They also had to adjust their external tariff to the Community CET level by 1977.

The aim of this progressive removal of tariffs and other barriers to trade and the creation of a custom union was to reconcile conflicting economic interests and to promote a common economic prosperity. It was hoped that such co-operation would prevent the reoccurrence of the economic nationalism of the interwar years. After the Wall Street Crash of 1929 individual states had increased tariffs and quotas, action that had aggravated the world slump.

Although customs duties between Community countries have been abolished, widely differing tax structures, especially VAT and excise duty, have tended to distort trade patterns within the Community. Therefore the Community in recent years has been giving attention to the harmonisation of indirect taxes. It has also been aiming at other areas where action is needed to ensure freedom of movement of goods. There still exists a large number of technical restrictions of international trade within the Community. Agricultural produce, processed foodstuffs and manufactured goods are often subjected to national controls and specifications. (The French are most prone to taking this kind of action but they are not alone as the example of the British ban on Breton turkeys demonstrates.) Such restrictions constitute in effect a barrier to trade and the Community aims to remove such barriers by harmonising technical standards. In the last ten years it has adopted about 200 harmonisation directives. It has started to grapple with the problem of trade marks. There are 1.8 million trade marks in the Community, a quarter of which are similar to each other but relate to entirely different products. This causes confusion for exporters, can create a barrier to trade and result in limiting consumer choice. Consequently, the Commission has set up a working group in 1981 to tackle this question with the idea of creating a Community system of trade mark law and a Community trade mark office.

Another method of securing free movement of goods is through Community competition policy under Articles 85 and 86 of the Rome Treaty. These ban certain types of cartel agreements or concerted practices that could affect trade between member states. For example Article 85 bans price fixing and Article 86 bans abuse of a dominant market position by a firm (see chapter 5).

However the Community does not aim at free movement for goods alone. Article 3 of the Rome Treaty lays down as an important Community objective, 'the abolition as between member states, of obstacles to freedom of movement for persons, services and capital'. A national of any member state has an absolute right to enter another member state for the purpose of working or doing business, and he or she must be employed on the same terms as workers of the host country. There are certain exceptions; public service employment is excluded from this arrangement and it has been a difficult and complex task to arrange mutual recognition of qualifications for professional jobs but progress has been made. In 1977 the 450,000 doctors in the Community became free to practise in any of the member states subject to certain training qualifications or experience. The Commission continues to try to extend the principle of the free movement of labour to other professions but progress has been slow.

Positive Integration

The removal of barriers to the free movement of goods, services, persons and capital by such devices as a customs union is called negative integration. But the Community wishes to go much further than this; in the words of A. M. El Agraa, 'The EEC is a common market aspiring to become a complete economic and political union.' It has always aimed at economic union, at what is sometimes called positive integration. The Treaty of Rome was less specific here but the objective was the development of co-ordinated or harmonised Community policies which would in certain fields replace national policies. Article 3 of the Rome Treaty pointed, for example, to the establishment of common policies in the spheres of agriculture, transport and balance of payments control. The Treaty of Rome provisions should, however, be considered in conjunction with later developments particularly the Bremen Declaration of 1978 which reaffirmed Community commitment to complete monetary union by adopting the European Monetary System (EMS).

The only form of positive integration on which the Rome Treaty was specific is the contentious Common Agricultural Policy (CAP). Its aims as stated in Articles 38–47 of the Treaty of Rome are: (1) to increase agricultural productivity by promoting technical progress and the best uses of the resources of land and labour, (2) to ensure a fair standard of living for the agricultural community, (3) to stabilise markets, (4) to assure availability of supplies and (5) to ensure a reasonable price for consumers. However, the huge amounts of money needed to carry out agricultural policy have consumed most of the Community funds, it has normally meant higher level of food prices in the Community than on world markets and has led to an accumulation of surplus products like the butter mountains and wine lakes (see chapter 4).

Although not an explicit objective of the Rome Treaty, the concept of monetary union became in 1969 an accepted element of Community policy for the achievement of economic and political union. Early attempts to implement this faltered in the difficult economic climate after 1973. But the importance of creating a European zone of monetary stability as a condition for continuing the process of European integration was recognised and in 1977 the then President of the Commission Roy Jenkins launched a new initiative for a revival of a debate on monetary union. At Bremen in 1978 the European Council established a framework for a system for the creation of closer monetary co-operation and the European Monetary System was introduced in 1979. The unit of account used by the European Monetary Co-operation Fund was changed from a gold value to that of a basket of member states' currencies—the European Currency Unit (ECU) (see chapter 10).

Common policies are evolving, albeit often slowly, in many other important fields. In recent years Community industrial policy has been worked out to grapple with the problems of declining industries in the Community, for example steel and textiles. The Community has been working on a Common Fisheries Policy (CFP) since 1970. This aimed at restructuring the industry and allocating catches to member states and only in 1983 was a CFP finally agreed. Community policies for Consumer Protection only really began in 1975 with the aim of giving the consumer five basic rights: (1) effective protection against hazards to health and safety, (2) protection of the consumer's economic interests, (3) adequate facilities for advice, help and redress, (4) information and education and consultation and (5) representation in decision-making. A second consumer protection programme was adopted in May 1981 by the Council of Ministers. The Programme saw the need for progress in four main fields. In the first place the consumer should be protected against unfair sales practices and terms of contract and extortionate credit terms. Second he should be protected against the consequences of defective products and poor services, and third against misleading promotion and advertising of goods and services and inadequate and inaccurate labelling of goods. Fourth, he should be entitled to reliable after-sales service and provision of spares.

The development of other common policies—on the environment, on energy, transport and research and development—has been rather tentative but is beginning to have some impact on British economic life, for example the vexed issue of the fitting of tachographs on lorries (see chapter 12).

Improvement of Living Standards

Because Europe reflects world trends in its disparities of wealth, fluctuations in economic activity and inflationary tendencies, the founders of the Community have attempted to bring in machinery to provide all with a fair share of wealth. The first Social Fund was set up in 1958 to retrain workers from declining industries. Its scope was widened after 1972 through pressure from the West German Chancellor, Willy Brandt, so that it could deal with other social problems—migrant workers, women and the young. With the horrendous rise in unemployment in the Community to over ten million by 1982, the emphasis has been on help to the young unemployed and their training.

The Community is also pledged under the Treaty of Rome to reduce differences between the various regions of the Community. In fact this task has become more urgent since 1957 because the prosperity gap in the Community has been widening. The inhabitants of the Community's ten poorest regions now earn on average a quarter of the amount enjoyed by their counterparts in the ten richest areas. At the beginning of the 1970s the ratio was less than 3 to 1. There are two main types of poor areas: (a) rural areas on the periphery like Southern Italy and (b) areas with declining industries like South Wales where wages are low and unemployment high. The Community, therefore, in 1974 agreed to set up a Regional Development Fund to tackle its regional problems though so far it has not had a sufficient share of the Community budget to implement its policies to the full.

The Encouragement of Trade with Overseas Countries

Article 3 of the Rome Treaty states that Community activities should include 'the association of overseas countries and territories with a view to increasing trade and to promoting jointly economic and social development'. Under Article 113, the Commission was given the responsibility, once authorised by the Council of Ministers, to negotiate trade agreements with non-Community countries. This it has done, with such a will that nearly every country in the world has some kind of trading link with the Community. It has made a series of association agreements with various European and Mediterranean countries like Turkey and Spain. A particularly important development has been the creation of the two Lomé Conventions of 1975 and 1980 with over 60 countries in Africa, the Caribbean and the Pacific (the ACP countries). These agreements provided for duty free entry into the Community of all industrial goods and all agricultural produce not covered by CAP. A fund called the Stabex Fund was created to stabilise the export earnings of the ACP countries, earnings which are often volatile. Investment funds for the ACP countries have been made available through the Community's financial institutions— the European Development Fund (EDF) and the European Investment Bank (EIB)—though the ACP countries have been disappointed at the amount.

With some countries there are trading problems, especially with Japan and the United States. The Community is seeking to reduce the growing trade deficit with Japan while relations with the Americans have been exacerbated by a number of issues including steel and agriculture (see Chapter 13).

The Theory of Customs Unions

As the European Community and its trade policies are based upon the creation of a customs union, it may be of use to consider the theoretical advantages and disadvantages of customs unions. Only since the Second World War has much work been done in this field by economists. The pioneer study of the subject was done by Professor Jacob Viner in the United States in 1950 and his efforts were soon followed by contributions from R. G. Lipsey and J. E. Meade. A more detailed analysis of the problem than is given in this book can be found in Dennis Swann's *The Economics of the Common Market* (1978).

It has usually been assumed that a customs union will lead to a liberalising of trade and that its creation is therefore automatically advantageous. In fact customs unions by themselves are not as beneficial as universal free trade. Classical economists like David Ricardo were able to show that the universal elimination of protection would lead to a great increase in world welfare because each country would specialise in the production of those goods for which it was best suited or (in economists' language) in which it had a comparative advantage. World production levels would be higher than when the countries protected their industries and produced most of the goods which they needed.

Naturally, the setting up of a customs union which leads to a removal of tariffs may also have an effect on economic welfare and this may be illustrated by using supply and demand analysis. Figure 2 shows the demand and supply curves in a free market for a particular good (good A) in a certain country.

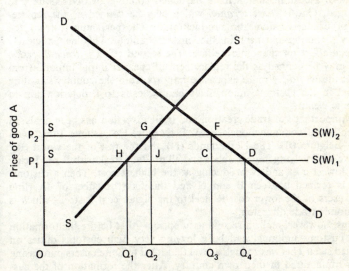

Fig. 2. The welfare effects of a tariff.

DD is the domestic demand curve; SS represents the domestic supply curve. $SS(W)_1$ is the supply curve of imports of good A from the rest of the world. If there is no tariff on good A then its price will be OP_1 and domestic demand will equal total supply at OQ_4. Total supply will be composed of domestic supply (OQ_1) and imports (Q_1Q_4).

Suppose then that the government of the country imposes a tariff on imports of good A, resulting in the raising of the price to OP_2. Domestic demand will equal total supply at OQ_3 with total supply being composed partly of home production (OQ_2) and imports (Q_2Q_3). The country will now be supplying an additional amount of good A (i.e. Q_1Q_2 at increasing marginal costs because the new amount (OQ_2) is being supplied at the price OP_2 when in fact imports can be supplied at the lower cost of OP_1). Thus the production cost of protection is represented by the triangle GHJ which is the difference in cost between supplying the quantity Q_1Q_2 at home and importing that amount. As consumption falls by Q_3Q_4 consumers also experience a loss of economic welfare which is represented by the triangle CDF.

If the country's government subsequently removes the tariff, then the reverse occurs. Production of good A will rise by the amount GHJ and consumption will rise by the amount CDF. Thus it may be argued that the removal of tariffs appears to result in an increase of economic welfare.

However a customs union is not so clearly beneficial in practice as might be assumed from this analysis because it represents free trade only within a bloc, a bloc which in fact discriminates against the rest of the world's goods by imposing tariffs on them. Therefore in estimating the consequences of a customs union for a particular country, two effects have to be gauged. One is *trade creation* which may be defined as the replacement of expensive domestic production by cheaper imports from the country's trading partners in the customs union. This has a clearly beneficial effect on economic welfare. The second effect is *trade diversion* which may be defined as the replacement of cheaper initial imports from the outside world by more expensive imports from the country's trading partners in the customs union. This clearly leads to a deterioration in economic welfare.

The importance of trade creation and trade diversion has been analysed in supply and demand models by J. E. Meade. He assumes three main areas—Belgium (B), The Netherlands (N) and the rest of the world (R). All have been levying import duties and all produce steel, with R producing at the lowest cost and N producing at the highest cost. Then a customs union is formed between B and N and this has the effect of diverting Dutch users of the lower cost R steel to the higher cost B steel—which is uneconomic trade diversion.

Let us, however, make a second assumption—that before the formation of the customs union N had been levying very high customs duties on imported steel. This was so high a level that it led to Dutch users purchasing steel manufactured in their own country. After the formation of the customs union with B, Dutch users would no longer buy high cost Dutch steel but would move to the lower cost Belgian steel. This would create more trade between the two countries, would mean the more efficient use of resources and mean the replacement of expensive domestic production by cheaper imports, i.e. trade creation.

The effects of trade creation and trade diversion are seen in Figure 3 which shows N's demand curve (DND) for and supply curve (SNS) of steel. The supply curve of imports of steel from B is SB_1 and from the rest of the world is SR_1 which is the lowest cost supplier.

In the days before the customs union between B and N is formed, N imposes a tariff of PP_1 on imports of steel. As a result both supply curves

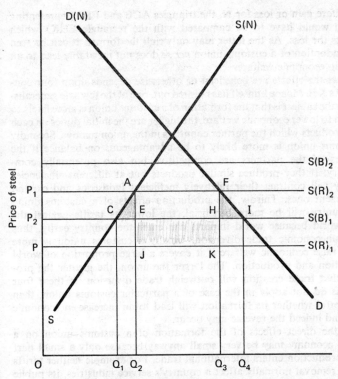

Fig. 3. Trade creation and trade diversion.

shift up to SB_2 and SR_2 respectively. The relevant supply curve is now $SAS(R)_2$ which intersects the demand curve at F so that the price is OP_1 and total supply is OQ_3 which is composed of domestic production (OQ_2) and imports (Q_2Q_3), all of which come from R.

Now the customs union is formed between N and B but steel from R continues to have a tariff imposed on it. B can now supply steel to N at the price OP_2 while R continues to supply at price OP_1. The actual supply curve becomes $SCS(B)_1$, the price falls to OP_2 and the quantity supplied increases to OQ_4. Domestic production decreases to OQ_1 and imports increase to Q_1Q_4, all of which come from the higher cost external supplier B.

This results in some trade creation because on the production side the triangle ACE represents a production gain as more costly home production is replaced by lower cost imports. The consumption gained is represented by the triangle FHI. But there is also some trade diversion because N has switched its imports from the lower cost supplier R to the higher cost supplier B and this loss is represented by the rectangle EHKJ which is the increased cost of the imports Q_2Q_3.

To estimate whether the formation of the customs union has resulted in a net welfare gain or loss for N, the triangles ACE and FHI (representing the gain) would have to be compared with the rectangle EHKJ which represents the loss. As the latter may outweigh the former, it can be seen that the adoption of a customs union *per se* does not inevitably lead to an increase in economic welfare.

Whether the effects are beneficial or otherwise depends upon four conditions. As J. E. Meade himself has pointed out, one of the few safe generalisations on the subject is that the formation of a customs union is more likely to raise than to lower economic welfare, the higher are the initial duties on each other's products which the partner countries in the union remove. Secondly the customs union is more likely to be advantageous on balance if the economies of the partners are competitive but also potentially complementary. If they produce similar products but at different efficiencies then they will contract their relatively inefficient industries and expand their efficient ones. Thirdly, the production effects of a customs union for a country will be more beneficial, the lower its tariffs against the outside world because world imports can enter the country easily, thus limiting uneconomic trade diversion. Finally a customs union is more likely to raise economic welfare if it covers a large proportion of world consumption and production. The larger the union, the greater the probability that trade creation will outweigh trade diversion. If these four conditions do not apply in the case of a particular customs union, then it is doubtful whether its formation will lead to an increase in economic welfare and indeed the reverse may occur.

Often the direct effects of the formation of a customs union on a country's economy may be very small anyway because only a small part of total production enters international trade. For example neither tariffs nor their removal normally affect a country's service industries, its public sector or its building industry. Secondly if the general level of tariffs is already low, the welfare effects of removing them will obviously be small. If gains from the formation of customs unions are so minute or uncertain, it may well be asked why so much attention has been given to this issue. Dennis Swann suggests that the answer is partly political in that more economic integration by way of a customs union may be preparing the ground for political unification at a later date. This certainly can happen as it did in the case of the Zollverein, a customs union between the German states in the nineteenth century. But in addition certain *dynamic* economic effects have to be taken into account. The formation of a customs union creates a larger market which may well encourage the greater use of economies of scale by producers. National markets may not be large enough for firms to use the optimum level of plant and machinery or mount the necessary research and development efforts to compete successfully with rivals outside the customs union. The larger market of the customs union would encourage such developments. Secondly the formation of a customs union would lead to increased competition. Such competition would tend to keep prices down, eliminate inefficient firms and give a greater incentive to managers to modernise their production methods. Indeed a considerable psychological change may take place. Firms can no longer rely on their own national markets being as secure as in the days before the customs union was formed and such uncertainty will necessitate more enterprising attitudes. Finally, the creation of a larger market will not only encourage more domestic investment. Its existence will usually lead to more foreign investment from countries outside the customs unions.

In practice, exact measurement of the direct and indirect effects of the formation of a customs union like the Common Market is difficult, but over the years economists have attempted this task. Most economists in the 1950s, for example the Dutch economist P. J. Verdoorn and the American Bela Balassa, estimated that the direct effects of West European integration would be small. Later studies which took into account the dynamic factors at work saw the effects of integration as being potentially more significant. J. H. Williamson in 1971 thought that British entry into the EEC would increase her Gross National Product by 1.5 per cent per annum by 1978. N. Kaldor writing at the same time gave a much more gloomy forecast, pointing out several disadvantages of membership, for example the loss of trading preferences given by the Commonwealth.

A decade later, opinion was still sharply divided on the precise impact of membership on the British economy. Christopher Johnson of Lloyds Bank calculated in 1983 that when Britain was outside the EEC, her growth rate was 64 per cent of the Community's. From 1973 on Britain's growth rate rose to 70 per cent of the Community's. Had Britain continued to grow at 64 per cent of the Community rate from 1973 on, her growth rate would have been 0.15 per cent less than it actually had been. The cumulative gain over the decade meant that £19 billion at 1982 prices had been added to the GDP in the years 1973 to 1983. According to this line of argument, Britain's gains from the rapid expansion of freer trade with the Community more than offset the losses to Britain from the CAP and the Community budget contributions.

There were of course alternative viewpoints, especially from left-wing writers like Stuart Holland. In his book *Uncommon Market* Mr Holland stressed that Community policies enriched the more prosperous central areas (West Germany and France) at the expense of the more peripheral areas like Britain.

Further Reading

El-Agraa, A. M. (ed.)., *The Economics of the European Community* (Chapters 1–3), Philip Allan, Deddington, 1980.
Holland, S., *Uncommon Market* (Chapters 1–3), Macmillan, London, 1980.
Swann, D., *The Economics of the Common Market* (4th edition), Penguin, Harmondsworth, 1978.

Questions

(1) Explain the term 'Political Co-operation' and find some current examples of this policy from the newspapers.

(2) What is the difference between 'negative' and 'positive' integration in a Community context?

(3) What is meant by the terms 'trade creation' and 'trade diversion'?

(4) What dynamic effects may the creation of a customs union like the EEC have on a particular country?

3
Community Institutions

The European Community functions in accordance with a constitution enshrined in a series of basic treaties which define the powers of the main institutions and their relationship with the member governments. The Treaty of Paris establishing the European Coal and Steel Community (ECSC) was signed in 1951 and was followed by two separate Treaties of Rome (March 1957) which established the European Atomic Energy Community (EURATOM) and the European Economic Community (EEC). It was agreed to create a single Assembly, Court of Justice and Economic and Social Committee for all three Communities.

In April 1965 it was further agreed by a Treaty signed at Brussels to create a single Council of the European Communities replacing the Special Council of Ministers of the ECSC, the Council of the EEC and the Council of EURATOM. A Commission of the European Communities was to replace the High Authority of the ECSC, the Commission of the EEC and the Commission of the EURATOM, a single Audit Board being created for all three Communities. This so-called Merger Treaty came into force in 1967 and the term European Community was increasingly used to refer to the unified Communities.

The fifth major treaty—the Treaty of Brussels of 1972—brought about the enlargement of the Community from six members to nine with 1975 seeing important decisions concerning direct elections to the European Parliament.

The European Council

At their meeting in Paris in 1974, the Community Heads of Government decided to meet three times a year under the name of the European Council with a view to making more rapid progress in Community policy, particularly in the field of Political Co-operation. These meetings have become formally organised, with the Commission being represented at the European Council by the President of the Commission and one of the vice-presidents while Heads of Government are accompanied by their foreign ministers. There had been occasional summit meetings in the past with the first major one being the Hague Summit of 1969 in which the Six re-committed themselves to the Community.

When Giscard d'Estaing advanced the idea of a European Council in 1973 the hope was that the summits would be occasions for tranquil reflection on the longer term issues facing the Community. In practice the government leaders have rarely found time at their meetings to discuss long-term strategy, free from the pressure of detailed decision-making. In fact the European Council has become the Community's highest court of appeal and its supreme decision-making institution. It has had to arbitrate on major disputes like Britain's net financial contribution to the Community budget and farm price increases which are technically complicated issues.

There are two chief reasons for this development. Firstly there have been more serious disputes among the member states in recent years owing to the worsening economic climate. Secondly, other Community institutions have personnel who have lacked the political influence in their own countries to force through any solutions to the problems dealing with major issues. They are then forced to pass the problem over to the European Council.

Difficult questions have led to acrimonious meetings of the European Council, particularly in the long disputes over Britain's contributions to the Community budget. At the Dublin Summit in December 1979 Mrs Thatcher's refusal of the terms offered led to Herr Schmidt's banging the table and Giscard d'Estaing refusing to take any further part in the proceedings. A similar impasse resulted at the Brussels Summit of March 1982. Another unfortunate feature is that the Summits have become media circuses with more than a thousand journalists present from the press, radio and television. The pressure on the national leaders to be seen to be taking a 'strong' line is therefore great and some have been unscrupulous about using press leaks and 'off the record' comments as part of their tactics in Community disputes.

The Summit meetings seem to have strengthened the intergovernmental structure of the Community at the expense of the supra-national element. However the meetings are enlarging the subjects in which the Community is seen to have a legitimate interest. Perhaps in the future the main political initiatives will come from the national political leaders rather than from the Commission.

The Council of Ministers

The Council is the principal decision-making body of the European Community and the only institution which directly represents the governments of the member states. The Council takes the final decisions on policy for the Community on the basis of proposals from the Commission, after taking into account the opinions of the European Parliament and the Economic and Social Committee. Normally the Council cannot enact any measure without a Commission proposal.

The office of President of the Council is held for a term of six months by each member state in turn. It has become the practice for each member to try and establish a particular style of work and to single out certain matters to which it wishes to give priority. Given that the Chairman can influence Council business, the President may exercise an important, if temporary, influence. For example, when Britain held the Presidency from June to December 1981, Lord Carrington successfully imparted an edge to the search for a more coherent Community foreign policy.

For major decisions the Council consists of the Foreign Ministers of the member states but on a day to day basis membership depends upon the subject before the Council and as Community affairs have developed, so a wider range of national ministers has attended to Council business. Three groups of ministers meet most frequently—those for foreign affairs, agriculture and finance. This large number of ministers involved has created difficulties for member governments because if Community issues are handled by various politicians it becomes more difficult to see their European policy as a coherent whole. There is even a danger that a national minister in pursuit of a Community policy may distance himself from his own national colleagues. The greater specialisation of the Council creates problems because as individual issues become compartmentalised, so it becomes more difficult to negotiate package deals acceptable to all parties. The Council of Agricultural Ministers in particular appears to have developed an independent existence of its own.

Under the Rome Treaties, the Council may take decisions in any one of three ways: by unanimity, by simple majority or by qualified majority. On matters regarded by a member state as being of vital interest, it has been until recently the Council's practice to proceed only on the basis of unanimity. Some Council decisions have, therefore, to be taken by unanimous vote, but abstention by one member state does not invalidate an otherwise unanimous vote.

In practice many issues are settled on the basis of consensus. In order to improve the work of the Council, the Heads of Government agreed at the Paris Summit of 1974 that the practice of requiring unanimity for agreement on issues which were not of vital concern should be abandoned. Decisions on most matters are taken by majority vote, often by the system of 'qualified majority'. The vote is weighted, giving a total of 63, of which 45 are required for a 'qualified majority'. Germany, France, Italy and Britain have ten votes each, Belgium, The Netherlands and Greece five votes each, Ireland and Denmark three each and Luxembourg two. This means that the four large countries cannot force a decision on the six smaller ones and that any two large countries can block a decision.

However, the whole question of voting procedures in the Council of Ministers was opened up on 18th May, 1982 when the Council took what might turn out to be an historic decision by forcing through farm price increases against British wishes—the first majority vote on a matter of importance since the Luxembourg Compromise of 1966. It arose from the row over British contributions to the Community budget. The British agricultural minister Peter Walker had co-operated in preparing farm price increases for 1982 but he made it clear that he would veto the final package until an acceptable offer was made to Britain over her budget rebates. The British believed that he was entitled to do this under the Luxembourg Compromise which General de Gaulle had forced his five partners to agree to in 1966. The Compromise allows a member state to veto a proposal if it affects a 'vital national interest' and up to 18th May several member states had used the veto for almost anything. The British thought that they were entitled to use the veto as a weapon for putting pressure on their partners to agree to their budgetary demands even though they were not against the agricultural price increases as such.

What the British had underestimated was the intense anger caused by such tactics and what finally swayed the issue was the attitude of France, the arch defender of national interests and the instigator of the Luxembourg Compromise. Thus, despite Peter Walker's protests, the decision on farm price increases went through by majority vote. It could be argued that the use of the majority vote helped to clear the air; the farm price increases were soon followed by a budget settlement for Britain and a decision to continue economic sanctions against Argentina until the end of the Falklands War by seven of Britain's nine partners (Italy and Ireland being the two opting out).

Yet the majority decision of 18th May opened up a grey area for the future on the issue of voting procedures. All member states were quick to stress that the power of the veto remained but it had become far from clear precisely when in the future it would be possible for a member state to invoke the Luxembourg Compromise. Obviously the practice of 'linkage' will be less easy, i.e. when a member state holds up a decision on one issue to get its own way on another. Normal Community business may now be speeded up while major new Community initiatives will still probably require unanimity but some uncertainty now exists about voting procedures. Nevertheless the principle of unanimity does constitute a stumbling block to orderly decision-making and one wonders how efficient the activities of any national cabinet would be if it had to approve every decision unanimously. Speedier methods of reaching a decision are needed and will become even more essential when the Community is enlarged to twelve.

The Council faces further problems. It tends to leave much of the details to COREPER (see page 35) and concerns itself with major political issues. Unfortunately, as with the European Council, members have had to put up with excessive pressure from the media and national groups who often lobby with a violent zeal, for example the French farmers. Meetings of the Council attract much media publicity and are portrayed by the media in terms of victory or defeat for national interests. The problem is made worse by Council ministers themselves leaking information to the press to gain a political advantage. As a result, agreements have become more and more difficult to achieve.

Decision-making is in any case difficult without the problems pointed to above. Ministers are dealing with delicate problems, already have too much business and can only attend part-time to Community affairs. Consequently there is often a time-lag in reaching a decision and the Council has become a major bottleneck preventing the efficient expediting of Community business. Reform has been suggested, including the more general use of majority voting, the creation of an inner group to handle important decisions and the holding of Cabinet meetings in all member states on the same day to allow ministers to attend Council meetings. Such suggestions have been so far rejected because they are seen as a threat to national sovereignty. It may well be that for European integration to continue, other Community institutions, especially the Parliament, need to take away from the Council at least a portion of its power.

The Committee of Permanent Representatives

As the Council of Ministers only met at intervals and in any case faced acute problems in expediting Community business, it was decided in 1965 to set up the Committee of Permanent Representatives (generally referred to as COREPER after the French acronym). It is an organisation of senior officials who prepare Council meetings and handle business between Council meetings. It meets regularly either to consider matters referred back to it by the Council of Ministers, on which the ministers have been unable to reach agreement, or to give a preliminary view to ministers on Commission proposals formally submitted to the Council but for which its timetable has left no time for discussion. In 1966 COREPER gained fresh influence when it was agreed that the Commission would work through it to make contact with national governments before deciding on the exact form of any intended proposal.

The importance of this institution has grown since 1965 because, with its links with both the Commission and the Council of Ministers, it is involved in all the major stages of Community policy-making from early discussions to the final Council decision-making and it forms an essential link between the Commission and the national governments. Many decisions are now made by COREPER in advance of a Council meeting, the Council merely giving formal assent.

The permanent representatives have, therefore, considerable importance. They have assistance from specialist subordinate committees, they hold ambassadorial rank and are effectively the member states' ambassadors in Brussels. Thus they act as the deputies to the ministers and in that capacity may attend Council meetings.

The European Commission

The Commission, which is based in Brussels, consists of 14 members—two each from Britain, France, West Germany and Italy and one each from Belgium, Denmark, Ireland, Luxembourg, The Netherlands and Greece. These 14 commissioners are chosen by agreements between the governments of the member states for a period of four years with renewable appointments. Both the President and the five vice-presidents are chosen from the 14 for a two year renewable period. In practice an individual can expect two terms as president and several have been men like Roy Jenkins, president 1977–80, significant in national politics and able to meet the Council ministers on more or less an equal footing.

Under the terms of the Treaties, the members 'shall be chosen on the grounds of their general competence' and according to Article 10 of the Merger Treaty 'in the general interests of the Communities be completely independent in the performance of their duties ... neither seek nor take any instructions from any government or any other body and refrain from any action incompatible with their duties'. They must also when taking up their office as commissioners 'give a solemn undertaking that, both during and after their term of office, they will respect the obligations arising therefrom'. Thus, though he is initially appointed by the national government, the commissioner does not represent that government nor is he allowed to be influenced by it. He is, in theory, supposed to be completely independent, a servant of the Community rather than the national interest.

The Commission heads an administration of about 10,000 international civil servants organised in 20 directorates-general, each responsible to one of the commissioners. Each commissioner has responsibility for one or more Community policies and in practice is given a large measure of influence in framing policy. Nevertheless, despite this division of responsibilities, the Treaty of Rome set up the Commission as a collegiate institution and therefore all measures, including proposals to the Council, have to be adopted by the Commissioners as a body. Unlike the Council, however, the Commission uses majority voting as the only way of dealing with the large volume of work. In practice only important matters, particularly politically delicate issues, are discussed by the commissioners themselves at their weekly meetings. More routine proposals are usually dealt with by 'written procedure'. The proposals are circulated to each member of the Commission and if no objections are raised within a specified period, they are adopted automatically.

A commissioner has help from two sources: (1) a chef de cabinet, a French phrase meaning a small personal staff which includes an assistant normally of the same nationality as himself; (2) the Commission staff of the particular General Directory which he heads. Their work can be complex because Commission proposals have to be integrated into ten national economies and there is of course the problem of using seven official languages. As a result half the Commission staff are translators and many are from Belgium, Italy or Luxembourg as it is in these states that most of the institutions are based. However, the General Directories are composed of staff from all the ten nationalities in the Community and care is taken to prevent any national viewpoint becoming too dominant by ensuring that the holders of the higher posts are drawn from several member states and that each Director (the head of the General Directory) is of a different nationality from the Commissioner to whom he is responsible.

The Commission has four main roles:

(1) It acts as a Community watchdog. As the guardian of the Treaties, the Commission has the function of ensuring that member states abide by their obligations. It can investigate circumstances where a breach of obligations is suspected either by a member state or a firm and issue a reasoned opinion. If matters are not set right within a stated period, the Commission can refer the matter to the European Court of Justice. The Commission has few direct sanctions but it can fine firms for breaches of the rules, especially the rules relating to fair competition (see chapter 5). In practice member states usually accept their obligations to abide by Community decisions. In 1979 for example the British government having been taken to the Court by the Commission accepted the Court's ruling on the installation of tachographs.

(2) The Commission's main function is that of initiator of policy. The Treaty of Rome was never a full guide to future policy and therefore the Commission has a great deal of influence in shaping Community develop-

ments. The directorate which is making a proposal will enter into discussion with government departments and other interested groups before the proposal is formulated. It is then discussed with COREPER, the European Parliament and the Economic and Social Committee before it reaches the Council of Ministers. The Commission can then mediate at meetings of the Council, frequently amending its own proposals to help reach a compromise acceptable to all member states.

(3) The Commission administers policies previously agreed by the Council or derived directly from the provisions of the Treaties. It administers the funds of the common programmes which account for most of the Community budget. It is particularly involved in the running of the Common Agricultural Policy because of the daily management of the markets which are necessary.

(4) Operating upon a mandate from the Council, the Commission negotiates on behalf of the Community in certain external matters. Under Article 113 of the Rome Treaty, it has negotiated trade agreements with foreign countries. An important example of this function is the Lomé Convention which the Commission agreed with 46 African, Caribbean and Pacific States (ACP) in 1975, with a second Lomé Convention being signed in 1979 (see chapter 13). In fact the Commission has negotiated treaties with many areas of the world including the countries inside the European Free Trade Area (EFTA), several East European states and many countries in North Africa and the Middle East.

To a considerable extent the commissioners have charge of areas which are of particular concern to their own countries. Thus the Danes, after the untimely death of their Commissioner for Agriculture Finn Olav Gundelach in January 1981, moved quickly to ensure that Poul Dalsager replaced him. The Greeks are immensely dependent on tourism; it was therefore natural that they would wish their representative on the Commission to have charge of this portfolio. Similarly the British who wish to restructure the Community budget and are only too aware of employment problems were anxious that their commissioners should be given the relevant portfolios.

Naturally this can lead at times to a rather undignified scrambling for jobs. When in 1981 Gaston Thorn, President of the Commission, wanted to give Michael O'Kennedy a post commensurate with his status, he suggested a special appointment related to budget restructuring. This appeared to cut across the powers of Christopher Tugendhat who was provoked into persuading Mrs Thatcher to intervene directly, a move contrary to convention. Mr O'Kennedy (who was subsequently replaced by Richard Burke) was given a post with less influence but Mr Tugendhat may have created some ill feeling among the other commissioners.

The Commission suffers from an invidious reputation; it is supposed to be bursting at the seams with too many interfering bureaucrats. In fact the Commission has a staff which is really quite small relative to its considerable responsibilities and while it may on occasions commit absurdities in the search for harmonised policies, most stories about it are simply untrue.

The Court of Auditors

The Court is made up of independent experts appointed by member governments. It is a recent creation, beginning work in 1977 when the European Parliament demanded a closer audit of the Community budget. It is intended that the Court of Auditors should monitor expenditure much more thoroughly than in the past, checking on the use made of Community revenue by member states and the Commission and on their methods of collecting duties and levies. Thus it is the Community's financial watchdog.

At times the Court has been able to compliment the Commission on its activities but it has certainly not been afraid to bark. It has criticised the Commission on aspects of its food aid to developing countries, claiming that one firm which had made deliveries of dubious quality continued to be awarded contracts. It has continually called on the Commission to develop a system of accounts which is more complete and more informative. It has particularly condemned the Commission's record in dealing with fraud in the Common Agricultural Policy and has indeed helped to uncover these frauds in the first place. In its 1982 report the Court, for example, pointed out that the Commission had recovered only £1 million out of £12 million in farming subsidies fraudulently claimed. The Court also singled out the building of a fitness centre for the free use of Commission staff in Luxembourg, claiming that this had not been properly authorised.

The European Parliament

Origins

The European Assembly as it is called in the Treaties, has its origins in the Assembly of the Coal and Steel Community established in 1951. When the Treaties of Rome were signed in 1957, that assembly was merged with the two assemblies of the EEC and EURATOM, thus creating one assembly. Until the enlargement of the Community in 1973, the assembly (now known as the European Parliament) consisted of 142 delegates chosen by the respective national parliaments from their own members. When Denmark, Britain and Ireland joined the Community in 1973, the Parliament was enlarged to 198 delegates.

At the Copenhagen Summit of 1974 it was decided to hold direct elections to the European Parliament and by 1976 it had been accepted that the Parliament should be enlarged from 198 seats to 410. In June 1979 the present parliament, except for the Greek members who were appointed by their political parties, was elected in the first ever European direct elections for a five year term. The European members of Parliament (MEPs) represent the member states in the following proportions: Britain, West Germany, France and Italy have 81 members, The Netherlands, 25 members, Greece and Belgium 24 members, Denmark 16 members, Ireland 15 members and Luxembourg 6 members.

The Powers of the European Parliament

The European Parliament acts as a consultative body on most Community affairs and in recent years its power has grown. It has, in theory, the power to dismiss the Commission though in practice perhaps this is of ttle value as to do so would bring the Community to a halt and the Parliament has no right to appoint a new Commission. However, it might continue to dismiss Commissions of which it disapproved until it obtained a satisfactory one. A vote of censure can also be a way of expressing Parliamentary opinions on a Community policy so that the Commission or other institutions may amend it.

The Parliament has also become more effective in using its power verbally or in writing to keep the Commission and Council of Ministers on their toes. It considers and gives opinions on the Commission's proposals before they are examined in the Council and although not obliged to do so the Commission does often change its proposals on parliamentary advice. It also receives and comments on reports from the other two bodies. Since 1974 the foreign ministers have been meeting four times a year with the Political Committee of the European Parliament to discuss foreign policy issues.

An important development in the Parliament's power occurred in 1970 when it was agreed that if the Community were to become independent in financial matters, then some kind of parliamentary control over Community revenue should be established. The practice has now evolved for a draft budget to be prepared by the Commission and then sent to the Council of Ministers for approval. It is then discussed by the Parliament. To understand the Parliament's budgetary control it is necessary to explain that the budget is made up of compulsory and non-compulsory expenditure. Compulsory expenditure (about 80 per cent of the total budget) may be amended by Parliamentary majority but the Council can reject any changes proposed here. The Parliament has more real control over non-compulsory expenditure because it can suggest changes in this section up to a certain limit and though the Council may amend the decision, the Parliament must receive the total draft budget back and at this point can reject the Council's amendments in the non-compulsory section. If there is considerable disagreement the Parliament has the right to reject the draft budget entirely and demand a new one.

It is clear, therefore, that the powers of the Parliament are significant and growing but as yet in some important respects inadequate.

Political Groups and Organisation

The June elections of 1979 were a remarkable achievement because they were the first ever international elections. They resulted in the creation of six main political groupings. Including the later addition of 24 Greek members, the line up of groups is as follows:

Socialists (including 18 Labour)	124 seats
European People's Party (Christian Democrats)	117 seats
European Democrats (including 61 Conservatives)	63 seats
Communists	48 seats
Liberals and Democrats	39 seats
European Progressive Democrats	22 seats

The remaining 21 seats are divided among minor parties and independents.

The existence of these groupings demonstrates that members take their seats in the House according to political conviction rather than nationality.

The European groups which they have formed usually make common caus in debates and vote together.

The European Parliament is run by a Bureau comprising the Presiden and twelve Vice-Presidents who are elected by secret ballot to serve for tw and a half years. The main task of the Bureau is to draw up the dra agenda for each Parliamentary session. The President elected in 1979 wa Mrs Simone Veil of France. After a poor start when she seemed too muc the choice of Giscard d'Estaing and exhibited little knowledge of parlia mentary procedure, she improved as a chairman and became an impressiv and respected figure with the courage to be independent. In 1982 she wa succeeded as President by the energetic Dutch Socialist, Pieter Dankert.

In addition to its President and Vice-Presidents, the Parliament als elects five Quaestors who deal with administrative and financial matters o concern to the European Members of Parliament. They too are elected fo two and a half years.

The Parliament has 15 specialised committees, each dealing with par ticular areas of the Community's activities, for example agriculture an regional policy. The membership of the Committees broadly reflects th political and national balance of the House as a whole. The Committee usually meet in Brussels so that they can make easier contact with th Council and the Commission.

Problems

Given the political will, the Parliament could become one of the mos important Community institutions in the next decade. However, it doe face a number of severe problems, five in particular.

(1) In the direct elections of 1979 each country was entitled to use it own electoral system but for future elections it is hoped to adopt a uniform system. However, only in 1984 will the Community decide on this problem and agreements on such procedures have been difficult to reach in th past. The salaries of MEPs also have been a problem. Most countries o the Ten pay MEPs on scales similar to senior civil servants, but other (including Britain) pay considerably less generously.

(2) Because of the need for interpretation into several languages, debate in the European Parliament lack the cut and thrust of the better sessions i national parliaments. The language barrier is in fact a major obstacle t European unity. A number of suggestions have been made to improve th problem—that everyone should speak French or English, that there shoul be official languages (all eight) but certain working languages (the fou chief ones) or that interpretation be given in only two or three. All ideas however, come up against the same stumbling block; it is politically un acceptable that those speaking minority languages should be put at a dis advantage in the work of the Parliament. The enlargement of the Com munity to include Portugal and Spain will make the problem even mor intractable.

(3) At present the Parliament meets in Strasbourg and Luxembourg, th Parliament's secretariat is based in Luxembourg while most meetings o the Parliament's committees are held in Brussels. This three-site mode o operation imposes an absurd strain on a conscientious European Membe

of Parliament who already has a large constituency in which he will wish to spend time, who will have to attend sessions of the Parliament in Strasbourg and Luxembourg and who may also be a member of a specialist committee meeting in Brussels. When the Parliament debated the problem in July 1981, they agreed to hold parliamentary sessions in Strasbourg only until the Community governments agreed on a single site, a decision that disappointed Luxembourg.

(4) The Parliament now possesses more moral authority than ever before and this was symbolised when in 1981 it was addressed by the late President Sadat of Egypt. Nevertheless it still has insufficient practical power to be an effective instrument of democratic control and certainly the Council of Ministers has little sympathy for the pretensions of the Parliament, because the ministers see it as a threat to national sovereignty. It is a serious weakness that the views of the Parliament may be legally disregarded by other institutions and it needs to receive a bigger share in decision-making with the Council of Ministers. Perhaps one way in which this may occur is if the Parliament gained a greater say in budgetary matters because this would then lead to the growth of Parliamentary powers in the policy-making field.

In the 1980s it is this strategy that the Parliament is pursuing as it tries to force increases in Community expenditure, particularly on the non-CAP sections of the Budget. In so doing it is frequently at loggerheads with the Council. For example in December 1981, the Parliament approved the Budget for 1982 and the Council replied by saying that the figure was £125 millions higher than the amount by which the Parliament was entitled to increase the total. The row stemmed from differences in interpretation over who had the final say—Parliament or Council—over Community food aid spending.

(5) Finally, it has to be admitted that the work of the Parliament is treated with overwhelming apathy or hostility by the publics in the Community. It has received bad publicity, particularly over its overseas expenses like the Great Bogota Scandal when 38 MEPs visiting South America took 58 interpreters with them. In fact some visits abroad are by no means luxurious and the cost of the Parliament per citizen works out at 27p a year. It is also condemned as a talking shop which is without influence and Walter Ellis of the *Financial Times* once described the MEPS as walking down the corridors of weakness. Again, this argument may be countered by pointing to the growing powers of Parliament but nevertheless it does need to rid itself of its rather depressing image.

The Economic and Social Committee (ECOSOC)

This body was created by the Rome Treaty with advisory status and its role is to represent the various categories of economic and social life in the Community, such as employers, unions, farmers, the self-employed and the general public. Members are appointed by the Council from national lists, each member being appointed for four years and acting in a personal capacity. There are 156 members in all, 24 each from France, Germany, Italy and the United Kingdom, 12 each from Belgium, The Netherlands and Greece, 9 each from Denmark and Ireland, and 6 from Luxembourg.

In practice members come from three main groups—employers, unions and those representing the general interest.

The opinion of the Committee is sought on all major policies by the Council and Commission and particularly on issues relating to transport, agriculture, harmonisation and the free movement of workers. However, it has not really had an effective voice in Community affairs for a number of reasons: (1) It only has a consultative role and its opinions can be ignored by the more powerful institutions within the Community. (2) The varied membership makes it difficult to produce a single point of view except of a very general and bland nature. Sometimes it has to produce a series of reports reflecting the differences of opinion. (3) Often reports appear too late to be useful because of the search for agreement. (4) Members involved in the Committee have too many commitments in their home countries and the amount of time they are able to spend on Committee affairs is therefore limited. Senior trades union officials, for example, are unlikely to achieve regular appearances at meetings of the Committee.

On the other hand, the views of the Committee can be useful to the Commission and to the Council in their policy-making and its work does help quite a large number of influential individuals and their assistants to familiarise themselves with the workings of the Community.

In addition to ECOSOC, there are more than 70 consultative bodies helping the Community's work such as the Consultative Committee for the coal and steel industry and the Standing Committee on Employment.

The European Court of Justice

The European Community is such a complex body that a Court is necessary for several reasons. It must ensure that the institutions of the Community act in a constitutional way, fulfilling their Treaty obligations but it also has to ensure the observance of Community rules by member states, firms and individuals within the Community. For these reasons the European Court of Justice was established by Article 136 of the Treaty of Rome. It is based in Luxembourg and is not to be confused with the International Court of Justice at the Hague or the European Commission on Human Rights. It operates independently of all other Community institutions and is the supreme arbiter of Community law. Article 193 of the Treaty of Rome stipulates that 'member states undertake not to submit a dispute concerning the interpretation or application of this Treaty to any method of settlement other than those provided for therein'. This clause effectively prevents other international tribunals being brought into Community affairs.

The ten judges who hold office for six years are drawn one from each member state and are assisted by four advocates-general who are responsible for the preliminary investigation of a matter and for submitting a reasoned opinion to the judges to help them to come to a decision. The deliberations of the judges are kept secret. Their judgment, with reasons, is given publicly in open court but there is only one judgment: no dissenting judgments are given. Whatever differences of view there may have been among the judges are therefore concealed and subsequently no judgment can be weakened by the charge that it is only a majority view.

The Court will hear cases brought by the Commission against member states or against the Council, cases brought by member states against each other or against the Council or Commission or by a person against a Community decision which affects him. The Court can enforce penalties for the infringement of the regulations. It is also responsible for the interpretation of the Treaty of Rome and subsequent legislation. Curiously, there is not a great deal that the Court can do to enforce a judgment. However member states and Community institutions have in practice always complied with its judgments. It seems unlikely that any defiance of the Court will take place because the Court has been given so central a place in the Community structure that such defiance would be tantamount to a fundamental breach of the Treaty itself.

The Court has successfully disposed of a large number of cases since it was set up despite the complexity of many of them. By the end of 1978, 1860 cases had been brought before the Court since 1953 (when it commenced its duties as part of ECSC). Of those, 1369 had been decided, 229 had been withdrawn and only 262 cases were still pending. The three fields of Community activity which created most work for the Court were agriculture, competition policy and social security for migrants, areas where the member states had pre-existing policies of their own and where the integration of two sets of law was difficult. Indeed the universal application of Community law is a slow business since it must be incorporated into ten different legal systems.

In terms of cases brought against member states in recent years, Italy heads the league table with 23 cases, followed by Belgium, France and Britain with 14, 9 and 5 respectively. In November 1981, for example, the Commission decided to take Britain to the Court over measures which Britain had taken to ban imports of poultry, an action which had brought speedy complaint from France.

In 1981 the Court dealt with 323 cases and passed 149 judgments. Through its judgments, the Court of Justice is contributing to the emergence of a veritable European law applicable to all Community institutions, member states, national courts and individuals, with the authority of the Court's judgments in the field of Community law surpassing that of national courts. In cases of non-application of Community law by the Council or member states the Court has been approached for help by individuals and upheld important principles contained in the Treaties, for example equal pay for men and women.

The European Investment Bank (EIB)

Based in Luxembourg, the European Investment Bank was set up as one of the institutions of the EEC under Article 129 of the Treaty of Rome. It is a public institution within the Community and has an independent legal status. It operates on a non-profit basis and its task, as stated in Article 130 of the Rome Treaty, is to contribute to the balanced development of the Community by making loans and giving guarantees to facilitate the financing of: (1) projects in less developed regions; (2) projects for modernising or converting undertakings or for developing fresh activities made necessary by the evolution of the Community; (3) projects of common interest to several member states.

Each member state has one representative, usually the finance minister, on the Board of Governors. The Bank is useful as an additional source of finance; it is not a grant-aiding fund but a bank operating normal banking criteria; its capital is contributed by member states and by its own ability to raise money on the normal markets.

In recent years the EIB has been by far the biggest source of finance within the Community for energy projects. In 1980, for example, 40 per cent of its lending went to energy projects such as nuclear energy stations and energy saving schemes in an effort to reduce the Community's oil requirements by 12 million tons.

In 1981 the Bank's lending capital was doubled to £8 billions with the funds earmarked mainly for regional development and employment schemes. Most of its loans (80 per cent) within the Community go to three member states—Italy, Ireland and the United Kingdom. In 1981, for example, the Bank loaned £15 millions for industrial projects in South-West England and £46 millions for a Leeds mini-computer factory. It also lends money outside the Community to developing countries or associated states like Portugal.

The Bank does not normally provide more than 40 per cent of the cost of any project. Since the Bank is a non-profit making organisation, interest rates charged are close to the rates on the markets from which it obtains its funds. For industrial projects, the term of the loans is normally seven to twelve years, for infrastructure projects up to twenty years. As the Community's principal source of investment finance, the EIB lent 14.4 billion ECU between 1958 and 1980, the amount showing a rapid growth in later years.

Community Law and the Legislative Process

Community law is either embodied in the Treaties themselves and is called the primary legislation of the European Community or it is derived from the Treaties and referred to as secondary legislation. Some Community law may have direct internal effect as law in the member states from the Treaties though to a considerable extent the Treaties only laid out the basic framework of Community law and left the Community institutions to work out the details later.

The Community makes use of five kinds of legal instruments—Regulations, Directives, Decisions, Recommendations and Opinions. Regulations have direct internal effect on the member states. They are legally binding and must be applied directly like national laws. They prevail over national law if any conflict arises between the two. Directives are equally binding on member states as regards the aim to be achieved but it is left to the national authorities as to how these aims are to be carried out. Decisions are usually concerned with specific problems rather than with the Community as a whole. They are binding in every respect on those to whom they are addressed. When a Decision is addressed to a government of a member state they impose binding obligations but do not have direct internal effect as law in the member state; when a Decision is addressed to individuals, it does have direct internal effect in relation to the individuals to whom it is addressed and is binding on the party concerned. Recommendations and Opinions have no binding force.

Community law in the fields covered by the Treaties takes precedence over the national law of the member states and in the case of conflict with national law, Community law is supreme.

The procedure for preparing and adopting Council instruments is as follows. The first stage in the creation of a policy depends on the Commission. The staff of the relevant director-general compiles a first-study report after consultation with national governments, professional bodies and other interested parties. The report is then examined by the commissioner and general guidelines decided. At this stage the commissioner may consult the relevant committee of the European Parliament for its views. Then the Commission staff prepares a draft proposal which it sends to the Council

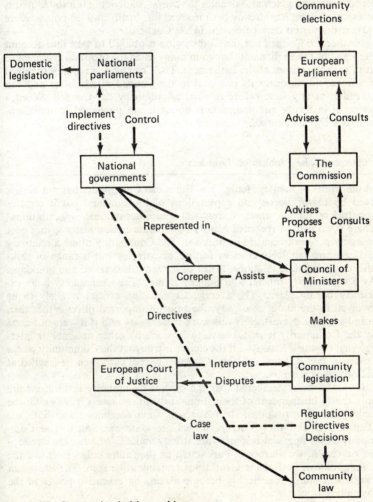

Fig. 4. The Community decision-making process.

and usually to the European Parliament and ECOSOC as well.

The draft proposal is considered in the Committee of Permanent Representatives by one of its specialist working parties and in both the European Parliament and the Economic and Social Committee by specialist committees. The appropriate committee of the European Parliament prepares a draft report on the proposal which the Parliament itself debates, votes on it (including any amendment to the original proposal) and sends its opinion to the Commission and Council. The Economic and Social Committee also sends its opinion to the Commission and Council.

Only when the above opinions have been received can the Council take a decision. It will take notice of the advice of the Committee of Permanent Representatives which also debates the proposal, dividing it into 'A' points where agreement has already been reached informally and 'B' points where further discussion may be needed in the Council.

Neither the Council nor the Commission is obliged to take into account the views of the Parliament though in many cases the proposal is altered to fit in with the wishes of the Parliament. The Commission remains involved in the consideration of its proposal in the Council of Ministers and can amend it at any time before its final adoption by the Council. When a proposal is finally adopted, details about it are published in the Community's *Official Journal*.

Conclusion: The Problem of 'Lourdeur'

In the words of Stanley Henig, 'The European Community has not always lived up to the hopes and expectations of its founders, but it remains nonetheless unique amongst regional and international organisations.' There is no case in recorded history of separate nation states giving over so many powers to central institutions. The Community offers a relatively civilised and relatively efficient forum for carrying out a range of tasks affecting inter-state relations. Much of the work is detailed and mundane. As a Community official told Stanley Henig, 'The Community is an extremely boring place.' The average Commission official is likely to be involved in the minutiae of, say, the price of imported olives rather than grand strategy. Nevertheless this work is necessary and if it were not done by the Community it would have to be done by other national or international organisations. And if the charge is true that the Community works slowly in evolving policies, then the same charge can often be levelled at national governments.

It should be remembered that the central Community institutions are only partly independent of the national institutions (see Figure 4). Of the major central institutions, the Council is state dominated and both the Commission and the Court personnel are state appointed. The Community's own financial resources are strictly limited. Whether the developing powers of the European Parliament or the future enlargement of the Community will affect the institutions remains to be seen. The European Parliament could conceivably become a curb on executive power in the Community.

However, increased Parliamentary power and the growing number of member states could make decision-making in the Community even more difficult. The problem of 'lourdeur' or weighing down of institutions would be aggravated because there would be more institutions and more countries to consult in every decision-making process and the whole process could grind to a halt. Another problem which contributes to 'lourdeur' is siting. It is an administrative nonsense for the Commission to be based mostly in Brussels but partly in Luxembourg and for Parliament to have three sites. The Community needs a capital proper. Decision-making, anyway, has been made more difficult by the recession which has added vigour to a new form of lobbying—Euro-lobbying. Powerful interest groups like COPA (The Committee of Agricultural Organisations) put pressure on the Council and the Commission as was clearly seen in the Brussels Summit of March 1982 when irate French farmers agitated for hefty farm price increases. This was hardly the right atmosphere for co-operative decision-making.

The final factor contributing to 'lourdeur' is of course language. The Community has seven official languages—Danish, Dutch, English, French, German, Greek and Italian. Since Greece joined, translators have had to cope with as many as 42 language pairs since each of the seven official languages may have to be translated into the other six. As a result the institutions now generate between them more than a million pages of translation a year and over 40 per cent of Community administrative costs are made up by translating and interpreting with their back-up services. In 1979 language-related costs were around £214 millions and by 1982 had reached £250 millions.

This problem is not merely a financial one. As the number of languages grows, so do the pressures on efficiency. It is easy to find good translators to work with language pairs such as French or German but there are not enough qualified translators to do the same between, say, Greek and Danish. The result is that the work of the institutions suffers because essential documents have not been circulated in time for meetings which have then to be postponed. The problem is now an urgent one and the Commission is investigating the possibility that computer-based technology may be the means of easing the burden on the language services. It has proposed a research programme aimed at developing a European machine translation system.

Further Reading

Henig, S., *Power and Decision in Europe*, Europotentials Press, London, 1980.
Kirchner, E., *The Role of Interest Groups in the European Community*, Gower, London, 1981.
Palmer, M., *The European Parliament*, Pergamon, London, 1981.
Noel, E., *The European Community: How It Works*, HMSO, London, 1979.

Questions

(1) Why have the European Council and the Committee of Permanent Representatives become more important in recent years?

(2) Describe the main powers of the Council of Ministers.

(3) What are the chief functions of the European Commission?

(4) Explain how a Commission proposal becomes part of Community law.

(5) Define and account for the problem of 'lourdeur' in the running of Community institutions.

4
The Common Agricultural Policy and Fishing

The Common Agricultural Policy (CAP)

The Underlying Problems of Agriculture

At the time of the signing of the Rome Treaty too many people in the original Six depended on farming for their main source of income; indeed 25 per cent of the total labour force was employed in agriculture compared to less than 5 per cent in the United Kingdom. The British did not face such problems because farms in Britain had been restructured by the enclosures of the eighteenth century while the repeal of the Corn Laws in 1846 had drastically exposed agriculture to the cold winds of competition and cheap food from overseas after 1873. These developments had pushed workers out of British agriculture but at the same time the process of industrialisation attracted rural workers into the factories where they could gain higher wages.

Such factors had not operated to the same degree on the Continent where the agricultural labour force remained worse off than most groups. Many farms were uneconomically small; about two-thirds of farms were between one and ten hectares in size compared to one third in the United Kingdom. Those who worked on the land were subject to forces that were often beyond human control. The effects of drought, flood or livestock disease could result in smaller production than hoped for by the farmers. On the other hand, favourable conditions could result in production far in excess of that planned by farmers. When actual agricultural output deviated from planned output, fluctuations in agricultural prices resulted with the individual farmer liable to lose out either way. Excess output reduced the prices which the farmer could obtain while though a shortage in output increased prices the individual farmer would often not have much to sell. Thus a sort of 'Catch 22' situation arose.

Other factors militated against living standards in farming. In advanced economies, as his income rose, the consumer tended to spend a smaller proportion of it on agricultural products. In economists' jargon, the income elasticity of demand for food was low. Therefore in Western Europe there was a historical tendency for a relative fall in demand for farm products with farming incomes lagging behind the incomes of groups engaged in non-farming occupations. Also as agriculture became more efficient, overall supply of food increased but this tended to keep agricultural prices down, especially when the competition from outside Europe (for example cheap American grain) became fierce from the 1870s on.

It was partly for these reasons that the founding fathers of the Community felt it necessary to introduce agricultural stabilisation policies. It was believed that farm prices should be stabilised and farm incomes raised to the national average on grounds of equity, especially as increases in agricultural productivity were not normally as great as in manufacturing. Strategic considerations also affected the statesmen's thinking in the 1950s; it was believed that reliance on supplies of foreign food in an uncertain world was unwise. Finally, practical political interests helped to bring about the adoption of important safeguards for agriculture in the Rome Treaty. The French government, influenced by its powerful farming lobby, agreed to free trade in industrial goods, which would help West German industrial exports to France, only if French farmers could be materially assisted to boost their agricultural exports to West Germany. Therefore in 1957 it was agreed under Article 38 of the Treaty that the development of a common market for agricultural goods should be accompanied by the establishment of a common agricultural policy.

The Aims of the CAP

Articles 38 to 45 of the Treaty of Rome were designed to ensure that a common market could extend to agriculture and agricultural products. Article 39 set out the aims of the CAP: (a) to increase agricultural productivity by developing technical progress and by ensuring the rational development of agricultural production and the optimum utilisation of the factors of production, particularly labour; (b) to ensure, thereby, a fair standard of living for the agricultural population particularly by the increasing of the individual earnings of persons engaged in agriculture; (c) to stabilise markets; (d) to guarantee regular supplies; (e) to ensure reasonable prices in supplies to consumers.

It can be seen that these objectives are mutually contradictory as El-Agraa has pointed out: 'Any policy which aims at providing adequate environmental conditions, secure food supplies and agricultural incomes equal to the national average interferes with the economy's natural development . . . the provision of stable farm incomes, let alone rising farm incomes, is not compatible with the promise of stable agricultural prices.' Perhaps sensibly the Treaty of Rome left unresolved the detailed methods by which these incompatible goals were to be achieved but Articles 40 to 47 pointed to the need for common competition rules, market organisation and price policy; the setting up of the European Agricultural Guidance and Guarantee Fund (EAGGF, often known by its French initials FEOGA); joint research; consumption and promotion measures and the granting of aid.

It was left to the Commission to put flesh on the skeleton. This took from July 1958 to December 1960 when the Council adopted the fundamental principles of CAP. The main components are: (a) A single market, implying common prices, harmonisation of relevant legislation and free movement of produce. (b) Community preference implying protection of the single market from world market fluctuations through a levy system. When world market prices are lower than those of the Community, a variable charge or levy brings the price of produce imported from third countries up to the level of common prices. This makes possible free access to the Community market without disturbing European farmers. When Community prices are below the world market, the system can go into reverse so as to protect European consumers by discouraging exports. In times of shortage the Community also protects consumers by lifting import levies temporarily. (c) Common funding of the CAP by the EAGGF.

The operation of CAP really falls into two areas: (1) price policy and (2) policies to improve the structure of Community agriculture.

The Price Policy and the Green Currencies

The price policy is concerned with fixing internal prices for EEC farmers. Separate price levels or regimes are established for most major products and they are decided annually by the Council of Ministers. For each product covered by CAP, a common market organisation has been introduced and it aims at fixing a common price for each commodity throughout the Community. In the absence of a common European currency, common prices were expressed in agricultural units of account (UA) because the EEC did not wish to make any particular country's currency seem to be more important than any other. It was not an actual currency but a common measure of value of agricultural products. The initial value of the UA was equivalent to one United States dollar or 0.888670888 grams of fine gold.

A target price level representing a desired market price is set for most products annually. Should the market price fall, a 'floor' price (or intervention price) for selected major products becomes operative in the domestic market. In the event of surplus production, commodities may be bought by intervention agencies to maintain a minimum wholesale market price level.

A common barrier operates in the form of minimum import prices (threshold prices) set annually for goods from third countries. Variable import levies compensate for the difference between fixed Community prices and fluctuating world prices. This protects the Community market from price fluctuations and from competition from low-priced imports. In the event of an EEC surplus in a particular commodity, the relevant management committee may authorise subsidies on exports of that commodity to third countries. This export subsidy allows Community produced goods to be competitive in world markets even though EEC domestic agricultural prices are usually above world prices.

The negotiation of prices is subject to an established procedure. The Director-General for Agriculture in the Commission works out a draft proposal with the help of experts from national governments. The draft is submitted for discussion to farmers' representatives, e.g. COPA (Comité des organisations professionelles agricoles des pays de la Communauté economique européenne) which is the federation of all farmers' unions and the representative of the farming lobby. The Economic and Social Committee and the Agricultural Committee of the European Parliament are also consulted. The proposal which may be amended at any stage is finally submitted to the Council of Ministers for decision before implementation by the Commission and member governments. The annual price review as a regulation is legally binding on all member states.

From 1962 responsibility for financing common measures was vested in the European Agricultural Guarantee and Guidance Fund (EAGGF). The Guarantee section has to finance price support measures and the Guidance section is concerned with structural reform. Up to 1971 the Fund operated by reimbursing expenditure already incurred by member governments. Now estimates of future expenditure are submitted and member governments are awarded the necessary finance in advance. By 1977 Community spending on agriculture had reached 6952 UAs, the great bulk (6662 UAs) being spent on the Guarantee section. The major part of this spending is on dairy products.

Expenditure on market support measures keeps increasing and far exceeds the revenue generated by CAP's duties and import levies. It is the major reason why by the 1980s the Community was finding it difficult to balance its budget.

During the 1960s it was possible to envisage the successful operation of the pricing policy in a period of stable exchange rates. However, in September 1968 following the 'French Revolution' the French franc was devalued and in October 1968 the Deutsche Mark was revalued. When a country devalues, its farm prices in terms of national currencies rise (in 1968 for example one UA became equivalent to more French francs). Also the price of imports rises and the price of its exports falls. In the case of a revaluation the opposite occurs. To prevent her enjoying the unfair competitive advantage of lower prices of her agricultural exports, France had to levy duties on those exports. To protect the French consumer from the higher price of agricultural imports a subsidy called a Monetary Compensation Amount (MCA) was paid.

Revaluation reduced farm prices and incomes in Germany in terms of Deutsche Marks because one UA became worth fewer Deutsche Marks. The price of German food exports was increased and the price of food imports reduced, thus making German farmers vulnerable to competition from French farmers benefiting from the devalued Franc. Border taxes were therefore levied on agricultural imports into Germany while German agricultural exports received subsidies. This system of border taxes and subsidies (MCAs) has become a regular feature of the CAP in the 1970s owing to further changes in exchange rates by member countries.

This was the origin of the green currencies which are the working currencies in the farm sector and now each member has its own 'green' currency for example the 'green' pound. Farm prices for producers are fixed in UA and then converted into national currencies at the 'green' currency rate. A 'green' pound, therefore, is used for buying farm products from EEC countries or selling farm products to them. The 'green' currency or representative rate is fixed annually by the Council of Ministers; the decision requires unanimous support so that if a country does not want to change its green rate, it does not have to. For a time British governments refused to devalue the 'green' pound in line with the fall in sterling so that the gap between the rate for the 'green' pound and the sterling market rate widened to more than 40 per cent by 1976. By using the 'green' pound Britain operated a dual exchange rate—the market rate for the great bulk of her purchases and the overvalued representative rate for her farm products. This meant that prices for British farmers were kept down while the British consumer benefited—at least until 1979.

The use of MCAs expanded in the 1970s in an effort to maintain unity of markets after all European currencies 'floated' in 1971 and were no longer tied by a fixed exchange rate to the US dollar. The UA itself remained tied to the US dollar until 1973; it was then revalued using an average of several European currencies (those of Germany, Denmark, Belgium, Luxembourg, The Netherlands and originally France—the 'Joint Float' currencies).

MCAs have allowed Community trade to continue in the absence of common pricing but they have permitted the real level of prices to vary among member countries. They have allowed growing distortion of production as farmers in countries with strong currencies are paid more than farmers in countries with weak currencies. Also MCAs have taken an increasing share of the EEC budget, about one quarter of the total expenditure of CAP. Nevertheless some elements of pricing unity remain. Changes in UA prices apply to all countries and the Community can still give preference to its own producers as against third country suppliers.

The annual price-fixing exercise has posed major problems for the Community and negotiations have often been most acrimonious for several reasons. The exercise is itself difficult because it requires estimates of future production and markets. The tendency has been to fix prices which lead to overproduction rather than underproduction so as to guarantee adequate supplies and give the small farmers a high enough level of prices. But the policy means transfer of income between member states and those who gain from the policy (e.g. France) are anxious to resist change, those who lose (e.g. UK) demand reform. The individual governments are also influenced by the strength of the farm lobbies in their countries. Thus in 1981 the French government with an election in the offing held out for a substantial average 9.5 per cent increase in farm prices (higher than the average inflation rate expected among the Ten). The French farmers had made their feelings clear by demonstrations in Brussels and throwing rotten eggs at the Conference building itself.

Another problem of the price-fixing exercise is the bias in the way the Guarantee section spends its money. Most of it is spent on commodities produced in the northern sector of the Community, for example beef, cereals and milk products whereas products from the Mediterranean zone have received relatively little support. Yet the southern region contains most of the poor farmers. This issue will become more difficult now that Greece is a member and especially so when Spain and Portugal join the Community.

Structural Improvements in Agriculture

In 1960 there were many small marginal farms in the Community. About half the six million farms were under five hectares (i.e. just over 12 acres) although many of the farmers were part-timers. In 1960 the average size was just under 11 hectares (just over 27 acres). During the 1960s the agricultural working population decreased by about one third (approximately four million people), but the agricultural sector did not streamline its structure in terms of size of farms.

In 1962 the Community set up a guidance section in the agricultural fund to finance individual farm projects submitted by each member state and find solutions to specific problems in an individual state or on a Community level. The projects had to further the basic objectives of the CAP.

However, the agricultural structure showed little improvement by the late 1960s and in 1968 Dr Sicco Mansholt who was the Agricultural Commissioner at the time brought out a memorandum on agricultural reform known as the Mansholt Plan. He emphasised that market supports by themselves would not solve the agricultural problem. His plan aimed: (a) to reduce the number of people engaged in agriculture by offering older people early retirement benefits and offering younger people training and education so that they could opt for alternative jobs; and (b) at merging the large number of uneconomic small farms to create larger farm units and also to reduce the area of cultivated land.

The Plan encountered shocked criticism and only in 1972 did the Council adopt a much watered-down version in the so-called Reform Directives. These directives were aimed at promoting farm modernisations, encouragement to specific farmers to leave farming and to allocate their land for the improvement of remaining holdings and guidance and training of farmers.

These directive were however 'blanket' measures and were likely to create problems in poorer farming areas, for example rural depopulation. Therefore in 1975 a further Directive was adopted on hill-farming to compensate farmers for the natural handicaps with which they have to contend. The aim was to persuade farmers to continue farming in these regions, carry out modernisation, keep the population at acceptable levels and conserve the countryside.

In 1978 certain measures were adopted to correct the bias in favour of northern products. These measures were called the Mediterranean 'package'. These included the provision of more finance in the Mediterranean regions for promoting better marketing structures, help for irrigation works in the Mezzogiorno in Southern Italy, improvement of public amenities in certain rural areas and the faster restructuring of vineyards in some Mediterranean regions of France. These measures demonstrated that one objective of CAP was now social.

Is the CAP Good for Britain?

Some commentators, including the Conservative Farm Minister after 1979, Mr Peter Walker, have claimed that the CAP has its virtues and has on balance been 'good' for Britain. They have used three main arguments to defend that position. Firstly they have stressed that food prices did not soar as a result of British membership of the Community and it is true that between 1973 and 1977 they rose only 3 per cent. When sterling was weak between 1975 and 1979, the Labour Farm Minister, Mr John Silkin, kept British food prices below Community levels by not adjusting the green pound's exchange rate in line with the real pound. As we saw on page 53, an overvalued green currency keeps farm prices down, and at one point British farm prices were 40 per cent lower than official Community farm prices.

But from 1979 when its value as a petrocurrency was seen, the value of sterling soared. At this very time the new British Farm Minister, Peter Walker, chose to devalue the 'green' pound. As we saw on page 52, the devaluation of the green pound has the effect of raising food prices nearer the Community level. As the green pound continued to rise against other currencies, British food prices actually rose *above* the Community level by 1981. Mr Walker was unwilling to counter this by an upvaluing of the green pound because farming incomes would then have been reduced. Had he done so, he would not only have benefited the consumer but would have reduced British contributions to the Community budget because food imports would not have been taxed so heavily.

Defenders of the CAP have also pointed to Britain's growing self-sufficiency in food since 1973 and again this is true. In 1972 for example Britain produced 65 per cent of its cereal needs and by 1982 was producing 96 per cent. In the same period production of milk powder rose from 64 per cent of what was needed to four times more than was needed. Such increases helped the British balance of payments because less food was imported and more food, particularly processed food, was exported. Against these arguments it should be pointed out that Britain was still importing 40 per cent of its food and that the CAP raised sharply the cost of these imports.

The third argument has been that British farmers should receive generous treatment as their economic performance has been impressive. Between 1973 and 1982 British farm output rose by 15 per cent and labour productivity by 29 per cent. Certainly British farmers have done well out of CAP, particularly since 1979. They have been protected from the worst ravages of the recession and from the effects of the over-valued pound which, were it not for the existence of the green currencies, would have made food cheaper. The decline in employment on British farms has virtually ended; in 1972 there were 298,000 farm workers and in 1982 there were 294,000, although more of them worked part-time. In 1982 British farmers increased their incomes by an astonishing average of 45 per cent.

The Community price support system has encouraged farmers to change the shape of British farming. Horticulture, beef production and milk sales have declined but several other sectors have expanded. The production of oilseed rape (used in vegetable oil) has increased from 11,000 tonnes in 1972 to 300,000 tonnes in 1982, as a result of Community subsidies. Cereals output has switched from barley towards wheat and in 1981 Britain exported 1.1 million tonnes of wheat compared with 21,000 tonnes in 1972.

There has been a big expansion in the manufactured sales of dairy output—that is cheese, yoghurt and butter—because liquid milk does not attract a Community subsidy. Finally lamb price support, introduced in 1980, has encouraged sheep farming in the hilly areas of Wales and Scotland.

However, the CAP has been directly responsible for damaging British interests in several ways. In recent years the steep rise in British food prices to above the Community average has obviously hindered the government's attempts to control inflation. Secondly the CAP's gargantuan appetite has meant that there has been little cash left over for those Community policies from which Britain could hope to benefit, for example the Regional and Social Funds. Nor has the CAP proved to be an unmixed blessing for British farmers. Some farming sectors have benefited, especially dairy produce, meat and cereals. Other sectors, in particular fruit and vegetables, have been subject to intense competition from other Community countries. The classic case has been that of the notorious and despised French Golden Delicious apple! This high-yielding, blight-resistant, easily-marketed, if completely tasteless product had by 1981 grabbed one third of the British market and as a result many English apple orchards were turned over to other uses.

But the main argument against the CAP in terms of British interest is that it has always been the fundamental cause of Britain's excess contributions to the Community budget (see also chapter 16). Because Britain's farm sector is small, the British taxpayer pays far more into the Community farm fund than is paid back to British farmers. There is also a substantial transfer of funds from Britain to the Community food exporting countries like France because Britain has to import food at high Community prices rather than at lower world prices. In 1982 a group of agricultural economists at the University of Newcastle, L. Hubbard, D. R. Harvey, A. Buckwell and K. Thomson, calculated that the overall financial cost of the CAP to Britain in 1981 was 2.5 billion ecus (£1.4 billion). This figure was made up of Britain's excess contributions to the Community farm fund and the financial transfer due to buying high-priced Community food rather than food at world prices.

Small wonder then that British governments, Labour and Conservative alike, have since 1973 attempted to reduce the British budgetary contributions caused by the CAP regime. Yet it is these very efforts that have caused British unpopularity in the Community, especially in French circles. In March 1982, the French Farm Minister, the fiery Edith Cresson roundly accused the British government of using terrorist tactics in its negotiations.

Unfortunately the CAP regime is now a major French interest and every French government, be it Socialist, Gaullist or any other, wishes to demonstrate that it can defend the well-being of French farmers. Anglo-French relations seem doomed to remain clouded by this issue. However, in conclusion it should be remembered that the CAP has created bad relations between several member countries and not merely between Britain and France. In Edith Cresson's first year as French Farm Minister (1981–82) the French were at loggerheads with the British over lamb and turkeys, with Italy over imported Italian wine, with Spain over fruit and with the Commission over Madame Cresson's illegal plans for national subsidies to French farmers.

Nevertheless the main quarrels over the CAP have been between Britain and France. What is worrying for the future of British farmers is the new export drive by French agriculture which started in 1980. France had already been Europe's biggest food producer, enjoying one quarter of the Community's food exports between 1973 and 1979. In 1980 the French government set a new ambitious target for a $6 billion food export surplus and created a new ministry for the food processing industry which gave food processing companies priority access to regional aid and tax rebates in return for bold export plans. The row over turkeys was a result of this kind of expansion. The company that opened a huge turkey factory in Brittany had been awarded regional aid subsidies and local rate rebates because its main market would be Britain.

France's export expansion was also increased throughout the Community by a marketing agency Sopexa which is partly government financed. In the future, Anglo-French relations could well be strained by French exports to Britain of cheap long-life milk from, among others, the Union Laitière Normande, another firm helped by the French government.

Evaluation—the Successes and Failures of the CAP

Despite criticism, the CAP has some successes to its credit. The various agricultural support systems that existed in EEC countries before the formation of the Community have been replaced by a common, albeit complicated, system. To a certain extent, also, intra-EEC free trade in agricultural products has been accomplished through the removal of intra-EEC trade restrictions.

The EEC has become more and more self-sufficient in many basic farm products even though the Community depends a great deal on imported agricultural raw materials such as fertilisers and animal feed, i.e. the aim of secure food supplies has been achieved. By the late 1970s the EEC enjoyed virtually complete self-sufficiency in pork, beef, veal and sugar, complete self-sufficiency in milk and dairy products and more than complete self-sufficiency in wheat and butter production.

Some progress has been made in reducing the size of the agricultural population and in increasing the size of farm holdings. The proportion of the population engaged in agriculture in 1955 was 26.1 per cent; by 1976 the proportion for the enlarged Community was 8.4 per cent with the numbers of persons engaged in agriculture falling from nearly 18 millions (for the 6) to 8.3 millions (in the 9).

If it is argued that this is still too large an agricultural sector, then one may counter by saying that agriculture should not be seen merely in economic terms but in terms of political and social considerations. It provides employment and can help to retain a pleasant environment; this justifies protection especially when most eminent competitors like Japan and the United States protect their agricultural sectors. Therefore the Community should continue to help the small farmers of France, Germany and Italy. Southern Italy, for example, has been called the Third World of European agriculture; farmers there are often desperately poor and excluded from the cash economy; there is no alternative employment nearby when towns like Naples suffer unemployment rates of 20 per cent. It can be argued therefore that it is better to keep such farmers going to offset urban over-crowding and prevent rural depopulation. Directive 75/268 dealing with mountain and hill-farming in disadvantaged areas means that special provision can be made for poor farmers and in 1980 they received £52 millions in aid.

The charge about mountains and lakes (the popular name for the surplus agricultural produce) is becoming less valid. As early as 1977 a *Which* Report pointed out that some of the so-called mountains were really mole-hills; the barley surplus would last only two days, the wheat surplus only a fortnight and the beef surplus less than three weeks. By 1981 considerable progress had been made in reducing the milk and butter mountains. The peak of the butter mountain was reached in 1979 and amounted to 590,000 tonnes; by 1981 it was a mere 39,700, only enough for a week's consumption in the EEC. Much of the surplus was sold abroad at cut prices but cheap butter was also made available to pensioners, hospitals, prisons, armed forces and schools within the Community. The tactic of subsidised sales has been attacked but such sales are cheaper than the alternative of storages. Other alternative methods of disposing of surpluses all have their drawbacks. If the surplus food was generally released for sale at knock-down prices, it would push down the prices offered for farm produce. EEC governments would then have to start buying farm produce again in order to keep prices up to the guaranteed levels.

Finally in this survey of the advantages of the CAP may be mentioned some comments of the Commissioner for the internal market, Karl-Heinz Narjes. In October 1981 he pointed out that by the end of the 1980s there will be twice as many people in the world as in 1957. Developing countries by then will have a grain deficit of 100 million tonnes and will need to raise their agricultural production by 4 per cent per year merely to meet their most pressing needs. As their current rate of increase of agricultural production is only 2.9 per cent, a world food crisis seems imminent. In the view of Narjes, such considerations justified a protected European agriculture which guaranteed security of supplies.

In this connection, the CAP has been successful in that its protection has spurred a dramatic growth in agricultural productivity. European farmers have had the confidence to make use of improvement grants and technical aid to become competitive with continents blest with more sun and land. The average 'Euro-cow' now pumps out twice as much milk as it did in 1957. Overall quality has also improved as the organisation of product markets is now virtually complete. This has had enormous consequences for harmonisation in the food-processing industry. For example common standards now exist for conditions under which animals are slaughtered as well as for the grading of grains and eggs. Much remains to be done for by 1978 only 7 of the 40 directives planned as part of the 1973 food harmonisation programme had been adopted. However food manufacturers are slowly finding it more easy to move their products across national frontiers without the hindrance of technical barriers to trade, such as different provisions in each country governing the safety, composition or labelling of food.

There are of course alternative farming policies to the CAP system of high guaranteed prices, for example the purely national farm policies advocated by the Labour Party, but such policies would not necessarily be cheaper overall. Before Britain joined the EEC British governments used to support farmers through deficiency payments—subsidies to top up incomes rather than through high guaranteed prices. The big advantage of a deficiency payments system is that prices are fixed by the market, not by governments. This would normally ensure that unwanted surpluses are not produced. Prices would normally be lower and British consumers might save £1.8 million if Britain returned to such a system. However the cost to the taxpayer would be high if such a return took place. Various estimates have been made of this cost for 1981, though they are all informed guesses because they depend on the level of prices chosen. Mr Christopher Tugendhat, then the Community's budget commissioner, suggested a figure of £2 billion; the Labour Party estimated the cost at £1.7 billion, the assumption being that production and farmers' incomes would be at 1980 levels. This compares with the direct budgetary cost of the CAP to Britain in 1981 of just over £1 billion according to the Newcastle study mentioned earlier. It is perhaps significant that British governments were already moving away from a deficiency payments system *before* 1973 because of the high level of Treasury spending involved.

Against the alleged advantages can be ranged a formidable array of problems and failures. The CAP has failed to achieve real progress on structural aspects. For example, even though the drift from the country to the town is a natural one it is hard to see how the CAP has encouraged farmers to seek alternative occupations. Many farmers on low incomes have indeed preferred to stay in farming because they are remote from alternative employment and because they have some status and property in their own community. And though their income may be poor, their land has appreciated making them relatively rich in terms of capital. Many farmers are old and find it harder to retrain or adjust to urban life.

The problem of small farms remains a difficult one; in 1977 the number of holdings under ten hectares in size comprised 53 per cent of all holdings in West Germany, 35 per cent of all holdings in France and 30 per cent of all holdings in Denmark.

Though the CAP has helped to raise the general level of farm incomes, there are some very unsatisfactory features. The CAP is a policy of high prices and therefore those who produce most gain the most benefit from the policy. However, farmers in poor areas produce little and derive little benefit from the policy. Thus the CAP makes rich farmers richer and increases regional income disparities.

The CAP also gives greater price support to products produced in the north than in the south. Livestock and cereals receive more support than fruit, vegetables and wine. In terms of fairness, this is unfortunate because many of the farmers in the south (the Midi in France, the Mezzogiorno in Italy) have very low incomes and depend heavily on products which receive the least support.

In global terms, the CAP can be seen as undermining the interests of the Third World. By disposing of surpluses to countries behind the Iron Curtain, the EEC has deprived the developing countries of potential export earnings. And by protecting its own agriculture, the EEC is competing unfairly against the imports from these countries. In this context it should be remembered what a massive exporter of food the Community has now become. It is the world's chief exporter of dairy produce, the world's second largest exporter of sugar behind Cuba, the world's second largest exporter of beef behind Australia and the world's largest exporter of poultry.

The CAP has failed to provide reasonable stable prices for the consumer. Indeed the initial prices were set at the high German level of farm prices. The consumer who is hit worst by this high food price policy is the poor consumer because he has to spend a higher proportion of his income on food than has a wealthy consumer. A policy which increases the price of food therefore represents a higher proportional tax on the expenditure of the poor, even though the total amount of tax collected per head will be higher from a rich family than from a poor family. Therefore the CAP has an adverse effect on the distribution of real incomes. For a period in the 1970s, food prices, it is true, did rise less than the average rate of inflation but this trend has been reversed in recent years with average price rises in food in 1981 and 1982 being 9 per cent and 10.5 per cent respectively. Such price rises are not only socially unjust; they may well encourage the creation of record food mountains in the mid-1980s.

It is the mountains and lakes and the expense involved in guaranteed support prices for farmers that remain the major criticisms of the CAP. Surpluses have been embarrassingly large particularly in respect of dairy products and wine even though such surpluses were being better controlled in the 1980s. The CAP consumes a huge proportion of the Community budget. In 1980 it swallowed up three quarters of total Community expenditure. As a consequence other areas of Community activity were starved of funds; Development Co-operation was allocated 11 per cent of the Budget fund, the Regional Fund 6 per cent, the Social Fund 5 per cent, Administration 5 per cent and Energy, the Environment and Transport a paltry 1 per cent.

The CAP is indeed a very expensive policy to operate. In 1981 it required financing to the tune of 13 billion ECU (£6.5 billion). On top of that, national governments have still handed out extra money from their own budgets. In 1977, the latest year for which the Commission has complete figures, the then nine governments spent a further 13.6 billion ECU on farming. The Rome Treaty forbids such national subsidies but they have become more common as the CAP has become short of money.

Only 10 per cent of CAP expenditure has been spent on the Guidance Section. Ninety per cent (and in 1981 more than 95 per cent) was spent on the Guarantee Section. Much of this money has gone on export refunds which enable traders to sell high-cost Community food on low price world markets. From 1977 to 1982 the cost of these refunds more than trebled to just under 5 billion ECU (£2.75 billion). To this item should be added storage charges of over a billion ECU. As a result the overall cost of disposing of surpluses outside the Community is accounting for half of all expenditure on the CAP. The chief beneficiaries of these subsidised sales of food have been Eastern Europe and the Middle East. In 1980, for example, the Russians bought 164,000 tonnes of surplus meat, 142,000 tonnes of butter and 832,000 tonnes of sugar from the EEC.

The worst and most costly surpluses are in the dairy sector which consumes more than a third of CAP spending. Output of milk has been increasing by 3 per cent a year but consumption of milk products inside the Community is static. The Commission has estimated that by 1985 European farmers will be producing 110 million tonnes of dairy produce a year but that Community consumers will only consume 82 million tonnes.

In the most notorious year of Community surpluses, 1978, Europe's stores were filled with more than a million tonnes of skimmed milk powder and 250,000 tonnes of butter. Only by subsidised sales to third countries were these mountains reduced and now the EEC accounts for 60 per cent of world exports of butter and milk powder, 71 per cent of condensed milk exports and 40 per cent of cheese exports. Perishable products like fruit and vegetables were simply destroyed.

Good harvests in 1982 in cereals, fruit and sugar plus rises in the production of dairy and beef output have coincided with good harvests in other food exporting countries outside the Community. Such a situation seems likely to increase the cost of disposing of the new Community farm surpluses and to increase also the proportion of the Community budget swallowed by CAP expenditure. Since 1977 when the cost of CAP absorbed 74 per cent of the total Community budget, the percentage figure had fallen each year, reaching 63 per cent in 1981. The estimated figure for 1983 is 68 per cent.

With such amounts of money available, it is not surprising that irregularities have occurred. In 1980 thirteen such cases were discovered and one at least was spectacular—the great Italian tomato scandal. In 1978 the Community had decided to help tomato canning in Southern Italy. Tomato processors falsified the certificates which stated how many tonnes of tomatoes had been bought for canning, in some cases merely by adding an extra zero to their figures. The processors were already buying the tomatoes at below Community minimum prices. The Commission's motives were no doubt laudable; tomato production in the region had been very high and the farmers were dependent on the canneries to buy up their tomato crops. But a hundred people were arrested for fraud in a case which cost the Community at least 130 million ECU. In 1983 news broke that the Mafia were involved in an olive oil fraud which was costing the Community 200 million ECU a year.

Canny farmers have also profited from the green money system by smuggling. When Britain had a negative MCA, Irish farmers could load their cereals into trucks, drive into Northern Ireland and collect an import subsidy. They would then drive out along a road without border controls, pick up new papers and drive through again (with the same load of cereals) to collect another MCA. The swing in recent years to a positive MCA has simply meant that the smuggling has had to be in the opposite direction.

Such devices are of course not confined to the Irish. Belgian farmers have walked their cattle or pigs into Holland at dead of night, to have them slaughtered there so as to disguise the livestock's origin. They then have imported the meat back into Belgium. The reason for resorting to this practice is that Holland had a positive MCA of 5.4 per cent (equivalent to an export subsidy) while Belgium had a negative MCA of 3.1 per cent (equivalent to an import subsidy). As a result Belgian farmers picked up a total 8.5 per cent subsidy (the sum of the Dutch and Belgian MCAs).

Finally the CAP has begun to damage trade relations with the United States (see also chapter 13). European farm exports into America's traditional markets, helped by export subsidies worth $2.2 billion, had by 1982 helped to intensify the worst incomes crisis which American farmers had suffered since the 1930s. Community exports had soared to a point where they were violating an agreement made with the Americans in the GATT Tokyo round. In 1980 the Community then agreed that subsidies for agriculture should continue but only if they were not used to expand markets beyond traditional shares. By 1982 the Americans claimed with justice that the Community had increased its share in both cereals and sugar, as well as other markets. The American government therefore opened cases for arbitration in GATT against Community dumping of flour and sugar and was considering similar action over pasta, canned fruit, poultry, pears and raisins. It gave a clear warning against Commission proposals to cut back on imports from the United States of soya and corn gluten feed. It promised retaliation if the Community continued to expand its export of cereals on the world market.

It seems clear that if the CAP is not to bedevil the future of the Community, a number of changes are urgently required. The question of state aids is in general a vexed one and increasingly so in agriculture. The Community needs to strengthen its hand in this area to restrict such aids particularly in view of the fact that such aids are usually motivated by a desire for increased exports.

Even more urgent is the need to reduce the cost of the CAP, thus allowing a fairer share of funds for other important Community policies. Community farm prices should be brought closer to those received by farmers in competing third countries and the prices guaranteed for farmers should not be so high as to encourage surplus output. Too often prices for Community agricultural products have been much higher than prices abroad; for example prices for Community cereals have been 20 per cent higher than the American level. Therefore, whether the agricultural produce is consumed in the Community or exported with the help of large subsidies

Table 1. Europe's Farmers

| | Agriculture's Share in: | | Share in | |
	Employment % (1981)	GNP % (1981)	EEC farm output % (1980)	National Farm Spending million ECU (1977)
Britain	2.8	2.3	12.2	2,188
Holland	4.9	3.5	7.9	378
Luxembourg	5.6	2.0	0.1	43
Belgium	2.9	2.9	3.4	328
France	8.4	3.8	26.6	5,703
Italy	13.0	6.7	20.8	1,315
West Germany	5.9	2.2	18.8	1,974
Ireland	18.9	12.0	2.1	270
Denmark	8.4	6.0	3.7	417
Greece	30.3	14.2	4.4	n.a.

to bring its price down to the world levels, the burden on the Community budget is considerable.

Community farm prices should be related to strict production targets which should be seen as a level of output above which official price support would cease or at least be progressively reduced. Indeed it would make sense to have penal taxes on overproduction of agricultural goods in considerable surplus. But such measures, though they may make economic sense, seem unlikely to be politically viable, given the strength and influence of the farming lobby.

Towards a Common Fisheries Policy

The Problems of Fisheries in the Community

Article 38 of the Rome Treaty defines agricultural products as 'the products of the soil, of stockfarming and of fisheries and products of first stage processing directly related to the foregoing'. Fish are therefore included as agricultural products and the same objectives apply to fishing as were set out for farming in general on page 50.

The Commission first published a report on the proposed Common Fisheries Policy (CFP) in 1966. The central idea was that there should be equal access for all member states to the territorial waters of other Community members and the report provided for a Common market organisation, assistance for restructuring the industry and incentives for the establishment of producers' organisations. At the same time they established the system of support, guidance and guarantee prices for withdrawal of supplies under an intervention scheme, similar to that already operating under the CAP.

Discussions on these issues in the Council were lengthy and a common policy for fisheries was not established until 1970 when agreement was hurried through. The agreement happened rather conveniently for the Six as the final series of negotiations for enlargement of the Community were about to begin and the prospective new members—the United Kingdom, Denmark, the Republic of Ireland and Norway—had most of the fish. It remains unclear whether the introduction of the CFP at that time was a deliberate manoeuvre or an unfortunate coincidence. Hardly surprisingly the candidates for membership objected to the principle of free access for all EEC vessels to Community fish resources but it was part of the *acquis communautaire* taken on by them when they joined in 1973. However, it was agreed in Article 100 of the Treaty of Accession that all members could until 1982 restrict fishing within a six mile limit and in certain areas a twelve mile limit, to vessels which had traditionally fished in those waters and which operated from nearby ports. The door was thus left open for arrangements to be made which would protect the interests of member states with strong fishing industries.

Unfortunately the basic position of the fishing industry within the Community deteriorated in the early 1970s. As traditional fishing grounds became more and more overfished, non-EEC countries began to take a more exclusive approach to the waters around their shores. Iceland which had introduced a 50 mile limit in 1972 extended the zone to 200 miles in 1975. Norway which had opted out of Community membership partly because it had not obtained better conditions for its fisheries introduced trawler free zones of between 12 and 50 miles in 1975. In 1976 both the Faroes and Canada decided to establish 200 mile limits. These areas of the Atlantic had been the traditional fishing grounds of the United Kingdom and West Germany for cod, haddock and hake and these members had to turn increasingly to the already overfished North Sea. Technological advances contributed to the problem. Better navigational aids, new net designs, the growing use of purse seiners and pair trawlers all made fishing more effective and led to the Community waters being over-exploited.

In 1976 the Commission put forward new proposals for a fisheries regime that might meet the needs of the crisis. The major innovation was the Community total allowable catch (TAC). Each species of fish would be allotted a TAC on an annual basis. It would then be allocated to member states on the basis of historic catch levels while taking into account the special needs of certain areas such as Ireland and the northern part of the United Kingdom. The TAC would be a feasible objective as the Community would introduce its own 200 mile limit. It had been the intention to wait for an international agreement under the auspices of the United Nations Conference on the Law of the Sea before declaring the limit but not only were Community vessels being forced to fish more in territorial waters but so were third country vessels which had also been denied access to their traditional grounds.

These proposals and subsequent attempts to divide the TAC among member states provoked bitterly hostile disagreement. 'Innocuous though the subject of fishing may sound,' comments Dennis Swann, 'it has indeed inflamed strong passions among the Council of Ministers.' The British and Irish objected to the Commission proposals because no account had been taken of their claims for 50 mile exclusive zones. Eventually in October 1976 a compromise was reached in the Hague Agreement. The chief clauses of the Agreement were: (a) preferential rights of inshore fishermen in Ireland, north and south-west England and Scotland would be recognised; (b) member states would be authorised to take unilateral non-discriminatory conservation measures, pending a full Community solution; (c) fishing zones within the North Sea and the Atlantic would be extended to 200 miles.

Britain and the Common Fisheries Policy

The Hague Agreement was merely a stopgap measure on which further debate was needed. Certainly the British felt dissatisfaction on three main counts.

The British were concerned about the conservation of fish stocks. The Community fleets having lost most of their rights in the rich waters of Iceland, Norway and Canada were driven back into the North Sea and what was now recognised as British waters. But there was not enough fish in the North Sea to meet demand and there was a clear danger that over-fishing would result in certain key species like herring being wiped out. The Community, it is true, did agree some conservation measures. It was arranged that in 1977 fishing should be at a 'standstill', i.e. that it should continue at 1976 levels. In 1977 also restrictions were put on the herring and Norwegian pout catches and measures passed to control the level of by-catches.

The British were dissatisfied with the strength of these temporary measures and invoking their rights under the Hague Agreement they intro-duced several unilateral measures in the interest of fish conservation. A ban was brought in on herring fishing in the North Sea, restrictions were put on mackerel fishing off the south-west coast of England and a ban imposed on all fishing in an area called the Pout or Shetland box. The Pout-box originally covered the area 56°–60° N and 3° W–0° E and is the part of the North Sea off the North East coast of Scotland. The British extended it in October 1978 temporarily. The box was important in that catching pout for industrial purposes (for turning into glue, fertiliser and animal feed) involved a high by-catch of immature haddock and hake. It was hoped that the ban on pout fishing would allow stocks of these human-consumption fish to regenerate. The British also took steps to enforce these measures, catching a number of trawlers from third countries and member states fishing illegally. After being brought before British courts, some owners of the offending vessels had their catches and fishing gear confiscated as well as enduring fines of up to £50,000. While initially the British measures were with the approval of the Commission, some of the later measures were claimed to be discriminatory and not given approval. The Commission therefore took Britain to the European Court, the find-ings of which went against her.

The second dispute concerned Britain's share of the TAC and was acri-monious. Every member state had lost out in terms of total catches by the mid-1970s and no country wanted to accept a reduced percentage of the catch that was left. British waters now provided 60 per cent of the Com-munity fish and British fishermen demanded first a 60 per cent and then a 45 per cent quota. The Labour farm minister John Silkin also stood out for a 45 per cent quota. This was unacceptable to Britain's partners for two reasons. They argued that British fishermen had never caught anything like that share of the total European catch and they also claimed that the British demand for a high TAC on the grounds that 60 per cent of the mature fish were found in British waters was specious. The migratory pat-terns of fish stocks showed that Britain relied very much on other state's waters for the maturation of the main species of fish. For example a survey of cod by the International Council for the Exploration of the Seas (ICES) proved that while British waters contained 13.6 per cent of one year old fish and 38.4 per cent of two year old fish, these same waters had 77 per cent of all three year old fish in Community waters as a whole. In West German waters, the corresponding shares were 54.1, 37.9 and 6.6 per cent and in Danish waters 20.3, 8.4 and 6.6 per cent.

As a result of this reasoning the Commission's early proposals on the TAC gave Britain only 28 per cent by weight, roughly equal to its share of catches in Community waters over previous years. The British objected to this, pointing out that Britain needed special treatment because their fishermen with the largest distant water fleet had lost the most from non-Community waters. When Britain's partners would not agree, John Silkin vetoed the entire body of proposals in 1977. In 1978 the Commission attempted to win British approval by increasing Britain's share of the TAC to 31 per cent. But this still fell far short of the 45 per cent demanded and was a larger share of a smaller total since the proposed 1978 catches were 7 per cent lower than the average catches for the years 1973 to 1976. Included in the British TAC was a quota of 100,000 tonnes of horse mackerel, a useless fish never caught by British fishermen before. Therefore, although the other eight member states agreed to the Commission's proposals, the British continued to block them throughout 1978 despite extra meetings of the Council of Ministers and indeed the raising of the question at the European Council in December.

Only after the accession of the Conservative government in May 1979 did Britain's intransigent position change. When the British gained an acceptable rebate on their contributions to the Community budget in May 1980, they also agreed to a declaration of principles on a Common Fisheries Policy. Finally in December 1980, the Commission offered Britain 36 per cent instead of 31 per cent of the TAC and Peter Walker accepted.

The agreement over the TAC still left, as *The Economist* put it, one fishbone of contention left—the precise place where the fish could be caught. Traditionally various continental countries had fished close to British shores, particularly France, Denmark, Belgium and Holland. The member states concerned regarded such fishing as a historic right which should continue, but Peter Walker was less accommodating on this issue. He wanted access to Britain's coastal waters to be restricted, so that local fishermen could catch their quota easily and cheaply. He demanded a twelve mile exclusive zone for British boats as well as preferential treatment for local boats in a large area to the north of Scotland, around Orkney and Shetland. In that area all boats longer than 80 feet would be excluded.

Such demands antagonised the French. Most of the French fishing took place inside Britain's twelve mile zone off Cornwall but this Mr Walker was agreeable to see continue. It was the preferential box around Orkney and Shetland that created a row because the militant Boulogne fishermen had traditionally fished in that area. As no agreement was forthcoming, the British tactics in early 1981 were to block a Community fishing deal with Canada. This proposed deal was admittedly one which concerned Britain. In return for access to Canada's waters for Community fishermen, the Canadians would be given reduced-tariff access to the Community market for 20,000 tonnes of Canadian fish of which most would be sold in an already depressed British market.

However, it is hard to applaud the British move when its price was the anger of the West Germans who had largely financed Britain's budget deal in the previous May. The Canadian deal would have enabled German trawlers to fish in Canadian waters and as negotiations dragged on in the Spring of 1981, the Canadian fishing season came to an end. The hostility of Helmut Schmidt towards Britain was therefore all too evident at the European Council of March in Maastricht.

Fortunately this issue was solved by September 1981. The Community ratified agreements providing fishing rights for German and Danish deep sea trawlers off Canadian and Swedish coasts in return for imports of fish from Sweden and Canada into the Community. But the imports were not to undercut the prices charged by Community fishermen and if they did the Commission would impose tariffs or an import ban in six days. The Commission would also continue to operate a price support system by which up to 20 per cent of the annual catch could be turned into fishmeal in the event of a glut.

That seemed to leave the question of French fishing rights in British coastal waters as the last remaining obstacle to a Common Fishing Policy. In June 1982 even this problem was solved by a Franco–British compromise agreement. Britain was given exclusive rights within a six mile coastal strip and Community boats were given only extremely limited access within Britain's six to twelve mile zone. The limited access zone was widened considerably in the fishing areas off northern Scotland.

With these access regulations agreed, the CFP now appeared complete. Its other principal elements included the following quotas for each country for each type of fish caught in Community waters.

Table 2. Community Fishing Quotas

	tonnes	%
Britain	464,000	36
Denmark	305,000	24
West Germany	186,000	14
France	162,000	13
Holland	92,000	7
Ireland	47,000	4
Belgium	25,000	2

There was also to be a three-year programme of financial aid to Community fishing fleets worth 250 million ECU (£150 million).

What now snarled up final agreement was opposition to the CFP from Denmark. For years the Danes had been able to cloak their opposition under the long-running Franco-British dispute. From June 1982, however, with Franco-British agreement close, the Danes were forced to come out into the open. They had been benefiting most from the absence of a CFP by increasing both their fleet and their catch. Although virtually all Community countries had been guilty of overfishing, Denmark had been most guilty. The Danes were dismayed at their allocation of 23.4 per cent of the total Community catch for the most valuable species of edible fish. They insisted that they needed an extra 20,000 tonnes quota for mackerel to save jobs in the mackerel-processing industry in North Jutland and extra licences to fish in the limited access zone off north-east Scotland, the so-called Shetland Box. This the British refused to concede and as no agreement was reached by the end of 1982 the British government with the Commission's approval applied its own regulations over limited access to British waters for other Community fishermen. In January 1983, the Danish Euro-MP Kent Kirk sought to challenge the legality of the British measures by fishing inside Britain's twelve mile limit, a gesture that cost him £30,000 in fines. 1983 thus opened with the possibility of a new fishing 'war'.

Fortunately in January a compromise was reached, closing in the words of *The Economist*, 'an inglorious chapter in the history of the common market'. Quotas were slightly revised (Britain 37.3 per cent, Denmark 25.5 per cent, France 11.6 per cent, West Germany 11.4 per cent) with Denmark being granted for 1983 only a speċıal quota of 7,000 tonnes of mackerel off the west coast of Scotland. From 1984 Danes were to find such extra catch elsewhere. Some element of ambiguity remained for the future. The Danes claimed that if enough fish could not be found in other Community or Norwegian waters, they could return to Scottish waters. The British denied this vigorously. However, such ambiguity seemed a small price to pay for a comprehensive CFP.

Overall, the British fishing industry had not done too badly since 1973. Those worst hit were the fishermen in Britain's four big deep-water fishing ports of Hull, Grimsby, Aberdeen and Fleetwood, many of whom lost their jobs owing to the expulsion of Britain's deep water fleet from its traditional fishing grounds off the coasts of Iceland, Norway and Canada. From 1972 to 1982 the number of deep-water trawlers operating from Hull fell from 92 to 12. The effect on employment in related industries like fish processing was not as drastic, because more fish were now landed at these ports by non-British boats.

Employment in the British fishing industry proper rose from 21,651 to 23,289 between 1970 and 1980, although most of the new jobs were for part-time fishermen. Coastal fishing enjoyed a boom, especially in Scotland which became the biggest fishing region in Britain. Peterhead with its specialist inshore fleet replaced Aberdeen as the busiest Scottish fishing port.

The 37 per cent of fish allocated to Britain was probably a fair compromise; it was a far bigger proportion than any other Community country enjoyed and represented a slight increase in amount on what Britain actually fished between 1973 and 1978. Under the new CFP British fishermen would benefit from the £150 million set aside for modernising Community fishing fleets. If Britain gained a quarter of this sum, it would be worth £1,500 per British fisherman.

The 1982 regulations concerning the rights of foreign fishermen to fish in British waters were complex but calculated to give British fishermen a real measure of protection. Foreign fleets were excluded from 73 per cent of the coast which they had formerly fished whether by historic right or EEC agreements. The Danes, for example, were excluded altogether from Britain's twelve mile zone.

On the other hand British fishermen found themselves competing against each other for diminishing stocks of fish in the middle of the North Sea. They were hit by rocketing fuel prices and a falling market; from 1979–83 the price of a tonne of cod dropped by £10 and haddock by £68.

The Need for a Common Fisheries Policy

After such a catalogue of bickering, it may well be asked whether the development of a CFP has been worth all the disputation involved. But fishing in Community waters requires a Community perspective. One issue in which Community supervision is needed is conservation of fish stocks which have fallen to a dangerously low level. For example, herring catches in the North Sea fell from 497,500 tonnes in 1972 to only 169,200 tonnes in 1976. The International Council for the Exploration of the Seas (ICES) estimated that herring reserves had fallen from 1.2 million tonnes in 1976 to only 300,000 tonnes in 1979. As only half of this reserve constituted breeding stock, the very survival of the herring was endangered.

Another area where Community supervision is needed is in enforcement of agreements made, an issue obviously related to the above problem. As Britain has 56 per cent of the Community waters the burden of policing has fallen on her, but the 200 mile zone covers 500,000 nautical square miles. With outlying areas included, the total area comes to about three quarters of a million nautical square miles. To police this area effectively really requires 300 vessels and some aircraft and Community assistance in policing is manifestly needed. Indeed more Community application of the rules in general is a matter of urgency. A major complaint of British fishermen in 1981 was that while the British government's fisheries inspectors enforced the rules on them, fishermen from other Community countries were able to flout the rules, for example by fishing over and above their permitted quotas—especially the Danes.

The most dramatic justification of Community as opposed to national action in fisheries came with the control of massive and destructive fishing by Soviet bloc trawlers. In 1977 the Commission passed a Regulation requiring fishing vessels from Poland, East Germany and Russia to be licensed if they wished to fish in the Community 200 mile zone. The negotiations resulting from this had the useful side effect of forcing the Soviet Bloc into a *de facto* recognition of the Community. In October 1978 was signed a new North Atlantic Fisheries Organisation agreement which Russia was persuaded to join.

Problems remain for the future, particularly over the future accession to the Community of Spain, which has the largest fishing fleet in Western Europe. At present Spanish ships need licences to fish anywhere within the Community 200 mile zone, although many Spanish fishermen have evaded such regulations by creating 'letter-box' companies in England, registering their vessels as British and fishing in British waters to the intense anger of fishermen in south west England.

Further Reading

Body, R., *Agriculture; the Triumph and the Shame*, Temple Smith, London, 1982.
Cipolla, C. M., (ed.), *The Fontana Economic History of Europe: The Twentieth Century* (2), *Chapter 8*, Collins, London, 1978.
Fennell, R., *The Common Agricultural Policy*, Granada, London, 1981.
Marsh, J. S., and Swanney, P. J., *Agriculture and the European Community*, Allen and Unwin, London, 1980.
Pearce, J., *The Common Agricultural Policy*, Routledge and Kegan Paul, London, 1981.

Questions

(1) Are there legitimate reasons why agriculture should be given considerable aid by the EEC?

(2) In what ways are the main aims of the CAP contradictory?

(3) What is meant by the 'green' currencies?

(4) Why has the CAP been described as the Community's 'prodigal son'?

(5) Why was the evolution of a Common Fisheries Policy so acrimonious?

5
Competition Policy

The Origins and Rationale of Competition Policy

The origins of Community Competition Policy lie in Articles 65 and 66 of
the ECSC Treaty and the roughly similar Articles 85 and 86 of the Rome
Treaty. The provisions in both treaties owe much to the American experience in trying to control the large trusts in the United States, as for example
in the Sherman Act of 1890. American thinking on trusts was indeed most
influential during the formative years of the Community when the prime
concern was control of a resurgent and more concentrated German heavy
industry. As a result the clauses in the ECSC Treaty are more stringent
than those in the Rome Treaty because by 1957 fears of a resurgent Germany were declining and there was more interest in creating a large unified
market in the Community with weaker supranational powers.

Nevertheless the Community has always demonstrated particular interest
in developing a Competition Policy with teeth because of the continued
process of concentration among firms in Community countries. A Commission report in 1973 illustrated this growth of concentration. Between
1962 and 1970 the annual number of mergers in the Community of the Six
rose from 173 to 612—an increase of 350 per cent. Since 1965 there had
been an increase in the number of mergers in Britain, a process that was
accelerating. The increasing interpenetration of capital had caused the
share of the 100 largest firms to rise from 26 per cent in 1953 to 50 per
cent in 1973 in Britain and from 34 per cent in 1954 to 50 per cent in 1969
in West Germany. In some sectors the concentration process had gone so
far that only four manufacturers were left in the Community but in many
other industries a very high degree of concentration had developed with
the four largest firms controlling about 80 or 90 per cent of sales or production. Obviously some firms enjoying such a degree of control might be
tempted to abuse their power through practices that exploited the consumer
or that limited fair competition.

Competition Policy in the Treaties

The concept of free competition is a fundamental element in the Rome
Treaty which embodies the premise that any restriction on free competition
is intrinsically reprehensible. There are in practice some exceptions but the

principle itself is that of positive general condemnation of any limits on competition.

Article 85 (1) of the Treaty declares: 'The following shall be prohibited as incompatible with the Common Market: all agreements between undertakings, decisions by associations of undertakings and concerted practices which may affect trade between member states and which have as their object or effect the prevention, restriction or distortion of competition within the Common Market.' The Treaty then goes on to illustrate the kinds of agreement that are prohibited by Article 85: those that directly or indirectly fix purchase or selling prices; those that limit production or result in the division of markets between competitors; those that lead to particular customers being treated differently to others. It is important to remember that the list is illustrative and not exhaustive. The principles laid down in the article apply to any arrangement that offends against those principles whether they are mentioned or not and they also apply not only to agreements that have as their object the restriction of competition but also to those that result in the restriction of competition.

All these types of agreement, prohibited by Article 85 (1) are under Article 85 (2) held to be automatically void but under Article 85 (3) the Commission can declare the prohibition inapplicable to particular agreements. Examples of such agreements are those that contribute to the improvement of the production or distribution of goods, those that promote technical or economic progress and allow consumers a fair share of the resulting benefit. However, such agreements must be unlikely to eliminate competition in much of the market for the goods in question.

Article 85 deals with agreements, between two or more parties, that constitute restrictive practices. Article 86 is concerned with the abuse by individual organisations of a dominant trading position enjoyed in the Community, that is to say monopolies. Article 86 of the Rome Treaty declares: 'Any abuse by one or more undertakings of a dominant position within the Common Market or in a substantial part of it shall be prohibited.' Again, as in Article 85, an illustrative list is given of the types of abuses that will be prohibited: directly or indirectly imposing unfair purchase or selling prices or other unfair trading conditions; limiting production, markets or technical development to the prejudice of consumers; applying dissimilar conditions to equivalent transactions with different trading partners, or imposing in contracts supplementary obligations on trading partners which have no real connection with the subject of such contracts. Article 86 is concerned essentially with the abuse of a dominant position in a particular market but there is no condemnation of a large share of the market as such. It is only when the dominant position is used against the interests of the consumer or trade generally that the Commission will be concerned. In practice the abuse of a dominant position takes one of two forms. (1) The firm involved adopts policies which hinder the development of other producers or suppliers who could be competitors. (2) In the absence of other competitors, a firm may use its power to adjust the production or price of its goods to the detriment of consumers.

Over the years many cases have gone to the Court of Justice under the competition laws and these have created precedents and led to the evolution of certain general principles. One principle is that neither in their terms nor by the interpretation put on them are the rules narrowly drawn and in many cases the Court has adopted a wide interpretation of the intentions of the firms concerned.

The first principle is, however, constrained by a second principle: the rules only apply to trade between member states. The Community competition rules are not concerned with restrictive practices or monopolies within one state alone which does not affect inter-state trade; the national law of the state concerned will deal with such cases. On the other hand if two or more traders within one member state make an agreement which could affect trade between member states, they will be subject to the rules. Indeed those making the agreement may be from states outside the Community entirely, from the example the United States, but if the agreements made have an effect on trade between member states of the Community, the competition rules will apply.

Indeed this leads on to the third principle—what counts is the effect of the agreements. The Commission is only concerned with agreements that have a serious adverse effect on free trade in the Community and may allow small agreements that affect only a small part of that trade.

The fourth principle is that the rules should be vigorously applied and the Commission has gained considerable administrative powers to fulfil this function. The principal regulation which defines the Commission powers in this field is Regulation 17 which was first put into force in 1962. It gives the Commission wide powers of investigation including exclusive authority to grant exemption from Article 85 (1), requires the co-operation of member states in the Commission's enquiries and gives the Commission wide powers to insist on the amendment of agreements or their cancellation. These powers are backed by a power to levy fines on firms that fail to comply with Commission instructions. As soon as the Commission has begun an enquiry, the case is taken outside the national courts, an important custom as it ensures that the same rules are applied consistently throughout the Common Market.

Regulation 17 is designed to make the powers of the Commission immediately effective. The Commission may prohibit the continuation of any agreement and that agreement must cease even though the parties concerned may intend to appeal to the European Court. It is therefore difficult for defendants to play for time and gain profitable breathing spaces. If they try to be unco-operative, companies can be fined for giving false or inadequate information as happened in the 1973 European Sugar Cartel case and the 1981 case of the French firm CCI which was fined £2,850.

The Decision-Making Process

The Commission can be alerted to the existence of a potential breach of the rules in a number of ways. Sometimes, as in the case of Hoffmann-La Roche, an individual may contact the Commission. Sometimes competitors will complain about a firm's unfair practices. Often the Commission itself from its own studies will see good reason to commence an investigation.

One practice that has developed has been that of giving publicity to any Commission decision in an attempt to influence and educate the market as a whole. Indeed to the annoyance of a number of firms, commissioners responsible for the competition rules have often called press conferences to inform the public both of decisions actually made, the state of investigations in progress and indeed those about to commence. In 1982 the Commissioner in charge of Competition Policy, the Dutchman Frans Andriessen made it abundantly clear that the Commission would be investigating why cars in Britain were a third dearer than in other Community countries.

Competition Policy is handled by the DGIV (Competition) and the Legal Service and there is an Advisory Committee on Restrictive Practices and Dominant Positions which has to be consulted. Care is taken over the initial stages of investigation and consultation also takes place with the whole Commission itself sitting as a collegiate body, because it is not necessarily the case that all the other work of the Commission is made easier by the application of the competition rules.

When an investigation is launched, the Commission is not required to ask for the co-operation of the company concerned. It can be brusque, enter premises of the company to examine books and other business records, take copies of extracts from these documents and ask for oral explanations on the spot. In 1979 such brusqueness in the case of National Panasonic (UK) Limited so aggrieved the company that it appealed to the European Court, complaining that the Commission investigation was carried out by officials who 'arrived at National Panasonic's sales offices and carried out the investigation without awaiting the arrival of the company's solicitors. They left with copies of several documents and notes made during the investigation.' The company was complaining that this approach was more hostile and abrasive than the circumstances warranted. The Court rejected all the complaints, ruling that the Commission had not exceeded its powers or acted unreasonably. In many cases the Court does endorse the actions of the Commission, in effect strengthening its practical power. In 1978 in the case of Unitel, the Court ruled that a company could not refuse to give information on an agreement to the Commission because it felt that the agreement did not affect trade between member states. The decision whether an agreement did affect such trade lay solely with the Commission.

However, the Court does remain an important form of appeal against the decisions of the Commission. The Court rarely reverses a Commission decision completely, though it did so in the 1967 case of the cement industry. Sometimes the Court, while upholding the Commission's conclusions in principle, has reduced the penalties imposed. When the Commission found that Hoffmann-La Roche had given rebates which were conditional upon buyers taking all their supplies from Hoffmann, a fine imposed by the Commission was subsequently reduced by the Court from 300,000 ECU to 200,000 ECU in 1976.

Sometimes the Commission will, under Article 85 (3), allow certain agreements to continue, either in their existing form or after some amendments recommended by the Commission. This procedure is called 'negative clearance' and is to be distinguished from exemption. Before an agreement can receive negative clearance, it must be notified to the Commission. If an agreement is kept secret and then the Commission stumbles across it, it cannot then be given negative clearance. There is therefore no incentive for a firm to gamble on never being discovered on the assumption that if they are, they may still obtain negative clearance. The term 'negative clearance' does imply very limited approval and if circumstances change, the Commission may review the situation and revoke that approval.

There are a number of agreements that may secure exemption from the competition rules. These include small agreements which have little or no effect on trade generally and sole agency agreements where the effect of such agreements is little different from the supplier having his own branch in the member state concerned.

The Widening Scope of Competition Policy: Dumping and State Aids

The Treaty of Rome refers to many aspects of competition, including patents, licensing agreements and trade marks; price discrimination and fixing; resale price maintenance; state aid; abuse of a dominant market position; dumping; quantitative restrictions on imports and exports; mergers and concentrations; and state undertakings. In practice the Commission has been most active in four areas: restrictive practices, dominant positions, dumping and state aids.

Many aspects concerning restrictive practices and dominant positions have already been discussed. But in addition to restricting unfair competition caused by the trading practices of private firms, the Community has also developed rules which regulate state aid within the Common Market to Community based industries and has also tried to protect the Community from unfair competition from outside the Common Market in the form of dumped and state subsidised goods.

Dumping

Dumping is the marketing of goods in a particular area at lower than their true cost. Very often the dumped price is lower than the price at which the goods are sold elsewhere. It was assumed by the creators of the Rome Treaty that dumping could not occur within the Community once a free competitive market had been established. Hence the Treaty only contained some transitional clauses to control dumping but no permanent provisions on dumping between member states.

The term 'dumping' is often misused. It is wrongly used to describe the disposal over a short term of surplus stocks by manufacturers. These may affect the market temporarily but their effect is limited. The term is also wrongly used in complaints about cheap imports from developing countries. In such countries lower production costs allow goods to be produced more cheaply than comparable goods manufactured in Europe. They are not dumped goods because the lower prices merely reflect lower costs. True dumping is long term. It arises when goods are sold consistently in export markets at lower than home prices and when the producers are in a protected home market or are helped by state aid which enables the price to be artificially lowered.

The Community has had to proceed carefully in its approach to dumping because any severe measures against it could be construed as protection by the Community's trading partners and could lead to retaliation. The Community is also restricted by its obligations under the General Agreement on Tariffs and Trade (GATT) which has worked towards freer world trade. The Community is bound to follow the GATT rules for dealing with dumping closely.

The Commission felt justified in taking an interest in the problem from Article 113 of the Rome Treaty which lays down that 'a common commercial policy shall be based on uniform principles, particularly in measures to protect trade such as those to be taken in case of dumping or subsidies'. The importance of this article is that it established the principle that any anti-dumping measures were to be adopted for the general Community interest and not merely for the benefit of a particular part of a Community industry.

At the GATT negotiations in Tokyo in 1973 it was recognised that a more formal code on dumping was needed and it was on the basis of the new GATT code that the 1979 Community Anti-Dumping Regulation was based. It came into effect on 1st January, 1980 and covers both anti-dumping control and the imposition of countervailing duties to compensate for state subsidies. An anti-dumping duty can be imposed on 'any dumped product whose entry for consumption in the Community causes injury to a Community industry or is likely to cause injury'. A product is defined as dumped if its export price to the Community is less than the normal price of the like product.

The application of the regulation requires a definition of three key phrases—normal value, export price and injury. For the term 'normal value' the Community has adopted the GATT definition. Normal value is 'the comparable price actually paid or payable in the ordinary course of trade for the like product intended for consumption in the exporting country or country of origin'. If the product is not sold in the country of origin, thus preventing any direct comparison with the dumped price, the normal value is defined as 'the comparable price of the like product when exported to any third country'. If there is no like product with which to make a comparison, then normal value should be the constructed value— that is to say, all production costs plus a reasonable margin for overheads and profit.

The establishment of normal value involves much research and the making of complex commercial judgments by the Commission. This area is particularly complex when dumping by Eastern bloc countries is suspected. The necessary information on costs will not be available and the goods have not been produced in a free market economy. Where goods originate in non-market economies, normal value is fixed by looking at the prices of like products in a country outside the Community where a free market operates.

The term 'export price' is easier to define. It is 'the price actually paid for the product sold for export to the Community'. The regulation on anti-dumping contains much guidance on what is a fair comparison between normal value and the export price, but even though such comparisons are made, the Commission may still exercise its discretion in individual cases.

Before any anti-dumping duty is levied, it must be established not only that dumping has taken place but has actually caused injury. Injury is defined in Article 4 of the regulation as 'causing or threatening to cause, material injury to an established Community industry or materially retarding the establishment of such an industry'.

When the Commission investigates an alleged dumping, it must examine the volume of imports and whether these have increased, the price of the goods and whether it significantly undercuts that of identical goods produced in the Community and the effect of the imports on the position of the Community industry involved. Such requirements place a heavy burden on the Commission unit which deals with dumping. The investigation must be thorough because if it were not, it could be condemned for failing to meet international requirements. Therefore it is difficult to act quickly and impose a duty.

The Commission could initiate action itself but normally acts on a complaint, usually by a trade association and occasionally by an individual company. The evidence in the complaint is referred to the Community anti-dumping advisory committee on which all member states are represented. If the committee believes there is evidence of dumping, the Commission begins its investigation. The interested parties can submit information and it is here that the European trade associations can help to protect the interests of their members by submitting persuasive evidence. If possible the Commission will visit the manufacturing plants both in the Community industry and those of the producers who are allegedly dumping goods.

If the Commission finds that goods have been dumped, it will impose a duty on them which should correct the imbalance brought about by the low price of the dumped goods. When the investigation begins and some evidence comes to light, a provisional duty may be imposed and held by the customs authorities of member states, pending the outcome of the full investigation. Provisional duties normally last for about four months to six months which is the period an investigation normally takes. If some compromise agreement is reached with the parties concerned, the Commission may remit any duty imposed.

A typical example of a complex dumping case was that of electric motors from Eastern Europe in 1979. In March 1979 a complaint was made by the relevant trade association that certain types of electric motors were being dumped in the Community by the USSR and six other East European countries. After lengthy and difficult enquiries the Commission noted that the imported motors had undercut like goods produced in the Community by between 10 and 51 per cent in price, contributing to the loss of 5,000 jobs between 1974 and 1978. Most East European countries quickly offered undertakings to the Commission and had no duty imposed on their goods. The USSR was less co-operative and only after a temporary duty was imposed did the USSR offer similar undertakings. The provisional duty collected was not returned to USSR exporters.

The Commission does not always uphold complaints about dumping but in a time of recession it is not surprising that the allegations of dumping have increased and the Commission has upheld most of them, in fields as varied as textiles, petrochemicals, American chemical fertilisers and East German alarm clocks. The cases show that dumping is indulged in by both market and non-market economies.

State Aids

As with dumping, state aids can result in an artificially low export price and the consequences to industry in the country where such goods are sold are the same as those caused by dumped goods. Like products may become uncompetitive and the industry suffers injury. The 1979 Community regulation deals with state aids in a similar way to the way it deals with dumping. When a complaint is received, the Commission will investigate and if it finds that goods have been subsidised, a countervailing duty may be imposed. Various practices are deemed to constitute indirect subsidies in a list that is illustrative, not exhaustive: currency retention schemes which involve a bonus on exports, government-sponsored schemes for cheaper freight charges for exports, reduced taxes levied on exports, some export credit guarantee systems and special low interest credit schemes sponsored by governments for exports.

In practice all countries give aid to their export industries and the Community must be aware that it cannot succeed in stamping out such practices. All it can do is to attempt to reduce the more blatant forms of state aid. The Commission is particularly vigilant in trying to remove state aid from inter-state trade in the Common Market because such an aim is a fundamental part of the Rome Treaty. Article 92 of the Treaty lays down that 'any aid granted by a member state or through state resources in any form whatsoever which distorts or threatens to distort competition by favouring certain undertakings or the production of certain goods shall, in so far as it affects trade between member states, be incompatible with the Common Market'.

The Commission has admitted that much direct or indirect aid of this kind is still being given by member states. In recent years it has asked the West German, French and British governments to stop giving grants that were designed to promote exports within the Community. It secured the ending of the special export credits offered by the Dutch central bank to Dutch exporters in the Community and refused to allow the Dutch government to grant aid to the cigarette manufacturers, Philip Morris Holland.

In trying to control such aid, the Commission is swimming against a strong nationalist tide because in a time of recession it is natural for member states to seek to encourage their own export industries.

Commission action is likely then to arouse resentment. For its part, the Commission has been prepared to pursue state aid of which it disapproved and take the member state to the European Court if necessary as it did with the Dutch government over Philip Morris Holland.

Nevertheless the Community does tolerate state aid in a number of cases. Three types of aid are specifically deemed to be compatible with Article 92: (a) aid of a social character to individuals where no discrimination on basis of origin exists; (b) aid for national calamities; and (c) aid to assist regions of the Federal Republic affected by the division of Germany. But in practice aid is also permitted to help underdeveloped regions, to promote projects with a European interest and to develop certain regions. Massive aid in fact has been granted by states to declining industries and regions and the Commission has found it difficult to control this area because of the level of aid and the difficulty of assessing its effect on the Community.

Problems of Competition Policy

Competition Policy has three established objectives. As the Commission recently stated, it aims to keep the Common Market 'open and unified' that is to say to create a single market for the benefit of industry and consumers. Secondly it must 'ensure that at all stages of the Common Market's development, there exists the right amount of competition'. By ensuring some degree of commercial rivalry, the Community can help European industry to be competitive in world markets as the competition will encourage firms to rationalise and change. The third objective is to ensure that competition is subject to 'the principles of fairness in the market place' by which the Commission means 'equality of opportunity for all operators in the Common Market'. In practice this means preventing companies from setting up restrictive agreements and cartels or from abusing a dominant position.

These principles are not always easy to accommodate together. The Commission itself has recognised that 'competition carries within it the seeds of its own destruction' because a free market may result in a concentration of economic power in the hands of those firms which have proved most efficient and have been able to put competitors out of business or take them over.

Competition Policy also seems to clash with other Community policies. One objective of Industrial Policy has been to establish cartels to protect certain Community industries in difficulty. Other major policies, for example the Regional and Social Policies which aim at protecting weaker regions and weaker groups seem difficult to reconcile with the objectives of Competition Policy.

There seem to be serious difficulties in the actual operation of Competition Policy. The process has been criticised as being excessively bureaucratic. Commission figures show that some cases can involve between 50 and 150 transmissions of drafts and notes. Not surprisingly an average case in the 1970s took from three to four years and the Netherlands Cement case which began in 1964 and was not concluded until 1972 is by no means unusual. The main reason for the length of time involved in each case is that proposals have to be passed along a lengthy chain within the Community machine several times before a decision emerges. In addition to this lengthy internal scrutiny the Commission also has to hear the opinions of the firms concerned as well as the views of interested third parties, for example the national experts from the member states.

The sheer complexity of the cases imposes a formidable strain on the Commission as the Continental Can decision demonstrated. The Continental Can Company, an American packaging firm, acquired, via its Belgian subsidiary, control of the largest German producer of packaging and metal boxes—Schmalbach-Lubeca-Werke AG of Brunswick. It later acquired a majority holding in a Dutch company, Thomassen and Drijver-Verblifa NV of Deventer, which was the leading manufacturer of packaging material in the Benelux countries. The Commission felt that these mergers produced such a dominant position for Continental Can that it constituted an abuse, a violation of Article 86. Continental Can, however, appealed against the Commission decision to the European Court. The Court delivered its decision in 1973. It agreed with the Commission's legal reasoning but found in favour of the company on the grounds that the Commission had got the facts of the case wrong. This decision highlighted a major weakness in operating Competition Policy since the Commission lost the case because it showed inadequate understanding of the market which it wished to regulate. It may be relatively easy to identify the degree of concentration among firms in a given market but it is much harder to analyse the behaviour of those firms to decide whether they are acting in the best interests of the Community. Some industries with research and development costs may need a high degree of concentration to perform efficiently and to deal with such cases requires expert economic judgment. It is impossible to apply a set of general rules and some criticism has been levelled at the calibre of Commission personnel who are accused of being too bureaucratic, of lacking a sophisticated grasp of economic realities and even of ignoring infringements of the rules in politically sensitive areas. Perhaps the essence of the problem here is that the Competition department is understaffed with only about 60 executive members.

Other criticisms have been levelled at Competition Policy. *The Economist* in April 1981 accused the Commissioners in charge of Competition Policy of being too timid and hoped that the new Commissioner Frans Andriessen would adopt a more aggressive approach. Certainly the fines imposed by the Commission have been too small. It was only in 1979 that it first imposed a really big fine when Pioneer, a Japanese hi-fi company was fined 4.65 million ECU (£2.5 million). But although this was the highest fine ever imposed, it still represented only 4 per cent of the firm's sales turnover, well short of the 10 per cent maximum. As *The Economist* put it, if the fines are to make any real impact, they must make sin unprofitable. In addition, appeals to the European Court by firms are too cheap. Firms can, by appealing, often make enough from the interest on unpaid fines, to finance a long case.

The Commission has even been accused of being too chauvinist. American companies have felt particularly aggrieved, alleging that when Directorate IV wishes to assert itself, it decides to harass a large non-European firm rather than looking at European culprits. But perhaps the explanation for this is that the culprits are often the American multinationals anyway!

A more just criticism is that the Directorate has dragged its feet in areas which are politically sensitive. One glaring example has been high European air fares where attempts to offer cheaper flights by independent air lines like British Caledonian and Laker have been thwarted by governments who have refused to grant landing licences. The Commission has also been slow in forcing governments to open up purchasing by their telecommunications monopolies. But the chief example here remains the vexed question of state aids. By the 1980s governments had become greater enemies of free competition than private companies. As unemployment has mounted, all governments have increased aid to keep tottering firms in business. The

Commission has the power to forbid governments giving out aids if it thinks such action will distort Community competition and it has successfully controlled member states' own regional policies and prevented regional aids from being applied to too large a part of each country. But in many other areas it has backed away from challenging the aids given, chiefly in the declining industries and in agriculture. All the Commission has been able to do in these cases is to negotiate the size and scope of the aids.

Conclusion

Despite the problems described above, it would still be true to claim that Competition Policy is a partial Commission success story. Over the years it has created in collaboration with the Court an unusually strong and effective body of law to control abuses by overmighty international companies. Before the development of a Community Competition Policy such firms had had little or no control exercised over them. As the process of concentration of firms continues, this branch of Community business will become even more important because such concentration does not necessarily help the public interest. Recent research organised by the Berlin based International Institute for Management covered a period of ten years and 765 mergers in a number of countries in the Community and beyond. The Institute concluded that mergers did not result in improved efficiency but rather that they were a form of empire-building which reduced competition without any compensations for the consumer.

Examples of successful Commission action in this field in the 1970s are the GEMA case of 1971, the Aniline Dye case of 1972 and the Commercial Solvents case of 1974. During 1971 the Commission issued its first decision under Article 86 and found that GEMA, a society dealing with musical copyrights, had a monopoly of the German market, a monopoly which it had abused by restricting the work of authors, composers and musical publishers. In the Aniline Dye case, the Commission found that the ten most important suppliers of dyes in the Community had all imposed similar price increases within a few days of each other. The firms were fined for concerted practices in respect of prices. It was a significant case because four of the ten firms (three Swiss and one British) were from outside the Community, demonstrating that the parallel price behaviour was international in character. The third example involved the American Commercial Solvents Corporation and its Italian subsidiary, the Instituto Chemioterapico Italiano. The American firm had a world monopoly in the production and sale of a chemical essential for a drug combating tuberculosis. It ordered its Italian subsidiary to manufacture the drug and simultaneously to cease selling the chemical to an independent firm ZOJA which also produced the drug. The Commission condemned such action as abuse of a dominant position under Article 86 and forced the subsidiary to resume supplying the chemical to ZOJA so that it could continue manufacture of the drug.

The Commission has continued to be active in this field in the 1980s. It has concerned itself with the issue of British car prices which have been up to one third higher than those in other Community countries. In 1982 a Ford Cortina costing £5,335 in Britain could be obtained for £4,100 in Europe. As a result British purchasers have tried to buy cars on the continent at the cheaper price but have found it difficult to do so owing to restrictive practices by motor manufacturers and dealers. The Commissioner responsible for Competition Policy, Frans Andriessen, has therefore investigated alleged abuses by eight manufacturers including British Leyland. Backed by the European Parliament, he has made clear his intention to draft legislation to guarantee that consumers should be free to buy a car anywhere in the Community. The whole issue was not only a potential infringement of Article 85 relating to restrictive practices but also of Article 3 which covers the free movement of goods from one Community country to another.

Nor is the Commission afraid to tackle the multinationals. Its zeal for trust-busting was seen in its pursuit of its case against IBM (International Business Machines). This American giant has enjoyed 63 per cent of the European market in big computers and in 1980 its data-processing revenue in Europe was $9.9 millions whereas its closest rival, the West German firm of Siemens could only boast a revenue of $1.5 millions. In 1979 a number of customers whom IBM supplied with software complained that the firm was putting pressure on them to buy all their software from IBM. The firm was able to turn the screw by building storage capacity into computers that tied the buyers to IBM and ensured that its competitors could not easily interface with their own equipment.

The Commission, which had already been investigating the firm, investigated the complaints and in December 1980 sent a list of objections to certain of IBM's business practices. IBM has made some moves towards meeting these objections and has stopped its discrimination against customers using software bought from other firms. However the Commission is as yet far from satisfied.

In December 1981 the Commission dealt a blow at restrictive practices in the wine trade when it fined Möet-et-Chandon's London subsidiary for banning the re-export of champagne from Britain. The firm claimed that it had the interests of British consumers at heart in this action. After three years of poor harvests, Möet imposed an export ban in January 1980 to stop champagne earmarked for Britain being diverted to the higher priced markets in West Germany. But this led to shortages and consequently higher prices in West Germany and was viewed as a restrictive practice by the Commission.

In October 1981 Michelin was fined $700,000 by the Commission for operating a system of financial incentives to its operators in the Netherlands which helped to exclude other manufacturers from the market for commercial tyres. The fine was not large but obviously Michelin and other tyre manufacturers indulging in similar practices were being warned that they should reform their marketing systems if they wished to avoid further fines. The fine set an important precedent since it was the first one to be imposed on the actions of a company in only one country where action could have been taken by the national government.

There is still much scope for development of Competition Policy in the field of state aids and mergers. As long ago as 1973 the Commission drew up a proposal for tighter control of mergers irrespective of whether they infringed Article 86 or not. In December 1981 Frans Andriessen revived the proposal the main points of which are: (a) All mergers that involved companies with a turnover of more than one billion ECU (£580 million) would have to be notified in advance to the Commission. (b) The Commission would have three months to decide whether to investigate the merger, during which time the merger would be suspended. If the Commission failed to decide within three months, the merger could go ahead. (c) Mergers that involved companies with a combined turnover below 500 million ECU (£290 million) would be exempted. Mergers worth between 500 million and one billion ECU could be investigated but would not need to give prior notification. (d) The Commission would have the power to ban or break up mergers that would hinder free trade between member states or would restrict free competition in the Community. The proposal did not cover mergers that only affected national markets; nor did it apply to mergers affecting less than 25 per cent of the Community market for its product. Mergers shown to be in the Community interest or needed to boost the industry's competitiveness against non-European rivals were also allowed.

In an attempt to make the draft directive more acceptable, Mr Andriessen also included provisions safeguarding the rights of firms under investigation. Firms would have the right to see some of the Commission files relating to their case and dawn raids by inspectors on firms suspected of breaching the competition rules would now be more controlled. Visiting officials would have to state precisely what they were looking for and limit their action to what was required to obtain it.

At the end of 1982 however, the draft directive on mergers had still failed to become Community law.

Further Reading

Beckerl, B., *EEC Competition Law*, ESC Publishing Ltd, Oxford, 1978.
El Agraa, E. M., *The Economics of the European Community, Chapter 6*, Philip Allan, Deddington, 1980.
Swann, D., *The Economics of the Common Market, Chapter 4*, Penguin, Harmondsworth, 1978.

Articles
'EEC Competition Law', *European Trends*, November 1980.
'Dumping and State Aids', *European Trends*, February 1981.
'Public Works and Public Supply Contracts', *European Trends*, August 1982.

Questions

(1) Why is a strong Competition Policy required in the Community?
(2) Explain the importance of Articles 85 and 86 of the Rome Treaty.
(3) Describe the powers of the Commission in dealing with contraventions of Articles 85 and 86.
(4) What are the chief obstacles to an effective Community Competition Policy?

6
Social Policy

The Acute Need for a Social Policy

A European Commission report on poverty in December 1981 proved, if ever one doubted it, the need for a Community Social Policy. The report showed that some 11.4 per cent of families or about 30 million people had incomes sufficiently below average national earnings to bring them within a relative poverty line. The growth of unemployment (12 million in 1982) was swelling the numbers, creating a category of new poor who had never before suffered poverty. Despite increased spending on welfare services by national governments in the previous 30 years, millions of people still lived in sub-standard housing; infant deaths in some countries were still twice as many among unskilled manual workers' children as in the professional classes; and between an eighth and a third of young people in different member countries were leaving school with few or no qualifications or vocational training.

The Community had already defined poverty in 1975 as 'individuals or families whose resources are so small as to exclude them from the minimum acceptable way of life of the member state in which they live'. The authors of the 1981 report found that certain groups of people were most vulnerable to relative poverty wherever they lived in the Community—immigrants, households headed by women, large families, one-parent families, the handicapped and the nomads or gypsies. Even when the breadwinner worked, he (or particularly she) was almost always badly paid. From the Commission evidence it was clear that once within the poverty bracket, disadvantage piled on disadvantage making escape very difficult.

In some respects the Treaty of Rome is weak on the social side because there are relatively few precise commitments and the Treaty does not contain a definite timetable for action as is the case with the introduction of the common market. It was believed at the time that social policy had little relevance to the immediate goals. Nevertheless the Community has over time evolved a wide-ranging social policy whose impact on some problems has been significant.

The three Treaties establishing the European Communities all refer to social policy. The ECSC Treaty includes provisions on the wages and mobility of workers in the coal and steel industries and the EAEC Treaty deals with the health and safety of workers in the atomic energy industry. The EEC Treaty provides a comprehensive basis for today's social policy, stating several general objectives of a social character. In Article 2 there is a commitment to an accelerated raising of the standard of living and to 'continuous and balanced expansion'. One part of the EEC Treaty (Part 3, Title 3) is devoted exclusively to social policy. To ensure the constant improvement in working conditions and employment this part of the Treaty makes provision for: (1) the gradual achievement of the free movement of workers, with guaranteed eligibility for social security benefits (Articles 48, 49 and 51); (2) encouraging the exchange of young workers under a joint programme (Article 50); (3) promoting close collaboration between the member states in social matters so as to encourage an improvement in living and working conditions and make possible their harmonisation while the improvement is being maintained (Articles 117 and 118); (4) the principle of equal pay for men and women (Article 119); (5) setting up a European Social Fund to promote employment opportunities and geographical and occupational mobility for workers within the Community (Articles 123 to 127); (6) establishing general principles for implementing a Community vocational training policy (Article 128).

Other parts of the EEC Treaty also refer to social objectives. In Article 39, for example, there is stated the aim of ensuring a fair standard of living for all the agricultural community.

To a considerable extent, these clauses reflected the concerns of the individual states in 1957. Because French industry was worried about the possibility of European competition, the French government insisted on certain Treaty provisions, notably on equal pay and holiday arrangements. The Italians sought and gained the prize of the principle of the free movement of workers.

The Early History of the Social Policy 1958–71

Given the rather imprecise clauses in the Treaties, it is not surprising that the development of Social Policy was rather slow. Member states were reluctant to allow the Community's responsibilities to develop beyond the strict legal commitment of the Treaties and even here, as in the case of the equal pay policy, objectives were sometimes fulfilled more in the letter than in the spirit. Employers were also reluctant to support measures which might incur extra costs. Most support for Social Policy came from the Commission and from Italy which stood to gain from a rapid implementing of the free movement of labour and Social Fund grants.

Some useful work was achieved in the first decade. By 1968 complete freedom of movement of labour had become a reality. Community workers had gained the same access to jobs as nationals, the only formality required being the acquisition of a residence certificate. The first European Social Fund had been set up in 1958 and by 1971 had contributed 210 million UA to the retraining and resettlement of 1.4 million workers. The Fund reimbursed governments with 50 per cent of any expenditure which they incurred in retraining labour, with the initiative for using the Fund lying with the member states.

Yet progress was disappointing and the Fund itself suffered from two major weaknesses. It could only intervene retroactively, that is to say, when the worker who had received vocational training had been productively employed for at least six months. Secondly the Fund did not have a budget limit; intervention from the Fund for a particular country depended mainly on the funds available in that country for vocational retraining and settlement. The ironical consequence was that the main beneficiary of the first European Social Fund was not Italy but West Germany.

The Reform of the Social Fund 1971

By the end of the 1960s a new concern for social issues became evident. The reasons for this were several. The immediate objectives of the transitional period had been completed by 1968 and there was a need for a renewed commitment to the Community. The relative failure of the Social Fund was too obvious and hardly a good advertisement for a Community which was considering enlargement from six to nine.

The first sign of greater concern for social affairs was a Commission proposal in 1965 to reform the Social Fund. No concrete action was then taken but at the Hague Summit of 1969 the existing six members asserted the need for a more concerted social policy which would include a reformed Social Fund. In 1970 the Council of Ministers agreed on the reform of the Fund's operations and by 1971 the details of the reform had been worked out.

It had been realised that the activities of the first Social Fund had lacked a unity of purpose because the initiative lay with the member states to introduce various and usually quite unrelated programmes with the Fund a relatively passive partner. What was preferable was for funds to be channelled into selected schemes which would fit in with Community policies and not merely with those of the member states. The 1971 reform of the Fund went some way to meet such needs. Instead of covering the expenditure of member states after the event, the Fund was henceforth to decide in advance how to allocate its own resources. It was also decided that aid from the new Fund would be given not only for operations carried out by public bodies but also to operations carried out by private bodies and business firms. The reformed Social Fund was allocated a much larger budget than its predecessor. During the first two years of its existence it had a total budget of more than 440 million EUA, which is more than the first Social Fund had in the whole of the twelve years it operated.

The Council decision of February 1971 on the reform of the Fund stressed two areas where the Fund should intervene. Under Article 4 of the new constitution of the Fund, it could intervene when the employment situation was affected by another Community policy or when the need arose for joint action to match labour supply and demand in the Community. This represented a new departure and in the years after 1971 the Council took action to help the retraining of farm workers who had been displaced by the restructuring of Community farming under CAP, migrant workers, the handicapped and the young unemployed. Under Article 5 of the new constitution the Fund could intervene without a specific Council decision to tackle certain difficult employment situations, for example areas where the predominant industries were in decline. Most of the Fund's resources (about 90 per cent) were for vocational training to promote occupational mobility and between 1971 and 1976 more than two million workers benefited from it.

The Social Action Programme

The reform of the Social Fund in 1971 was proof of a growing Community interest in social matters. Further evidence of this was seen in the Paris Summit of October 1972 when the Heads of State emphasised that they 'attached as much importance to vigorous action in the social field as to the achievement of the economic and monetary union' and thought it essential to increase 'the involvement of management and labour in the economic and social decisions of the Community'. It had become clear that not all sections of society had benefited from the increased prosperity of the preceding years and in stressing the quality of life as well as economic expansion, the leaders were trying to give the Community a human face to replace the image of a faceless economic machine in Brussels.

The Summit of 1972 called for an action programme and in 1973 the Commission published its 'Social Action Programme' which the Council adopted in a somewhat amended form in 1974. Some 40 priority objectives were to be carried out by the member states in pursuance of three major Community objectives: (1) the attainment of full and better employment; (2) the improvement and upward harmonisation of living and working conditions; (3) the increased involvement of management and labour in the economic and social decisions of the Community and of workers in the life of their firms.

Employment

Shortly after the Social Action Programme was adopted, the European economy went into recession and a sharp rise in unemployment occurred. The rag-bag of measures carried out under the Social Fund has failed to be anything more than a palliative. One useful measure was the collaboration at Community level between heads of national employment services to exchange experience and ideas. It has in fact gone further than this because since 1972 the labour services of each member state have exchanged, at least once a month, a statement of their own manpower needs for each occupation and a statement on job-hunters interested in working in another Community country. This created problems over language and the different nomenclature for the same job in different countries. Therefore the Community has compiled a system with a register of jobs and a coding to establish true comparability between jobs. It is called SEDOC (the European System for the International Clearing of Vacancies and Applications for Employment). It offered 25,000 jobs to British people in 1980 though only a 10 per cent matching rate was achieved.

The Commission particularly stressed the need for the vocational preparation of the young (under 25s) because young people now make up 42 per cent of Europe's unemployed. Many do not gain a job because they have no vocational training—and because they have no employment they cannot acquire vocational training. In 1978 the Council approved a Commission proposal for the introduction of a new form of aid from the European Social Fund for young people. Assistance of up to 30 EUA per person per week could be given for up to 12 months to promote recruitment in jobs with a vocational content and job creation schemes. In Britain the Manpower Services Commission operating the Youth Opportunities Scheme has received growing amounts from the Social Fund—£38 million in 1979, £47 million in 1980 and £67 million in 1981.

As unemployment has risen remorselessly, a larger proportion of funds from the Social Fund has been concentrated in regions suffering declining industries. To help the retraining of workers in such areas, the Fund has made cash available. A recent example is the contribution to the building of the Metro between Gateshead and Newcastle. To train staff for this venture, £2.9 million was made available from the Social Fund, a sum that amounted to 40 per cent of the cost of the training. By 1981 the Fund was helping one million people in the Community as a whole to retrain.

Living and Working Conditions

It has been recognised at Community level that more has needed to be done to improve the quality of life and a number of measures were planned under the Social Action Programme to improve the living and working conditions of the least favoured groups in society.

Certainly some progress has been made over the rights of working women. Although an equal pay policy had been written into the Treaty of Rome it was not until 1975 that the Commission produced a directive on equal pay. The member states were required within one year to repeal all laws incompatible with equal pay and take steps to ensure that it was adhered to in collective agreements and individual contracts. In 1976 a new directive laid down the implementation of equal treatment for men and women as regards access to employment, vocational training, promotion and working conditions to which the member states were to conform within two and a half years. In 1978 a directive concerning the progressive implementation of equality of treatment for men and women on matters of social security was adopted. Member states were given six years to integrate this principle into national laws because of the problems involved.

It is part of the Commission's work to monitor the progress made in member states on these questions and offending members have been taken to the European Court of Justice for failing to comply with the directives. But the Commission is not alone in having access to the Court. Private individuals may also claim their rights there. In 1981 two female employees of Lloyds Bank sued the bank, alleging sex discrimination in its pension scheme which allowed men more benefits than women. The case went to the European Court which upheld their claim ruling that pension arrangements fell clearly within Article 119 of the Rome Treaty.

With working women still poorly represented in the better jobs, the battle for full working rights is obviously an ongoing one. In December 1981 the Commission recognised this be drawing up a new Action Programme to improve equal opportunities for women in the Community between 1982 and 1985. The intended financial commitment was 550,000 ECU in 1983, rising to 750,000 ECU by 1985. A new permanent European Advisory Committee on Equal Opportunities for Men and Women was to be established, a consultative body, composed of the national equal opportunities bodies, to pool research and advise the Commission.

The first part of the new Action Programme was composed of eight measures to be tackled by the Commission and the member states. These aimed at strengthening the position of women in: (1) their means of redress against sexual discrimination; (2) their protective legislation against exploitation; (3) social security benefits; (4) taxation and employment; (5) their rights in agriculture; (6) the field of the self-employed; (7) parental leave; (8) maternity provision.

In the second part of the Action Programme the Commission hoped to tackle a rather harder target—'non-legal' obstacles to equal opportunities, that is to say existing attitudes to women and the traditional segregation of roles in Western society. The Commission is hoping here for funds to implement more positive discrimination in favour of women, for example more training to equip them for employment in the new technology industries and other non-traditional jobs. In the meantime, until such funds are available, the Commission can only try to educate public opinion through information campaigns and exchanges of information.

The Commission has also attempted to protect the interests of the whole working population in an age when large firms take over other firms and then proceed to cut down operations. In 1975 the Council adopted a directive on the procedures to be followed when an employer is contemplating mass dismissals; he was required to consult workers' representatives and observe certain time limits. In 1977 the Council adopted another Community directive on the safeguarding of employees' rights in the event of transfers of businesses, for example the continued payments of pensions. On working conditions as such the Commission has issued recommendations (rather than directives) on issues such as the 40 hour week and four weeks' paid holiday for all full-time workers. In fact these conditions had already been implemented in the member states.

It is estimated that each year some 100,000 Community citizens die and over twelve million are injured as a result of accidents. Therefore the Commission's Action Programme has included a number of measures to improve safety, hygiene and health at work. A number of directives have been adopted, including one in 1980 protecting workers from exposure to chemical, physical and biological agents at work.

Under the Social Fund, money has been made available for pilot projects to integrate the handicapped into working life and the first programme of this kind ran from 1974 to 1979. An anti-poverty programme was also started in 1975 after an Irish initiative; it set funds aside of 5.25 million EUA over two years and was later extended to 1980. Though eye-catching, the scale of the programme was too small to amount to anything more than an expression of Community concern for the problem.

Industrial Democracy

The Community has so far shown little interest in negotiating methods in industrial relations despite a reference to it at the Paris summit. It has, however, shown more interest in encouraging more active employer and union involvement in the Community decision-making process. Over the years it has become the practice for the Community advisory committees to contain representatives from both sides of industry and in particular the Standing Committee on Employment has discussed many questions and gained greater prestige.

The Community is also concerned to promote the idea of worker directors so that workers have a say in company decisions. In some countries, for example West Germany, this was already common practice, especially in the coal and steel industries. In most Community countries, employees merely had a say in working conditions and little or no say in major company decisions. When the Commission tried to bring in proposals concerning more employee participation it ran into considerable opposition from member states like Britain.

Community Social Policy in Action: The Case of the Migrant Workers

Articles 48 and 49 of the Treaty of Rome enshrine the principle of the free movement of workers from one Community country to another. In practice the migration of workers within the EEC has been relatively limited. Only Italy and Ireland have been large suppliers of migrant labour with figures of 700,000 and 450,000 respectively.

The Commission has explained this low level of labour mobility within the Community in several ways. The standard of living having become more evenly balanced in the Community, it was possible for workers in poor areas to move to richer areas of their own country. Differences in language and culture discouraged workers from taking jobs outside their own country. The existence of welfare benefits was perhaps another disincentive and, as the economics of the member states in the Community developed along parallel lines, it meant that where unemployment existed in one industry in a member state, it was almost certain to be the case for that same industry in the other Community countries.

What was ironic and unexpected in the growth years of the Community was the great influx of third country workers from outside the Community. The statistics on this question are unreliable but recent estimates suggest that there are now about six million foreign workers in the Community, of whom 4.5 million come from third countries. Many of them have been joined by their families so that the number of foreigners now living in the Community is estimated at 12 million, of whom about 9 million come from non-member countries.

As a result of this influx most Community countries experienced the creation of a migrant problem by the late 1970s. Many people from Surinam and the Moluccan Islands had gone to The Netherlands which by 1978 had 370,000 immigrants from outside the Community. Belgium recruited many Italians, Spaniards, Moroccans and Turks in the boom years and by 1978 had a total immigrant population of 160,000. Even Italy which had been such an exporter of labour in the early years of the Community experienced considerable immigration from Yugoslavia, Tunisia and several other countries amounting to something between 300,000 and

400,000. The British problem was different in character; there was considerable recruitment of labour from the Caribbean, India and Pakistan but these immigrants usually had citizenship status and political rights.

It was France and Germany that experienced the largest influx of foreign labour. Over three and a half million workers were registered in these two countries in 1979. The bulk of France's one and a half million foreign workers was composed of Algerians, Moroccans, Tunisians, Spanish and Portuguese. West Germany has been the largest post-war employer of foreigners who number about two millions. About half a million have come from Turkey and the remainder from Yugoslavia, Greece, Spain and Portugal.

In the years of expansion such migration could be seen to have positive benefits. The migrant workers would function as an economic safety-valve, reducing manpower bottlenecks, especially in certain jobs which the indigenous workers did not want, although the availability of a relatively cheap external source of unskilled manpower retarded the search for greater productivity in some sectors, e.g. transport and the automobile assembly industry. It could even be argued that such migration benefited the countries of origin by reducing domestic unemployment, by the sending of remittances home and by improving the skills of the migrants for when they returned home.

Today, however, with the depressed state of virtually all the Community economies, the migrants are seen as an unwelcome problem. Indeed since 1973 most Community countries have shut their borders to third country migrants. The whole question is a vexed one for a number of reasons: (1) there is a great deal of illegal immigration and the Commission has suggested that there are about half a million illegal immigrants in the Community. This is probably an underestimate because for many years most of France's immigrants entered the country clandestinely because the official route was so slow. Illegal migrants tend to suffer from more exploitation because they dare not complain. (2) In times of high unemployment, the migrant worker is given the sack and is at the end of the queue for jobs. However, unlike the Community migrant he has no right of free movement. A Turk resident in Germany cannot work in France. This is a disadvantage in economic terms because free movement could help to absorb the unemployed migrants who will, as stated above, often take on work which others do not want. (3) If the Community is enlarged to include countries that have been major suppliers of guest-workers, then the migrants will acquire freedom of movement as will all other workers from those countries. This consideration is a problem connected with the proposed enlargement of the Community in 1984. Community countries fear a kind of uncontrolled flood of migrants from Greece, Spain and Portugal, countries which have contributed over one million of the guest-workers. (4) The guest-workers are now seen as a burden on the social services. When they first came to the host country they were normally young and healthy and did not cost the social services very much. In time they have become older, need more care and attention themselves but have also brought over their families who need to be housed, educated and kept healthy. (5) The first generation of guest-workers tolerated evil conditions in ghettoes or shanty-towns like the French bidonvilles because they remembered the poor conditions back home. The second generation guest-workers are far less passive. They feel rootless as they cannot identify with a homeland which they have never seen or with the country in which they reside. They resent the fact that the best jobs are kept by the indigenous population while they suffer unemployment or have to put up with jobs with poor pay, bad conditions and unsocial hours. What was true for Britain in 1981 with the Toxteth riots may occur in other Community countries. The migrants form a sort of social time-bomb.

Such a situation aroused the concern of the Commission which proposed an Action Programme for Migrant Workers and their Families. This was the subject of a Council resolution in February 1976. It planned a number of measures relating to language teaching, vocational training, social security, housing, social services, schooling and economic and political rights so that the inferior position of third country workers could be improved.

Early in 1976 the Council adopted a regulation extending the trade union rights of migrant workers and in 1977 came a directive on schooling for migrant workers' children. Funds for this have been made available and a 1981 example was a Social Fund grant of £46,500 for the training of 100 language instructors at the National Centre for Industrial Language Training at Southall in Middlesex. However, such piecemeal reforms are unlikely to alter the position of migrants very significantly and a fully developed Community policy for the migrant problem remains a long way off.

The problem remains urgent as the events in West Germany in 1982 demonstrated. An upsurge of xenophobia led to action groups rallying to the banner 'Ausländer raus' ('foreigners out'). Their main targets were the Turkish 'gastarbeiter' and non-Europeans seeking political asylum in West Germany. Intolerance had grown in proportion with the rising rate of unemployment of which the two million gastarbeiter were seen as a major cause. With their families they formed 4.6 million, 7 per cent of the population. As a result new restrictions on the entry of their dependants were made law in 1981 and in 1982 the Turkish minority of 1.5 million was subject to violent attacks from neo-Nazi groups.

Conclusion

The work of the Social Fund can claim some successes in the 1970s. Increasingly Social Fund aid has gone to the regions and industries in most need of it (unlike the 1960s when West Germany was the main recipient of aid). Of the 436 million EUA granted by the Commission in mid-1980 for the first batch of approved applications 16.4 per cent went to Ireland, 25.4 per cent to France, 26.2 per cent to Italy, 22.5 per cent to Britain but only 2.9 per cent to West Germany and 4 per cent to the three Benelux countries.

There is some evidence that the equal pay directives have begun to have some effect. The average gross hourly earnings of women in industry compared to those of their male colleagues rose between October 1975 and 1978 to 62.8 per cent against 52.2 per cent in Italy, to 43.6 per cent against 38.6 per cent in Britain and to 27.5 per cent against 25.7 per cent in The Netherlands.

The improvements in the provisions over safety and health protection at work also seem to be bearing fruit though it would be absurd to claim that Community efforts are the only factor at work. Industrial accidents have decreased in number, particularly those resulting in death or serious injury. This is clear from the statistics on industrial accidents in the iron and steel industry, the only industry where statistics have been harmonised on a Community basis. Whereas in 1960 there were 0.19 fatal accidents per million hours worked in the Community of Six, by 1978 in the Community of Nine the figure was down to 0.06, less than a third of the previous amount. Over the same period the number of non-fatal accidents declined by more than 50 per cent. Similarly impressive figures occurred in other industries.

Nevertheless the Social Policy suffers from serious weaknesses. One severe constraint is the tiny proportion of the Community budget devoted to social work; in 1981 it gained only £568 million, about 4.6 per cent of the budget. At a time when unemployment was reaching 11 million, this figure was pathetically inadequate.

Even where the Community does influence employment issues, its action is sometimes unwelcome to member states whose policies conflict with Community ideas and who are concerned about their budgetary contributions. There is clearly a potential conflict in, for example, Mrs Thatcher's Britain where the government is attempting to restrict public spending rather than seeing it increased.

One pressing Community need is progress towards integration of Social Fund operations with other Community policies such as the Regional and Agricultural Funds since they may all be working towards solving the same problem. If they were all better co-ordinated, then the problem could be more effectively attacked.

So far the Social Policy itself has been a mixture of measures rather than a coherent whole, a reality tacitly admitted in June 1980 when the Council passed a Commission resolution on guidelines for a co-ordinated Community labour policy. This aimed at better integration of the Community labour market: (1) by increasing co-operation between the national and Community employment services; (2) by developing placement services like the SEDOC system; (3) by stimulating co-operation between both sides of industry for better manpower planning; (4) by more help for women, the young and industries facing structural adaptation; and (5) by the creation of employment in the public services, more work-sharing by limiting over-time and more flexible retirement.

But more needs to be seen to be done under the Social Policy for political reasons. Community unemployment figures have been unacceptably high since 1979 and high unemployment has now become the most important and intractable problem facing the Community. It seems likely that the position will become worse before it gets better for a number of reasons. (1) Until the middle of the 1980s the number of young people arriving on the labour market will be higher than the number of workers retiring. Not until 1984 will the number of first-time job-seekers start to fall and the number of workers retiring start to increase. The growing number of children of migrant workers will swell the numbers looking for work. (2) The continuing problems over energy, inflation and world recession seem likely to act as a brake on employment. (3) The use of new technologies such as microprocessors will eliminate many jobs throughout the economy. It is estimated for example that 4 million jobs will be lost in offices in Britain by 1990 as a result of the new processes. (4) A number of European industries, for example steel and textiles, will continue to face the problems of structural change because of increasing overseas competition and shifts in demand. Often the only solution is the adoption of the most modern techniques which will make the industries more competitive but will require more productive and fewer workers.

It goes without saying that this situation involves a social tragedy but it is also a test of the Community's credibility. If Community policies in the 1980s make a contribution towards diminishing unemployment, then the Community will gain credit and more support. If the Community fails to make a significant contribution, then many more critics will question its value. Unfortunately many unemployed may, albeit irrationally, blame the Community for their misfortune because it is still to many people a remote body and a convenient scapegoat.

For all its limitations the development of Social Policy is still one of the best hopes for the improvement of the present employment difficulties. Political obstacles, however, seem likely to slow its development. In 1982, for example, Ivor Richard hoped to expand spending under the Social Fund to £1 billion in 1983 and to have its rules made more flexible so that jobs could be created more directly. He wanted specific authority to finance training for the young unemployed, job-creation schemes and aid for new industry. Such ideas were criticised by the directors-general and other commissioners who felt that Mr Richard, in his attempt to expand the powers of the Social Fund, was cutting across their areas of responsibility.

Mr Richard also faced disappointment over another aspect of his work, this time at the hands of the European Parliament. The previous Social Affairs Commissioner Mr Henk Vredeling had proposed that multinational companies should consult their employees on all matters affecting their jobs (the so-called Vredeling directive). In considering this directive, the European Parliament thoroughly weakened it by proposing 35 amendments after lobbying by American-based companies. In addition the Social Affairs Commissioner can normally expect an uphill struggle against Community Governments, the majority of which are right of centre.

Further Reading

Barber, J. and Reeds, B., *European Community: Vision and Reality*, Croom Helm, London, 1973.
Coffey, P., (ed.), *The Economic Policies of the Common Market*, Chapter 6, Macmillan, London, 1979.
El Agraa, A. M., *The Economics of the European Community*, Philip Allan, Deddington, 1980.

Articles
'Migration in the EEC', *European Trends*, February 1979.
'Labour Migration in the EEC', *European Trends*, February 1982.

Questions

(1) Why has the need for a Community Social Programme increased since 1971?
(2) How was the Social Fund reformed in 1971?
(3) Describe the main areas of concern in the Social Action Programme.
(4) Why have migrant workers become a major social issue since 1971?
(5) What obstacles have blocked the development of a powerful Social Policy?

7
Regional Problems and Approaches

The Nature of the Regional Problem

It is not likely that all regions of a national economy will ever enjoy an equal degree of success. Certain regions are always likely to be more prosperous than others and today it is fashionable to point to the 'centre periphery model' as an explanation of regional diversity. This model postulates the existence of a national economic 'centre' and a surrounding periphery and suggests that resources will tend to move towards the centre by a kind of gravitational pull. The result is that the centre achieves high levels of growth while the periphery, especially those parts furthest away from the core, will become a backwater suffering poor levels of growth and remaining underdeveloped.

The origins of this phenomenon lie in a number of characteristics of a modern economy. Firstly the decline of agriculture has led to the depopulation of usually peripheral regions which are rather hostile to the development of urban life. A second feature has been the decreasing reliance of industry on natural materials such as coal. This development has harmed the prosperity of regions which relied on mining in earlier years and has left the environment in such regions unattractive. Thirdly, the increasing importance of the tertiary sector—the service industries—has increased the tendency for populations to concentrate in the major cities, especially the capital cities. Finally one must point to the replacement of the free markets of earlier periods by imperfect markets where prices are fixed for the whole country by government, businessmen or unions. This hits a declining region hard because when one of its industries is falling behind, it cannot solve the problem by reducing wages; its only recourse is unemployment. When the industry is heavily concentrated in a particular region, as is the case with coal, steel or shipbuilding, a depressed area is created.

In theory such uneven growth should lead to a movement of labour and capital out of the high-cost regions and into the depressed areas where resources are cheaper. In practice such developments occur too slowly and often the best labour, the youngest or the most skilled, will leave the depressed region causing it to fall even further behind. Such labour will move into densely populated areas, creating more problems of congestion while leaving behind relatively unused capacity in the declining region.

The creation of a form of economic integration like the European Community will tend to aggravate existing regional problems. The range of disparity between the richest and the poorest regions becomes greater and may have political consequences since attention is drawn to the wider disparity. More importantly, such integration may exacerbate the regional problem directly. More intense competition will result and this will tend to damage uncompetitive industries in the depressed regions. Also if the creation of the Community results in some equalisation of wages, it will increase the incomes of those in work in the less prosperous regions but at the same time it will increase their unemployment. Finally integration will lead to some regions being very remote indeed from the economic centre of the Community while some areas in fact become more central. Thus the Saar became more central after 1957 while the Mezzogiorno and Wales became even more peripheral than they had been in their national economies.

Regional Diversity within the Community

With a surface area of 1.6 million square kilometres, the European Community boasts a wide variety of climate, landscape, people and activities. The full range of its diversity is revealed when one examines its regions. The industrial concentration of the Ruhr, farming in the Po Valley, the docks of Antwerp, the fishing regions of Brittany, the tourist regions of the Mediterranean, vast conurbations like London and sparsely populated Alpine regions—all show a face of the Community which is diverse and changing.

By world standards, the Community may appear a prosperous whole but at regional level the disparities are enormous. Gross domestic product per person in the Community's richest regions like Hamburg is at least six times higher than in the poorest regions of Calabria in Southern Italy or the west of Ireland.

There are four main types of problem area within the Community: (1) underdeveloped rural areas; (2) regions suffering industrial decline; (3) congested cities; (4) frontier regions. Some underdeveloped rural areas are still very dependent on farming which often provides 20 to 40 per cent of all jobs, compared to an average of 8 per cent for the Community as a whole. Examples of such regions are the south of Italy, the west of Ireland, west and south-west France and even parts of Scotland, Wales and Bavaria. Much of the farming in such regions is based on tiny holdings far too small to be economically viable and in the last 25 years employment in agriculture in the Community has fallen by 60 per cent or by more than 13 million workers. This necessary exodus has, however, created problems of rural depopulation. Also it is usually the younger people who leave the land, leaving behind the old who are less likely to accept new ideas. In earlier years it was relatively easy for those leaving agriculture to find work in industry but since 1973 with rising unemployment this avenue of escape has disappeared and there is an urgent need to create alternative jobs in the rural areas themselves.

These rural areas suffer other disadvantages. They possess inadequate infrastructures and often labour from disadvantages of geography and climate—parts of northern Scotland for example. All tend to be on the periphery of both the national state and the Community as a whole as is the case with the Mezzogiorno and the west of Ireland. These features make it difficult to attract new investment.

The other main type of problem region is one suffering the decline of its traditional industries owing to shifts of demand, competition from other countries or the world recession. Steel, coal, textiles, shipbuilding have all felt the cold wind of recession and all are heavily concentrated industries. As a result particular regions like west-central Scotland, South Wales, Northern Ireland, southern and eastern Belgium and Lorraine have been gravely affected. These regions suffer high unemployment and face daunting tasks of improving the environment and creating new industries.

Some of the Community's more densely populated conurbations face problems of congestion, pollution and general environmental decline. These occur in the poorer regions in cities like Naples and Liverpool but they are to be found mainly in the richer and more central parts of the Community. The Paris region houses 19 per cent of the French population on 2 per cent of the national territory and the London metropolitan area comprises 23 per cent of the British population. Such congestion leads to decline in the quality of life and problems of inner-city decay.

Finally the problems faced by certain border regions within the Community should not be overlooked. For example the regions of Lorraine, the south of Luxembourg and the Saar form a contiguous area with similar problems stemming from the decline of the steel industry. West Germany has a particular border problem owing to its frontiers with East Germany and Czechoslovakia which run for 1,380 kilometres from Schleswig-Holstein to Bavaria. It is a peripheral area which understandably has not attracted investment.

In the last decade the problems of these regions have, if anything, become even more daunting and have real political implications. 'Since the onset of the internal recession in 1973, regional problems and regional crises have become the major underlying disintegrative tendency in the EEC' (J. Carney, R. Hudson and J. Lewis (eds), *Regions in Crisis*, 1980). The danger that the Community might break apart because of this problem was dramatically underlined by events in France in 1979. A crisis in the French steel industry from 1974 on led to savage closure programmes in Lorraine in 1977–78. Reaction was immediate; a series of general strikes was called early in 1979 and eventually the situation was so threatening that the CRS, the French riot police, had to be brought in to quell the rioters.

Particular Problem Regions

All the Community states have some kind of problem regions. West Germany, as we have seen, has a problem region bordering the Iron Curtain countries while in France some areas appear in danger of becoming rural deserts—Brittany and the Massif Central for example. In Belgium the decline of traditional industries has led to the south becoming a backwater and the whole of the south-west of the Irish Republic remains underdeveloped. Even the prosperous Danes and Dutch have claimed that peripheral regions in their countries away from the great cities are depressed areas. However, it is perhaps more instructive to analyse two regions—

Northern Ireland and the Mezzogiorno (Southern Italy)—in a little depth to illustrate the intractability of the problems.

Northern Ireland is one of the Community's five least prosperous regions and a 1980 Commission report on its prospects was bleak. Unemployment by the end of 1980 had risen to 16.3 per cent of the working population (and by 1982 had risen to over 20 per cent). This rate of unemployment was twice as high as the Community average and was worst in the rural areas of the south and west. Earnings are lower than elsewhere in the United Kingdom and are only 59 per cent of the Community average yet the people of the Province work longer hours.

There are 1.5 million people in Northern Ireland and the working population of 600,000 is increasing steadily, thanks to a birthrate which is one of the highest in Europe. Over 45 per cent of the population is under 25 years of age. Lacking energy resources, Northern Ireland has to pay considerably more for its energy than other parts of the United Kingdom and being on the extreme periphery of the Community it has to bear the additional cost of transport for its imports and exports, adding about 10 per cent to prices. As a result of these factors, the standard of living is well below that of most other regions in the Community. Less than 50 per cent of families in Ulster own a car and only one third of all homes have central heating, compared with 55 per cent in the United Kingdom as a whole. The standard of housing is very poor indeed with 20 per cent of all houses unfit for human habitation. In Belfast half the houses were found to be insanitary.

Given this grim catalogue of deprivation, it is understandable that many Ulster people have emigrated. In the 1970s about 18,000 people a year were leaving the Province, especially the young and the skilled. At the heart of the problem is the decline in Northern Ireland's basic traditional industries, shipbuilding and textiles with the consequent loss of jobs. In 1950 twenty-four and a half thousand people were employed in the ship-building industry; by 1980 this figure had fallen to 7,400. In the traditional textile industries in the same period, the number employed fell from 65,000 to 18,000. Changes in farming methods reduced the number of people employed on the land. In the 1950s, one in five of Northern Ireland's working population was involved in agriculture; it is now one in ten. Those who remain in farming face severe problems such as the high cost of feedstuffs for livestock.

The political troubles of the Province which have of course hampered economic activity in general have particularly discouraged foreign investment. On occasion even when such investment has occurred, the end result has been fiasco as witness the decline of the De Lorean car firm in 1982 despite aid from the Regional Development Fund of over £7 million.

The character of Italy's Mezzogiorno was brought home to British people in November 1980 after an earthquake had created havoc over an area of Italy stretching 100 miles inland from Naples and Salerno. The slow recovery from that disaster has illustrated the difficulty of improving a region which has been a problem for all Italian governments from the period when Italy was united in 1861.

The Mezzogiorno is probably the poorest region in the European Community. One of the main reasons for this is the large population which has one of the highest reproductive rates in the whole of Europe. With nearly 20 million people there, very high rural densities of population result. The natural environment is hostile with only one eighth of the region flat and suitable for cultivation; malaria, drought, thin soils, erosion and mountainous terrain have all played their part in reducing the capacity of the region to support its large population adequately.

The combination of a large population and a limited supply of suitable land conspire to keep agriculture in the Mezzogiorno rather backward. Southern agriculture possesses the largest proportion of small farms in the Community. For Italy as a whole the average farm comprises only 8 hectares of land. This compares with a Community average of just under 17 hectares and 65 hectares in the United Kingdom. Many Southern farms particularly in the hilly areas are under 3 hectares in size.

Agricultural incomes in these areas are low and there is little opportunity to add to them by part-time work in industry as regional development policies have failed to create a network of small and medium-sized industries. There have been large industrial projects in steel and petrochemicals but these have provided few jobs. As a result real poverty remains a disturbing characteristic of the South. Per capita income there was only half the national average in 1950 and this situation has not improved in subsequent decades. The striking growth of the North has had the effect of sucking capital, enterprise and labour from other parts of Italy. Much of the labour has come from the South, but usually the youngest and most productive elements.

The Development of the Regional Development Fund

The idea of a Community regional policy is implicit in the preamble of the Rome Treaty in which the contracting parties stress their concern 'to strengthen the unity of their economies and to ensure their harmonious development by reducing the differences existing between the various regions and the backwardness of the less favoured regions'. However, there is no explicit call for a common regional policy in the Treaty though a number of articles scattered through it relate to a regional problem. Thus Article 39 points to the need for the Common Agricultural Policy to have regard to 'structural and national disparities between the various agricultural regions'. The clearest reference to regional policy lies in Article 90 relating to state aids. This article allows state aids for regional development with the Commission exercising a general supervision of such aids.

Not until 1969 did the Commission begin to take a more positive interest in regional policy with its idea of a Regional Development Rebate Fund which would make grants by way of interest relief. This scheme was never implemented but the 1969 Hague Summit, in calling for the achievement of economic and monetary union, recognised that regional policy would have to be given more attention. The major breakthrough came at the Paris Summit of 1972 at which the British Prime Minister Edward Heath pressed strongly for the creation of a Regional Development Fund and won the agreement in principle of the Nine. The British knew that their terms of entry to the Community were such that they were likely to be net contributors to the Budget and a Regional Development Fund might correct the imbalance as the United Kingdom would be a net beneficiary. In the words of Denis Swann, 'the Regional Fund might do for the UK what the CAP had done for France'.

The Paris Summit also suggested that the Commission should prepare a report on the Community regional problem and in 1973 the Thomson 'Report on the Regional Problems of the Enlarged Community' was published. The report showed that although through the 1960s the Community had achieved an average annual growth rate of 5.4 per cent, the ratio between the richest and poorest regions, calculated in terms of gross domestic product per capita, remained constant at 5:1 and that overall patterns of unemployment remained the same. In other words, such intervention as had so far been attempted by national governments and the Community to tackle the regional problem in the form of grants or loans from bodies like the European Investment Bank had been woefully inadequate. The movement towards integration had not benefited the peripheral parts of the Community and more action was needed to distribute the economic benefits of Community membership more evenly.

In 1973 George Thomson, the then Commissioner for Regional Policy, proposed the establishment of a European Regional Development Fund (ERDF) of 2,250 million UA (£931.5 million) to be spent over three years. The Fund was intended to complement the efforts of national governments to assist underdeveloped regions. There were three criteria which would decide which regions would benefit from the Fund: (1) a gross domestic product per capita consistently below the Community average; (2) dependence on agriculture or a declining industry; and (3) a consistently high rate of unemployment or net outward migration.

Thomson suggested 31st December, 1973 as a deadline for the setting up of the Fund but this was not met due to disagreements between the member states as to the size of the Fund. While the British naturally wished for a large Fund, the Germans, whose views had been rather neglected and who stood to gain little from the Fund, wanted a considerably smaller Fund. Only at the Paris Summit of December 1974 did the Heads of State decide to set up a Regional Development Fund as from 1st January, 1975. But the size of the Fund was severely reduced from 2,250 million UA to 1,300 million UA (£541.67 million). The method of distribution was also changed. In place of the Community criteria mentioned above, aid was to be distributed on a rigidly proportional basis—for example 40 per cent for Italy, 25 per cent for the United Kingdom and 6 per cent for Ireland with national governments alone having the right to make applications and not the firms or authorities to whom the projects referred. This was a severe constraint on the potential value of the work of the Fund because even if the Commission believed that a member state's regional programme was unbalanced, nothing positive could be done to assist, since only projects suggested by national governments could be considered.

When the Fund first started Community aid could only be given to projects already in receipt of support from national authorities. The Community took the view that the purpose of the Fund was to give extra support to projects in the regions and that the Fund should ensure that not only was more money spent but that more projects should be undertaken (the principle of additionality). Under the original agreement establishing the Fund the Commission was required to produce proposals for the future of regional policy after a three year period. This was duly done in a document called 'Community Regional Policy—New Guidelines', produced in 1977. Its most important proposals were to keep a part of the Fund outside the system of national quotas for the Commission to spend on 'specific Community regional development measures' as opposed to the measures pursued by member states, to place member states under the obligation to produce and forward to the Commission details of their regional development programmes and to ensure that the Commission took fuller account of the likely effect on the regions of all Community policies.

These new guidelines were agreed in principle by the Council of Ministers in June 1978 and adopted in 1979. As a result, the Fund is now divided into two parts. The largest part continues to operate under a system of national quotas and a new 'quota-free' section has been created. The quota section is by far the larger part of the Regional Fund, accounting for 95 per cent of available resources. It is the instrument through which the Community provides additional financial support for regional development measures undertaken by the authorities of the member states. It is shared between the member states by a system of quotas which aims at directing the largest shares of the Fund towards the countries with the most acute regional problems. Up until the end of 1980, almost three quarters of the allocations from the section went to Italy, Ireland and the United Kingdom. With the entry of Greece into the Community in 1981, the quotas were slightly changed to cater for the regional problems of the new member state but the principle of sharing the resources between the countries most in need remains the same.

Each member state currently receives the following share of this section of the Fund:

Belgium	1.11%	Ireland	5.94%
Denmark	1.06%	Italy	35.49%
Germany	4.65%	Luxembourg	0.07%
Greece	13.00%	The Netherlands	1.24%
France	13.64%	United Kingdom	23.80%

Regional Fund priority areas are the same as nationally-defined priority areas. As a result most aid has gone to regions like Southern Italy, Northern Ireland, the west and south-west of France, special development areas in Great Britain, the eastern frontier regions of West Germany and the old industrial areas of Belgium.

It is essential for the welfare of the regions that Community and national regional policy measures are in some way co-ordinated. To provide this element of co-ordination, the Regional Fund continues to only help investments which are also receiving national funds. Under the 'quota' section, governments apply for help from the Fund after selecting a number of suitable projects. Such selection has to be made at some point because otherwise the Fund would face a barrage of applications if they came direct from firms or local authorities.

The 'quota' section makes grants for two particular types of investment: (a) investment aimed at creating or maintaining jobs in industry or in the service sector, for example the building of a factory. Aid from the Fund can extend to 20 per cent of the investment cost but must not exceed 50 per cent of the amount of national aid given to the project. (b) Infrastructure investments which help to develop the region, for example roads, ports, tourist facilities, telecommunications and water supply. The Fund aid normally goes up to 30 per cent of the cost of the investment but in exceptional circumstances can be as high as 40 per cent. When the Commission has approved a project submitted by a member state for a grant, the money is then paid over to the government concerned. The government can, according to the Fund rules, either pass the grant on to the investors or consider it as part-payment for its own national regional aid expenditure. In all member states, assistance for industrial investment is kept by the national authorities, while funds for infrastructure investment are usually (but not always) passed on to the local authorities concerned.

The second section of the Regional Fund, the 'quota-free' section, was only approved in February 1979. It is only a beginning of a new dimension in Community regional policy as it only has 5 per cent of the Fund's resources. Instead of merely providing support for national regional development measures, it will help finance, jointly with the national authorities and in co-ordination with other Community measures, specific Community regional development projects. Such projects are designed to help overcome problems associated with Community decisions in other fields, for example agriculture or consequences of the world recession. Unlike the 'quota' section which merely finances individual investment schemes, the Fund in this section will help overall development programmes including a variety of measures not eligible for aid before, such as management training, market research and help for small firms. The first five measures of this type were adopted in 1980 with a funding of 220 million EUA. The main aims were to help: (a) areas which might be unfavourably affected by enlargement of the Community (the south of Italy and Aquitaine, Midi-Pyrenees and Languedoc-Roussillon in France); (b) areas affected by the crisis in the steel and shipbuilding industries in the United Kingdom (Strathclyde in Scotland, parts of north and south Wales, the Tyne and Wear, Cleveland, Merseyside and Corby in England and Belfast in Northern Ireland); (c) the mountainous areas of Southern Italy which suffer from shortages of energy supply; (d) the frontier regions of Ireland and Northern Ireland.

An important element in the general running of Regional Policy is the work of the Regional Policy Committee. It is a consultative body made up of officials from the member states and the Commission. Its creation had been part of the Thomson proposals of 1973 and it began work in 1975. It concerns itself with all aspects of Regional Policy. Some of its work is linked with the Regional Fund itself, especially in deciding which infrastructure schemes should be given assistance. It also examines the regional development programmes drawn up under the 'quota-free' section of the Fund. It advises the Commission on its research programme in the field of regional development but it has an overall function of co-ordinating all the elements in Regional Policy. It was this Committee that drew up the Commission Report of December 1980, referred to later in this chapter (see page 105).

Since 1975 the Regional Development Fund has given some useful rather than outstanding aid to the United Kingdom. Between 1975 and 1978 it provided £194 million to just under 2,000 projects, mainly in Northern England, Scotland, Wales and Northern Ireland. This had risen to £532 million by 1980 and by the end of 1981 had reached £720 million. The regions gaining the lion's share of assistance from the Fund between 1975 and 1981 were Northern England (£147 million), North-West England (£108 million), Scotland (£178 million), Wales (£115 million) and Northern Ireland (£103 million). Two-thirds of the money (£467 million) was spent on infrastructure developments and the remainder on industrial projects.

Examples of infrastructure development may be taken from several regions. The water shortage suffered in any period of drought by the tourist areas of South West England is being tackled by the creation of three new reservoirs, the Wimbleball project on the edge of Exmoor, Colliford on Bodmin Moor and Roadford on the River Wolf. Grants from the Regional Development Fund for these schemes will total nearly £10 million. In Scotland the Fund made a grant of £600,000 to improve the water supply in Fife with a new reservoir at Castlehill. To assist the development of oil, the Fund has made a grant of a million pounds to develop Sumburgh, Shetland's airport and a similar sum was granted to develop harbour installations at Sullom Voe, Britain's biggest oil port. In 1981 aid from the Fund was given to road improvements in Falkirk and Stirling and port improvements at Frazerburgh and Peterhead. In Wales the Fund has tried to contribute towards eliminating a major weakness in the Welsh economy by grants towards improving the road system around Cardiff. In Northern Ireland a recent emphasis has been that of encouraging the revival of the tourist industry with grants to help the creation of youth hostels, an arts theatre, the improvement of the coastline and the expansion of Belfast's airport.

Examples of Regional Fund aid to particular industrial projects may also be taken from several regions. In 1981 the Fund granted £10 million to the Ford Motor Company, most of which was to be spent at Bridgend in the production of new Escorts. It was hoped that this scheme would create 1,800 jobs. In Scotland in 1981 the Fund granted £6 million to the Nippon Electric Company in Livingston New Town to manufacture computer components. It was hoped that this project would create 650 jobs by 1986. The firm of Tullis Russell and Co., a firm making paper and board, was also granted over £1 million. In the North East of England the firm of Findus Ltd in Newcastle-upon-Tyne was granted £3.5 million to help its production of frozen foods with a hoped-for creation of 436 jobs.

Other Community Instruments

The principal Community instrument to tackle regional development is the Regional Development Fund but it is only one of several funds which, though their aims are not exclusively regional, have made a contribution towards helping the less prosperous areas.

The European Coal and Steel Community (ECSC) had made loans totalling 7,200 million EUA by the end of 1980 to help modernise the coal and steel industries or to attract new job-creating industries in coal and steel regions. For example in 1978 the ECSC made loans of 80 million EUA to Peugeot-Citroën for a new factory near Hagondange and the extension of an existing one at Metz. Both these sites were in the troubled area of Lorraine. The ECSC made a loan of £2 million in 1981 to the Scottish firm of McKellar Watt, the largest sausage manufacturer in the United Kingdom so that it could develop its frozen food section.

The European Investment Bank (EIB) made available over 15,400 million EUA in loans by the end of 1980, most of it for regional purposes. In 1980 more than 1,900 million EUA (70 per cent of all loans made) were directed towards regional development. The British Steel Corporation has been a major recipient of such loans, receiving over 300 million EUA between 1973 and 1979. A noteworthy example is the Ravenscraig steelworks at Motherwell in Scotland. Distillers, the important whisky firm, was given a loan of £12 million for a new whisky plant in Glasgow.

A new Community intervention instrument (the Ortoli facility) has since 1979 given loans for modernising infrastructure and developing energy resources. By the end of 1980 four hundred and seventy million EUA had been granted, most of which went to the problem regions. In 1981 the Ortoli facility was used along with help from the European Investment Bank, to provide 1,000 million EUA to help the areas of Southern Italy devastated by the earthquake of November 1980.

The European Social Fund and the European Coal and Steel Community have together given grants totalling more than 3,400 million EUA for training workers. Aid distributed in 1980 reached a level of more than 1,040 million EUA, 80 per cent of which went to training schemes in the poorer regions (see chapter 6).

The Guidance Section of the European Agricultural Fund (EAGGF) had by the end of 1980 allocated aid worth 2,700 million EUA to modernise agriculture. Most of this aid had gone to the Mediterranean area, the west of Ireland, the Western Isles of Scotland and the Lozère department of France (see chapter 4).

In the framework of the European Monetary System, interest rebates totalling 400 million EUA were given to the least prosperous regions of Ireland and Italy. They were in effect given low-cost loans.

The Central Problems of Regional Policy

That European Members of Parliament who represent problem regions, such as David Harris for Cornwall and Plymouth and Mrs Winifred Ewing for the Highlands, find value in Community regional policy is significant. Transfer of resources from the Regional Development Fund to poor areas have been considerable and by 1981 had reached 4,500 million EUA.

However, the impact of all the funds on the essence of the regional problem has been negligible as a Commission Report of December 1980 demonstrated. The economic gap between different areas of the Community has not been reduced at all; on the contrary it has been widening. The inhabitants of the Community's ten poorest regions now earn on average four times less than their counterparts in the ten richest areas. At the beginning of the 1970s, the ratio was less than three to one. In Southern Italy, for example, average incomes which were at 39 per cent of the Community average in 1960 increased to 50 per cent in 1970 but then fell to 46 per cent in 1973 and continued down to 41 per cent by 1977. In Wales the percentage fell from 79 per cent in 1970 to 61 per cent by 1977. The Commission Report is therefore a disturbing one as it points to the basic failure of Community Regional Policy.

The Commission Report blamed the growing economic crisis as one factor causing the widening economic gap between different areas of the Community and it is true that in a time of recession large firms and state enterprises do tend to close down their operations in the peripheral areas first. They wish to concentrate their efforts only on those areas that remain profitable and they abandon areas that have become unprofitable. Capital, in the words of Felix Damette, has become hypermobile and this results in the acceleration of the pace at which industrial sites become obsolescent. As we have seen, such a process usually hits the depressed regions hardest. Damette himself cites two examples of this hypermobility of capital in France—the plastics and steel industries. The firm of Ugine-Kuhlmann set up a plastics factory at Mazingarbe in the Pas-de-Calais, using coal by-products. But eventually the firm found that using petroleum made for better profits and moved to the Basse-Seine area. As a result the collieries in the Pas-de-Calais all closed. But the irony was that Ugine-Kuhlmann could only have carried out the operation with State assistance. Indeed in the case of the French steel industry it was the state that closed down the steelworks in Lorraine and Valencienness and it is central to Damette's thesis that state intervention has created chaos of monumental proportions for the regions.

In the United Kingdom too there have been many examples of the flight of capital from the regions as a result of the recession.

It is hard to see any rapid end to the recession and even when there is a recovery in economic growth, it is likely to be extremely slow in the next few years. Its impact will be insufficient to reduce the gaps between poorer and richer regions. The situation is made worse because population growth—and consequently the need for new jobs—will be greatest in the peripheral rural regions where creating new jobs is the most difficult. Also employment in the older industrial areas will continue to be threatened by growing competition from outside the Community as Third World countries like Korea develop their own industries.

The task of diverting capital to the regions has become more difficult in the age of the multinationals, as Stuart Holland has shown. Governments would often prefer that a multinational setting up a new plant should locate it in the more backward regions of the national economy. In practice multinational companies can repudiate any pressure to do so by threatening to go abroad if not allowed permission to expand in the area of their choice. The example of the American computer giant, IBM, is illuminating. IBM wanted to expand at Havant in the relatively developed and prosperous South of England. When told by the British government that the necessary industrial permission for such expansion would not be granted, the firm threatened that if one were not granted it would locate the expansion outside Britain altogether. The government therefore granted the certificate to expand at Havant even though this ran counter to the policy of encouraging regional location of firms. As Stuart Holland suggests: 'Because they can locate multinationally, big firms can refuse to go multi-regional'. (But see chapter 16 for the other side of this issue.)

There is in any case a powerful incentive for large firms to locate multi-nationally. Many firms have located new plants in countries like Taiwan, Mexico, Brazil, the Philippines and Hong Kong because labour costs there are so much lower than in the Community. Such savings in labour costs dwarf even massive regional incentives in developed countries because foreign labour costs are often about a quarter of those in Britain. In other words, the Community would have to subsidise up to 75 per cent of wages to equalise the difference in labour costs and in practice national and Community incentives are often insufficient for leading companies to locate in the problem regions.

The growth of the multinational companies has certainly become one influence undermining the effectiveness of the Regional Fund. It is one reason why the bulk of aid from the Regional Fund so far has gone to infrastructure projects rather than to regionally mobile manufacturing firms. Leading companies are not sufficiently tempted by Community in-centives and locate in countries where the labour is cheaper and not un-ionised. 'Donning their seven league boots,' as Stuart Holland phrases it, 'they bypass Europe's problem regions.'

Ironically, other Community policies may have exacerbated the regional problems and the 1980 Commission Report stresses the importance in this respect of the Common Agricultural Policy, trade agreements with other countries and the free movement of factors of production. The CAP mech-anisms of intervention and price controls have increased the disparities in agricultural incomes between one region and another. As shown in chapter 4, the guarantees which farmers receive for their crops are most extensive for products grown in the Community's more fertile, temperate areas, while many Mediterranean agricultural products are less favourably supported. At the same time, the virtually open-ended commitment to provide farmers with guaranteed prices for certain crops has tended to help larger farmers who benefit from economies of scale and reap bigger rewards than their colleagues who work smaller farms. In addition, the Community's weaker regions have been handicapped by the many trade agreements which have encouraged agricultural imports from other Mediterranean countries. Finally, the Commission's regional policy experts argue in their report that the free movement of the factors of production—one of the crucial Com-munity objectives—has contributed to the growing disparity between re-gions. Labour has been the most mobile factor of production and Com-munity influence has accelerated the migration of labour from the peri-pheral regions. This last claim should perhaps be seen as the least important of the three policies in its influence on the regions because as we have seen in chapter 4 migration within the Community has been relatively limited.

In addition to these underlying problems, there are difficulties and lim-itations in the operation of the Regional Fund itself. As described above most of the grants from the Fund go to the governments of the member states. What is important is that the preamble to the Regulation setting up the Fund lays down the principle of additionality or complementarity. The essence of this principle is that aid from the Fund should not merely be a mechanism that would allow members to reduce their own regional expenditure but should add to those efforts. Giving extra assistance to projects already approved is called 'vertical complementarity' whereas if the aid is used to finance additional schemes, it is called 'horizontal complementarity'. Either way, there should be a genuine addition to regional development and the Regional Fund operators do prefer aid going to provide more numerous projects rather than merely providing more generous aid to a static number of investors.

Unfortunately the principle of additionality is difficult to supervise, given the complexity of national accounting procedures and there is a probably well-founded suspicion that the governments of some member-states have simply pocketed aid from the Regional Fund and used it as a means of reducing their own levels of expenditure. An inspection of a member's total expenditure by the Commission would not necessarily prove misuse of Community aid because even if that expenditure had fallen, the member state could still argue that it would have fallen further if Regional Fund aid had not been given.

What is clear in the years since 1975 is that the Finance Ministries in all governments have shown some reluctance to give a specific commitment to the principle of additionality with perhaps the exception of the Irish and Italian governments. The British government has been particularly ambivalent on this issue with continuing divisions between the ministries sponsoring regional development and the Treasury which opposed extra expenditure in the interests of controlling inflation.

A second major weakness in the Regional Development Fund remains its size. Since 1975 the assistance provided by the Fund has averaged only about £300 million a year and in the early years represented less than 5 per cent of the Community budget. Although the size of the Fund has increased significantly since 1979 it still represents only about 10 per cent of the Community budget and is inadequate to tackle the serious problems facing it. In fact it has often had only very small influence on the majority of regional development projects being undertaken. Its activities between 1975 and 1978 involved some 6,300 projects but the Fund only contributed 11 per cent of their total cost.

The need to increase the size of the ERDF is one of the most urgent of Community reforms but the issue faces political difficulties. The reason for the smallness of the Fund is the refusal of governments in the Council to increase its size, particularly in the past the governments of West Germany and France. The issue is likely to become more complicated in the 1980s when the potential accession of Spain and Portugal is taken into consideration. A Commission estimate based on 1978 data suggested that Spain and Portugal might receive respectively 190 million EUA and 125 million EUA from the ERDF. With three new members —Greece, Spain and Portugal—there would be strong pressure for an increase in the size of the Fund as all three countries have severe regional problems. Equally however, the richer member states would resist such an increase because the financial burden would fall on them. Conceivably enlargement could even turn the United Kingdom from a supporter of a larger regional fund into an opponent because in the revision of national quotas, the British proportion might be reduced well below the current 24 per cent level.

Aid to the United Kingdom might be reduced by internal developments. According to Fund rules, projects have to be in government scheduled assisted areas to be eligible. That means that the whole of Ireland and Luxembourg, most of Greece, 33 per cent of the West German population and a rather larger percentage of the Italian and French populations could be eligible for such aid. But the British government is planning in 1982 to declassify or down grade some scheduled assisted areas so that only 25 per cent of the United Kingdom population will be covered after August 1982.

What is indisputable is that enlargement will bring a dramatic widening of regional disparities within the Community. The average income in Hamburg is six times greater than that in Southern Italy. After Spain and Portugal have acceded to the Community, the richest area will be earning twelve times more than the poorest.

Conclusion

The 1975 Regulation establishing the Regional Development Fund required the Commission to re-examine the principles of the Fund by 1st January, 1982. Therefore in July 1981 the Commission proposed significant changes in a bid to step up aid to the Community's least prosperous areas. Instead of spreading its support among all ten countries as at present (the so-called 'sprinkler' system), it suggested that it concentrated its efforts on regions which suffered structural unemployment and where the per capita wealth was less than three quarters of the Community average. The whole of Ireland would meet these criteria, as would Wales, Scotland and the North of England. The other main beneficiaries would be Southern Italy, Greece (except for Athens and Thessalonika) and the French overseas departments.

The Commission also proposed that the 'non-quota' section of the Fund should in future be allocated 20 per cent of resources rather than the 5 per cent allocated since 1979. The non-quota section would be used to encourage new industry in areas where the decline of traditional industries had created high unemployment.

If the Commission proposals are adopted, aid will be shared out in the following way: Italy 43.7 per cent, United Kingdom 29.3 per cent, France 2.5 per cent, Greece 16 per cent, Ireland 7.3 per cent, Denmark 1.3 per cent.

Further Reading

Hodges, M., and Wallace, W., *Economic Divergence in the European Community*, Allen and Unwin, London, 1981.

Parker, G., *The Countries of Community Europe*, Macmillan, London, 1980.

Seers, D., and Vaitsos, C., (eds.), *Integration and Unequal Development*, Macmillan, London, 1980.

Swann, D., *The Economics of the Common Market, Chapter 7*, Penguin, Harmondsworth, 1978.

Questions

(1) Why is the centre periphery model often put forward as an explanation of regional diversity?

(2) Why are Northern Ireland and Southern Italy among the poorest regions in the EEC?

(3) How does the Regional Development Fund operate?

(4) What are the major obstacles to an effective Community Regional Policy?

8
Industrial Policy

The Origins of Community Industrial Policy

In the early days of the Community, industrial policy was more a state of mind than a specific programme as there was no call for a common industrial policy in the Rome Treaty. Of course many articles in the Treaty referred to issues affecting industry, for example Articles 12 to 37 covering the free movement of goods, Articles 48 to 73 covering the free movement of persons, services and capital and Articles 100 to 102 covering approximation of laws. However, the Treaty was not comprehensive in the areas covered nor did it explain how the different policies would be meshed together. The founding fathers of the Treaty seem to have assumed that, once a common market was established, either industry would spontaneously transform itself to take advantage of the market or industrial policies would develop as a kind of natural process.

In the first decade there was real indifference to industrial policy as such. The creation of a single market was the main Commission strategy for industrial development, backed up by legal and fiscal measures which would help firms to develop on a Community basis. Indeed in those early optimistic days, great stress was laid upon the need to create larger firms which could reap the attendant benefits of economies of scale and stand up to competition from outside the Community. In the Commission, in business itself, as well as in the governments of the member states, the view was widely held that any factors which impeded concentration should be abolished. The Commission therefore focussed its efforts in this period on the fields of taxation and company law.

Only in 1967 when the executives of the three Communities were merged was a separate Directorate for Industrial Affairs established (D–G III) but even then it was envisaged that its operations would be limited. However, the achievement of the customs union in 1968 was seen as an opportunity for the new Directorate to review industrial structures in the Community and it was asked to put forward priorities for action in the industrial field.

In 1970 the Commissioner for Industrial Affairs, Colonna, and his staff produced the Memorandum on Industrial Policy (often called the Colonna Report). It gave a survey of existing industrial structures in the Community, the obstacles to industrial adaptation on a Community basis and the role of technology in industrial development. Five broad themes were stressed: (1) the creation of a single market by the removal of remaining barriers, for example public contracts should be open to all firms on a non-discriminatory basis. (2) Work on the harmonisation and standardisation of the legal, fiscal and financial framework within which firms operated would be accelerated in order to help firms develop their activities throughout the Community. This section included the idea of a European company statute, the modernisation of the Community's banking system and the use of Community funds for financing transnational projects. (3) Active promotion of transnational mergers especially in the advanced technological industries. This was seen as necessary to enable European firms to withstand increasing competition from outside Europe. Oddly enough it was soon after this that Directorate IV (Competition) proposed bringing mergers under closer control, reflecting the lack of a coherent Community policy on concentration and competition. (4) Measures to assist industry to adapt to changing conditions especially in matters relating to employment. (5) Greater Community solidarity in external economic relations, particularly over control of multinational companies and technological collaboration.

Though the Colonna Report generated much discussion in the various institutions, it was never seriously taken up by the Council of Ministers and Industrial Policy remained in limbo until the Paris Summit of 1972. As a result of sustained pressure by the Commission and the Heath government, the final communiqué of the meeting contained a commitment by the member states of the enlarged Community 'to seek to establish a single industrial base for the Community as a whole' and to adopt by January 1974 a programme of action and a timetable to achieve it.

The Paris communiqué represented a breakthrough for Industrial Policy and in response to it the Commission in May 1973 produced a Memorandum on the Technological and Industrial Policy Programme. The programme included: (a) an acceleration in the moves to eliminate technical barriers to trade; (b) the opening up of public contracts, a much needed move in a Community where only 5 per cent of such contracts were being awarded to firms from other countries; (c) the monitoring of mergers; (d) the harmonisation of company law; (e) assistance for small and medium-sized firms; (f) the co-ordination of assistance to modernise certain industries. The Commission particularly emphasised the need to eliminate technical barriers to trade within five years and singled out four industrial sectors as immediate priorities—aeronautics, shipbuilding, data-processing and paper.

The Action Programme was adopted with minor amendments by the Council in December 1973 but subsequently the work of the Commissioner for Industrial Affairs, Spinelli, became frustratingly slow as proposals for changes in shipbuilding and paper were delayed by the other Community institutions. The only substantial progress made in the early and mid-1970s was in the fields of the internal market and competition which were not the main responsibility of Directionate III anyway.

Several factors militated against a rapid development of Industrial Policy. The Directorate for Industrial Affairs, lacking a political mandate in the Treaties, suffered from its lack of a direct and continual access to industrial policy-making in the member governments. Secondly, discussion of industrial issues brought to light some disagreements in fundamental economic philosophy. Whereas the French government favoured more Community intervention and planning (in line with its own 'dirigisme' at home), the German position was that industrial development could best be achieved by creating an internal market free from any obstacles with competition as the most effective means of achieving optimum industrial structures.

The creation of a real Industrial Policy was in any case difficult. It raised awkward questions about the distribution of resources among different industrial sectors and among different member states. Each member state tended to define Community Industrial Policy as those measures which served its self-interest and evinced little interest in overall industrial development on a Community basis. In this respect, perhaps, the two Commissioners responsible for industrial affairs between 1967 and 1976— Guido Colonna di Paliano and Altiero Spinelli—were too ambitious in their conception of Industrial Policy. It might have been wiser to implement limited objectives through more modest proposals. Spinelli in particular, in the words of Michael Hodges, 'cajoled governments for their lack of faith in the manner of an Old Testament prophet'. As a result his vision seemed to present a greater threat to national sovereignty than it really did.

The temptation for member states to pursue a narrow self-interest became stronger with the growing crisis in European industry after 1973.

The Community's Growing Industrial Crisis since 1973

The optimistic assumptions concerning steady, indeed spectacular, industrial growth were rudely shattered by a number of adverse factors which came to the fore from 1973 on. Certain external pressures affected European industry, chiefly the rising cost of oil and other raw materials. The Organisation of Petroleum Exporting Countries (OPEC) increased oil prices fourfold within a few months in the winter of 1973–74 and in late 1979 it again increased the price of oil threefold. When inflation is taken into account, the real price of oil was four and a half times higher in 1981 than it had been in 1973.

The rise in oil prices was an important factor provoking a world recession and as a consequence world demand for Europe's manufactures slowed down significantly. International demand rose by only 1.5 per cent in 1981 compared to 6 per cent per annum during the 1970s and 8 per cent per annum during the 1960s. Some Community export markets continued to develop well, notably the Middle East, Africa and the developing countries of Asia. However, exports to Latin America, the Eastern Bloc, the rest of Western Europe, Japan and the United States stagnated.

The third external factor was the chill wind of increasing competition from newly industrialising countries like Taiwan and South Korea as well as from more established competitors like Japan. Low wages and, in certain sectors, ultra-modern equipment enabled these countries to manufacture at prices much lower than their European counterparts. The rise of imported manufactures from Japan and East Asia (which accounted for nearly one third of all Community imported manufactures) was particularly worrying because it reflected a combination of cost and quality which European industries often could not match.

The Cambridge Economic Policy Group in 1981 saw these external pressures as the main cause of the crisis, creating a novel blend of high inflation and high unemployment. However, various internal pressures have affected Community industries adversely. Their competitiveness has declined owing to increased wage claims and high interest rates which have discouraged investment. Investment only increased by 0.7 per cent per year between 1973 and 1980. The development of competitive productive capacity has therefore been restrained, growth has dwindled and Europe has lost ground to its main industrial competitors.

As a result of these external and internal pressures the Community has experienced a severe recession which seems likely to continue at least until the mid-1980s. Its most depressing characteristic has been the dramatic rise in unemployment, itself a factor reducing home demand for Community manufactures. From 2.5 million in 1973, recorded unemployment drifted up by half a million a year to reach 6 million by 1979; by 1982 it had increased to 10 million. The Cambridge Economic Policy Group in 1981 forecast a total of 13.5 million recorded unemployed in the Community as a whole by 1985.

Since 1973 the recession has sharply reduced the growth of all major sectors of the Community economy with the exceptions of fuel and power. The manufacturing sector has been particularly hard hit because of the

Table 3. Inflation and Unemployment in the Community January 1982 (%)

	Unemployment	Inflation
Belgium	15	7.7
Denmark	8.6	11.8
France	9.8	14.0
Germany	6.2	6.7
Greece	2.3	25.4
Ireland	10.8	20.1
Italy	8.9	16.7
Luxembourg	1.1	8.8
The Netherlands	9.5	7.3
United Kingdom	11.3	11.9

Table 4. Recorded Unemployment in the Community (millions)

	1973	1979	1981	1985
Germany	0.27	0.88	1.28	1.78
France	0.39	1.35	1.84	2.92
Italy	1.00	1.65	1.93	2.88
The Netherlands	0.11	0.21	0.39	0.64
Belgium	0.11	0.35	0.47	0.62
United Kingdom	0.62	1.39	2.55	4.09
Ireland	0.07	0.09	0.13	0.18
Denmark	0.02	0.14	0.23	0.32
EEC	2.60	6.06	8.83	13.44

Table 5. Job Losses in Community Manufacturing 1973–85 (millions)

	1973–81	1981–85 (est.)
Germany	1.19	0.75
France	0.60	0.32
Italy	0.01	0.24
The Netherlands	0.27	0.14
Belgium	0.28	0.10
United Kingdom	1.76	0.84
Ireland	0.01	0.02
Denmark	0.10	0.05
EEC	4.22	2.47

Table 6. Community Exports 1973–80 (%)

	1973	1980
Japan	2.9	2.1
East Asia	3.3	3.9
USA	16.1	12.1
Eastern Bloc	9.1	8.4
Rest of Europe	35.3	33.6
Other developed	8.0	6.0
Other developing	16.0	15.9
OPEC	9.4	18.0
	100.0	100.0

cyclical volatility of the demand for its products. From 1973 to 1975 manufacturing output fell by 5 per cent in the Community as a whole and by 8.5 per cent in the United Kingdom. From 1975 to 1979 there was a partial recovery but output still rose by 2 per cent a year less than before 1973. From 1979 to 1981 there was another fall of 4 per cent in manufacturing output in the Community as a whole with a 15 per cent collapse in the United Kingdom. Overall the growth of manufacturing output in the Community averaged only 0.5 per cent a year between 1973 and 1981. In the United Kingdom the level of manufacturing output fell by nearly 20 per cent.

The Development of the Community's Industrial Policy

The critical industrial problems summarised above constrained and conditioned Community Industrial Policy in the 1970s. Nevertheless a three-pronged Industrial Policy has developed and its three areas of operation are: (a) the completion of the common market by the removal of technical and other barriers to trade; (b) the reorganisation of industries in crisis; and (c) the encouragement of new industries with growth potential.

The Completion of the Common Market

The Removal of Technical Barriers to Trade

The provisions of the Rome Treaty referring to the harmonisation of technical standards are found in Articles 100 to 102. Article 100 confers a general power to harmonise all kinds of rules that affect the functioning of the Common Market. Articles 101 to 102 confer an administrative power which enables action to be taken in respect of specific disparities in national legislation which could threaten the distortion of competition in the Common Market.

Technical obstacles or barriers to trade may be said to exist where free trade is impeded by national legislation which regulates such matters as the conditions under which goods are marketed. These include controls on the quality or the composition of goods. That Community action was—and is—necessary to deal with disparities in national legislation is indisputable because a generation after the signing of the Treaty of Rome, the Community is still far from being a genuine common market. Cars, televisions, fridges and cookers can cost twice as much in one Community country as they cost in another. How does this occur? One reason is that national governments maintain non-tariff barriers such as technical standards to help their own domestic industries indulge in price discrimination, as has occurred over the prices of cars in the United Kingdom. Technical standards are also used as a means of excluding from the domestic market the industrial products of foreign rivals.

A Commission report of 1978 gives us a good example of the misuse of technical standards. The Commission looked at the prices of some 100 electrical appliances, hi-fi and video products in major European markets. It found that the prices of these goods varied by over 56 per cent because the manufacturers exploited tiny differences in national safety standards to make reselling difficult. They also refused to service their products if they were bought in another country. They used different brand names in different countries to disguise the fact that the products were in fact one and the same so as to discourage consumers from making precise comparisons and shopping abroad. If common standards were introduced, such artificial obstacles to trade would be eliminated.

The removal of technical barriers are necessary for two other reasons. If common technical standards are introduced for a particular product, it can help to rationalise industrial production. Standardisation helps large-scale production, helps the marketing of interchangeable pieces and simplifies stock control. The savings gained should benefit the manufacturer and ultimately the consumer. Secondly the adoption of common standards helps to protect the consumers' health and promote user safety. Technical standards covering braking efficiency and headlight quality help to reduce the number of road accidents while those covering additives contribute to the improvement of the quality of food. Other common standards may protect the consumer by giving him necessary information, for example correct labelling on clothing.

However, even when member governments are not attempting to protect their home industries through the indirect barrier of technical standards, the problem is a difficult one because each country has over the years created its own set of technical norms, and rarely are these different national norms compatible with each other. The practice of adding vitamins to margarine may be compulsory in The Netherlands but banned in Italy. But the end result is that the area of worthwhile trade in the Community is restricted and it is clear that the Commission has an important role here in attempting to harmonise the norms in force in member countries so that technical barriers which restrict trade may be eliminated. Harmonisation of course has won the Commission itself a bad press because of short-lived proposals for Eurobread and Eurobeer, proposals which were in fact speedily withdrawn. However, it is not aiming at total harmonisation for its own sake but in important areas such as technical standards relating to cars, the creation of Community norms can lead to the realisation of a single European market serving the interests of both manufacturers and consumers.

By 1981 the Community had adopted nearly 200 directives aimed at eliminating technical barriers to trade with many others awaiting adoption by the Council. Nearly 150 of the directives in force applied to industrial products and the remainder to foodstuffs. About 40 of the directives referred to the car industry where the Community's principal concern was safety. On the initiative of the European Commission, for example, provisions for dual braking circuits have been introduced. A number of directives relate to measuring instruments; over 20 directives have been adopted by the Community relating to gas and electricity meters, devices to measure the alcoholic content of spirits and water counters. A directive of 1973 gave the Community a mandate to order the national standards bodies to draw up uniform safety standards for electricity for all member states.

Many directives have been introduced to protect the consumer against dangerous substances according to their degree of toxicity. Community labelling standards have been introduced for these substances as well as for solvents, paints, pesticides and fertilisers. Rules have been prescribed to limit the sale and use of certain dangerous substances. A number of directives relate to foodstuffs, with the particular aim of protecting the consumer. They regulate the use of additives such as colorants, preservative agents and emulsifiers which are incorporated in foodstuffs. A recent directive has defined common practices over the description of weight, last date of sale and additives which have to be carried on the labels of pre-packaged foodstuffs throughout the Community.

The progress of harmonisation, though significant, should not be over-stated. The process of the harmonisation of legislation is very slow because action is necessary over a wide range of areas and because debate over each directive tends to be lengthy. Even on matters of public safety, on which delegations could be expected to adopt similar points of view, national positions are often far apart through genuine differences of approach. The Commission has estimated that 300 directives will be needed to remove the most serious technical barriers in the field of industrial goods. This poses a serious problem of staffing. Up until the 1980s the Commission had been able to do its job with a relatively small staff of 30 in the industrial harmonisation field but as the technical complexities increase, this number is clearly inadequate. To reach the minimum number of 300 harmonisation directives in the industrial field will take 20 years if the average of ten new directives a year is maintained. But by that time many new barriers will have been created by industry and national governments, especially in a period of industrial stagnation. Small wonder that a Commission report of 1979 described the work of harmonisation as similar to emptying a bathtub with a teaspoon while the taps are full on! The pace of technological change itself also presents a problem for the harmonisation process because directives on technical standards for particular products may become outdated by the time they are finally adopted.

Public Procurement

Other aspects of the industrial environment have required legislation for the aim of a genuine common market to be realised. Under the Rome Treaty public contracts should be open to tender not only from national firms but from competitors in all Community states. In practice this has often not been the case as the Commission recognised as early as 1960. In 1971 it issued a directive concerning public works contracts. Common rules were established for the awarding of contracts so that contractors throughout the Community were guaranteed free and effective competition in all major public works offered by member states. This directive was followed up by a second one in 1976. This required that from 1978 certain types of public contract worth more than 200,000 ECU should be notified in the Official Journal of the Communities so that a company in one member state could tender for a contract in another member state. Most types of public contracts are included in this second directive but not military equipment, computers, aircraft or telecommunications.

In considering tenders the contract-awarding authority is supposed to treat all offers equally. If a firm suspects irregularities by public authorities it may make use of a complaints procedure which is the responsibility of the Advisory Committee for Public Contracts.

More Co-operation between European companies

In 1973 the European Commission set up the Business Co-operation Centre—nicknamed the Marriage Bureau—which has aimed to arrange contracts between companies in the Community that wish to co-operate. Between 1973 and 1978 the Centre replied to 3,000 requests for information on many aspects of transnational co-operation. It dealt with 576 requests for co-operation which led to agreements between 70 mostly middle-sized companies.

The Reorganisation of Industries in Crisis

Since the late 1970s Community Industrial Policy has concentrated more and more on sectoral issues and has begun to look like a macrocosm of national industrial polices with detailed planned approaches to different industrial sectors. The reason for this is that Community member governments have wanted to see the Commission contribute towards solving the problems of their declining industrial sectors such as steel, shipbuilding and textiles. The Commission is the natural channel through which member states can combine to ward off foreign competition where it hurts most.

As a result the Commission has become more protectionist since 1974–75 but it has also argued that the protection should be used to carry out a reorganisation of the Community's declining industrial sectors. It has cast itself in the role of independent umpire, attempting to ensure an equality of sacrifice in the necessarily painful re-adjustments.

The architect of the Commission's plans for industrial reorganisation was Viscount Etienne Davignon, the Belgian Commissioner for Industry and Energy, who has established himself as one of the most dominant personalities in the Commission. When Roy Jenkins was President of the Commission, Davignon was a member of his inner cabinet and remains one of the most influential Commissioners whenever a key decision is being debated.

Steel

In no field is the Commission more committed than steel. It has powers under the Paris Treaty setting up the European Coal and Steel Community to organise the internal steel market without having to obtain specific approval from the Council of Ministers.

In 1977 Davignon brought out a plan for the Community steel industry. Its first and less controversial aim was the reduction of the heavy losses being suffered by the steel companies through protection and the raising of Community steel prices. Initially the Commission set voluntary production quotas for the major Community steel companies in the hope that these would bring overproduction and sluggish demand into better balance. When this proved inadequate the Commission introduced guideline prices in May 1977 for a series of steel products and a compulsory minimum price for one product particularly in glut, concrete reinforcing bars used in the construction industry. The compulsory minimum price regime was extended at the end of 1977 to cover other basic steel products and in 1978 guideline prices were raised by 15 per cent. Further price increases were called for in subsequent years and in 1981 the Commission raised the price of crude steel by 25 per cent and special steels by 40 per cent. That such moves if successful would be inflationary did not seem to bother the Commission or the national governments too much because many steel firms, notably the British Steel Corporation, were making such horrendous losses.

On the external front, the Commission has imposed minimum base prices for steel imports and has imposed anti-dumping duties on steel shipments that enter the Community below those base prices. It has also demanded that third countries either negotiate lower levels of steel exports to the Community or run the risk of losing even these lower levels.

The second and much more controversial aspect of the Davignon Plan for steel concerned 'restructuring' or cutting down the industry to size. In 1977 the work force in the Community steel industry was 730,000 and Davignon then warned that 100,000 jobs would have to go because the industry was in a position of serious excess capacity. It was producing over 200 million tonnes a year with plans to increase the figure to 214 million tonnes yet the Community demand for steel in 1977 was only about 130 million tonnes with perhaps 15 million tonnes for net export. Therefore the Commission argued that there should be no modernisation of steel plant without a corresponding closure in capacity. Davignon's industrial department also believed that bigger steel companies were desirable, partly for reasons of economies of scale and partly for reasons of price discipline. In 1979 a voluntary cartel of the largest steel firms was established but was short-lived.

By 1980 the Commission was enforcing compulsory and steadily deeper cuts in steel production. Using the last quarter of 1979 as a base, quotas were set 14 per cent lower in the last quarter of 1980, around 16 per cent lower in the first quarter of 1981 and 20 per cent lower in the second quarter of 1981. For each company the quota was fixed in relation to its best last quarter production during the years 1977 to 1979. In 1981 the Commission called for further cuts of 20 per cent in steel capacity over the next five years and the loss of 150,000 more jobs.

The hope of the Commission was that it would produce a leaner but fitter Community steel industry but this hope has in part been thwarted by the continued plummeting of demand for steel and by the actions of the steel firms and national governments. Steel firms have unloaded excess stocks of steel built up before quotas came into force and they have also sold these stocks at lower than official prices. The next step would seem to be stronger disciplining of such firms by the Commission. Under Articles 60, 63 and 64 of the Community's steel treaty, the Commission can punish 'unfair and discriminatory pricing' with fines of up to double the value of the sale involved. In 1981 the Commission began to use its powers in this area when it fined the German steel company Klöchner 2.3 million ECU for exceeding output quotas. Additional fines seemed likely to be imposed on other German companies as well as Italian and French companies.

Another major obstacle has been the continuation of aid by several member governments to their own ailing steel industries. Ironically the worst offender (given Davignon's nationality) was found to be Belgium which had provided large subsidies to the Walloon steel industry. Plans to reduce Belgium's crude steel capacity from 11.5 million tonnes to 8.5 million tonnes had consistently been delayed. In June 1981, therefore, the Community industry ministers agreed that all member governments should phase out subsidies to their steel industries by 1985. Operational aid not directly linked to a reduction in capacity was to be withdrawn by June 1982; operational aid of any kind by the end of 1984 and financial aid by the end of 1985. Agreement on such a sensitive issue was a remarkable achievement but it remained to be seen how closely member states adhered to this agreement.

Another factor of concern is a flaw in Community steel policy itself; by imposing production quotas and price increases on all steelmakers, the efficient producers suffer in order to help the weaker ones.

The Community steel industry still faces a severe future. An area of growing concern is the trend towards greater protectionism. American behaviour may be cited as an example of this trend. The American government has contrived to restrict cheap steel imports with the result that Community steel exports to the USA fell from 7.4 million tonnes in 1979 to 3.9 million tonnes in 1980. In October 1982 the Community was forced to agree to limit its steel exports to the United States when the Reagan government threatened to impose heavy duties on such exports.

Table 7. Crude Steel Production (million tonnes)

	1960	1974	1975	1976	1977	1978	1979	1980
EEC	98	156	125	134	126	133	141	128
World	341	709	646	676	674	716	746	718

More seriously the Community steel industry still has a long way to go to return to international competitivity. It lacks the large scale modern production units of Japan with its technological superiority yet suffers higher wage costs and lower levels of investment than that country.

Perhaps in the end the world recession itself will produce, albeit painfully, the desired rationalisation of steel production in the Community. By 1981 only 508,000 people were employed in the Community steel industry compared to 730,000 in 1977 but further job losses were seen as inevitable. The social effects were disastrous. Towns heavily dependent on steel for employment have witnessed the forced closure of their steelworks, for example Corby and Shotton in the United Kingdom. Punitive Community quotas made further closures likely in all Community countries.

Shoes

Between 1972 and 1977 the production of shoes dropped by 8 per cent for the whole Community and was particularly serious in three countries— The Netherlands where output fell by 30 per cent, Ireland which saw a 36 per cent cutback and Belgium which experienced a 49 per cent drop. The main cause was a vast influx of low cost shoes from South Korea and Taiwan in particular. The situation tended to be aggravated by protectionist measures taken by Japan and the United States.

Here there have been only glimmerings of a Community policy. The Commission has made approaches to the countries concerned to reduce exports of cheap shoes to the Community and it has also brought in surveillance licensing for shoe imports.

Shipbuilding

By the mid-1970s shipbuilding in the Community was in a parlous state. Whereas in 1955 it had produced 70 per cent of the world total of shipbuilding, by 1976 its share had fallen to 22.6 per cent. Competition had been particularly strong from the Japanese and the future looked even bleaker with the rise of new rivals like Brazil and South Korea. In 1977 the Commission estimated that the Community shipbuilding firms which built 4.4 million tons in 1975 would only deliver 2.4 million tonnes in 1980, a drastic 46 per cent reduction. Its gloomy prognostication was that the workforce would fall from 165,000 to 75,000 by 1980.

In December 1977, therefore, the Commission sent the Council of Ministers a Community Action Programme to help the shipbuilding sector. It involved an ordered reduction in production capacity, the finding of alternative jobs for the unemployed and improved productivity in the surviving part of the industry. In 1978 the Council of Ministers adopted the directive. However, much of the programme was still-born because the Commission had little money available to persuade Community shipyards and governments to do its bidding. As a result, the main thrust of Commission activity has been the monitoring of state subsidies to shipbuilding and if necessary the forbidding of them. As with the steel industry, no state aid was to be allowed unless there was a compensating reduction in capacity. Davignon believed that such aid was doomed to failure and would only increase problems in the future. In December 1977 he said that the Commission would not allow a repetition of the large British government subsidy which had won a controversial £115 million Polish ships order for British yards. Member governments which had been subsidising their shipbuilding industries to the tune of 600 million UA a year were asked to produce restructuring plans for their shipbuilding sectors.

The Commission also tried to negotiate with Community rivals, notably Japan, so that the worst competition might be mitigated. The Japanese government agreed to urge its shipbuilders to increase prices by 5 per cent, to promise to cut back working hours in their yards and exercise some restraint in taking orders from Community member states which had been particularly hard hit.

By 1980 the Commission began to modify its policy somewhat because by 1979 there had been a 40 per cent cut in Community shipbuilding output since 1975 and a 35 per cent cut in employment. The Commission now suggested that some subsidies should be allowed but only where the aim was modernisation. It still opposed aid which only aimed at the temporary baling out of the shipbuilding sector in distress.

Textiles

The Community textile and clothing industry has been another sector hard hit by the economic difficulties common to European industry as a whole and between 1973 and 1981 textile production fell by 5.9 per cent and clothing by 6.3 per cent. This resulted in the closure of 15 per cent of all firms and a reduction in the workforce of 30 per cent (100,000 people). European textile companies have faced growing competition in their traditional markets both inside and outside the Community from a number of Asian, African and Latin American countries such as Japan, Hong Kong, and Pakistan. These countries offered similar products at much lower prices since they often produced their own raw materials and had a ready supply of cheap labour. Between 1973 and 1980 the share of the European market taken by non-Community imports rose from 21 to 44 per cent.

The other major cause of decline was stagnation in demand which had been adversely affected by the recession. The annual rate of increase in demand for textiles by 1981 was only 1 per cent; before 1975 it had been between 3 and 5 per cent.

The decline of the textile and clothing industry as an employer was all the more serious in that it primarily affected one category of workers, women, particularly in some of the poorest regions of the Community. Yet the industry remained important as it still employed 9.6 per cent of the total employed in European manufacturing in 1981 (1.3 million people). In areas already hit by the recession, it was crucial; for example in Northern Ireland it provided jobs for 18 per cent of the employed and 12 per cent in North-West England and Yorkshire–Humberside.

The Commission's attempts to improve the situation have revolved around the Multi-Fibre Agreement (MFA). The first MFA ran from 1974 to 1977 and was designed to liberalise the textile trade but by the time that it expired the Community found that textile imports had greatly increased. Therefore in return for extending the MFA for a further four years, the Commission insisted on bilateral agreements with 26 major textile suppliers so that they restricted their textile exports to the Community, especially in a number of sensitive areas. The agreed annual growth rate of textile imports ranged from 0.25 to 6 per cent.

The developing countries were taken by surprise by the Commission's moves in 1977 and were unable to co-ordinate their position prior to the negotiations. They complained bitterly that the protectionist clauses which they were forced to accept did not stop the imports of textiles into the Community. They pointed out that the restrictions merely benefited textile producers in more advanced industrialised countries who were able to increase their exports to the Community to a far greater extent than they could. The developing countries had some justice on their side on this point because American exports of MFA products to the Community had risen faster than those from the developing countries. The value of all United States exports of textile products to the Community virtually doubled between 1978 and 1980 from $537 million to $1,014 million. Overall, however, the 1977 MFA arrangements did help the Community by limiting the growth of textile imports. Between 1978 and 1980 they rose by only 23 per cent compared with a rise of 75 per cent between 1974 and 1977. Only countries which agreed to limit their exports to the Community could qualify for a reduced customs levy.

The Community synthetic or man-made fibre industry which produced nearly 50 per cent of all textile fibre consumed, faced particular difficulties by the mid-1970s and Community man-made fibre companies lost over £1,000 million between 1975 and 1978. Originally this was not due mainly to foreign competition; the problem was a purely internal one of excess capacity in the Community. Therefore in 1977 the Commission argued that as capacity utilisation in synthetic fibres was only some 68 per cent in 1976, no more state aid should be given to this sector for two years. It then approached the 13 major synthetic fibre makers in the Community: Montefibre and three other Italian companies, Rhône Poulenc of France, Bayer and Hoechst of Germany, ICI and Courtaulds of the United Kingdom, Akzo of the Netherlands, Fabelta of Belgium and two United States multinationals Monsanto and Dupont. Davignon was able to sign with these firms a cartel arrangement which froze market shares and cut capacity.

However, events overtook this arrangement because the Americans, who were increasing their textile exports to the Community in all ranges between 1978 and 1980, made their biggest advance in synthetic products. Their artificially low prices for crude oil and natural gas gave their synthetic fibre products a cost advantage of between 10 and 15 per cent. Combined with the depreciation of the dollar and American productivity, this gave American synthetic textiles a definite competitive edge over European synthetic products. American exports of man-made fibres to the Community rose from 75 million square yards in 1978 to 194 million square yards in 1980.

In dealing with this delicate problem, the Community had to move carefully. It did have safeguard clauses and anti-dumping procedures which it could use against unfair American competition but these could only be used with caution and in watertight cases because of the danger of American retaliation.

By 1982, the Commission wished to make changes in its overall textile trade policy. Given the weakness in the growth of demand within the EEC (about 1 per cent a year) and in the international markets, it felt that it could not return to a 6 per cent growth rate for textile imports as set out in the 1977 MFA. Therefore in 1981 it proposed: (1) differentiating more than in 1977 between the different categories of low cost exporters of textiles to the Community. It wanted to stabilise imports from the most advanced textile countries and then be able to grant more favourable treatment to the poor developing countries; (2) making access of Community textile exports to the markets of the advanced textile countries and East European states a deciding factor in the sort of treatment the Community was willing to give imports from those sources; (3) a five year renewal period for the MFA from 1981 to 1986 which would provide a framework for the Commission to conclude new bilateral agreements with individual supplier countries with a view to restricting textile imports into the Community; (4) urging the American government to give easier access to the American market for the textile exports of low cost producers.

After some difficulties the Council of Ministers reached a consensus on these proposals. The Germans had not wanted as protectionist a package as the British, French and Italians but dropped their objections. In February 1982 the ministers ratified the new MFA which had been agreed at Geneva at the end of 1981 but they stressed that the Commission should negotiate a 10 per cent cut in imports from the major producers of cheap textiles. The ministers also agreed on a ceiling of about 1 per cent for the average annual growth of imports of sensitive products like basic yarns and cloths, and unsophisticated garments like T-shirts and trousers. If the bilateral agreements with individual supplier countries could not be reached, then the Community would be likely to pull out of the MFA altogether.

By the end of 1982, the EEC had signed bilateral agreements with 25 major suppliers including South Korea and it was felt that the Community textile industry had gained a breathing space.

The Encouragement of New Industries

According to Davignon, 'the Community should not become a hospital for sick industries. Community action to help growth industries is as important as the strategy to restructure industries in trouble. In the aerospace industry, in data processing and in other areas opening up markets and pooling industrial capacity will be necessary to reach the scale required by international competition.'

These are fine words but the aim of developing new industry in the hope of giving the Community some level of economic and technological independence has proved even more difficult to achieve than that of helping crisis-ridden industries. Member states have co-operated to some extent over joint action for troubled industries but national interests have prevented much co-operation in the development of new technologies. This can be clearly seen in the case of the aerospace industry where the Commission has regularly proposed initiatives for action on a Community level yet has succeeded in implementing very few of its ideas. The major European companies involved have preferred to collaborate with American firms or between themselves on projects like the JET (Joint European Transport) scheme for a medium-range civil aeroplane or the long-range European Airbus.

Another example where Community action has so far been negligible is telematics. In a Europe where more than 90 per cent of advanced electrical circuits are imported from rivals like the United States and Japan, the Community is one hope for the survival of a European micro-chip industry. Since 1979 the Commission has been trying to develop a common European strategy in telematics (the fusion of telecommunications, micro-electronics, computers and information). In 1981 it put forward proposals for: (a) a programme to co-ordinate support for European micro-chip research and manufacture; (b) the development of common Community telecommunications standards with contracts being open for tender for all companies in the member states.

The Commission's goal was to increase the Community share of world production from 6 to 12 per cent by the mid-1980s and the reduction of the level of dependence on imported products. It seemed an ambitious, if not to say an unrealistic, programme. Despite large amounts of investment from European governments and corporate giants like Philips and Siemens, the Japanese had increased the value of their sales in this field fourteenfold between 1976 and 1980, establishing silicon-chip plants like Hitachi in West Germany. American firms like IBM were also strongly placed. So far Commission proposals have largely remained proposals with little money spent on implementing them. The slow-moving Council of Ministers was perhaps not the appropriate body to make decisions in such a fast-moving field.

However in 1983 the Community put forward ESPRIT—a research programme among 12 leading European companies, including three British firms GEC, ICL and Plessey. Between 1986 and 1990 about £2.5 billion is to be pumped into information technology research, half from the EEC and half from industry. ESPRIT is to concentrate on the next generation of computers, microchips, robotics and computer-aided design.

Further Reading

Swann, D., *The Economics of the Common Market*, Chapter 8, Penguin, Harmondsworth, 1978.

Twitchett, C. C., (ed.), *Harmonisation in the EEC*, Macmillan, London, 1981.

Articles
'The EEC Steel Industry', *European Trends*, May 1981.
'The MFA', *European Trends*, August 1981.
'The EEC response to the Microelectronics Challenge', *European Trends*, May 1982.
'The New Technologies', *European Trends*, August 1982.
'Shipbuilding', *European Trends*, November 1982.

Questions

(1) Why has the Community faced a growing industrial crisis since 1973?
(2) What progress has been made in recent years towards the completion of a common market?
(3) Describe the attempts of the Commission to solve the problems of industries in crisis?
(4) Which new industries should the Commission encourage in the 1980s?

9
Energy Policy

The Nature of the Problem

The World Perspective

The problems over energy in the final quarter of the twentieth century are not merely European; they are global. Given the developments in world energy in the twentieth century, a crisis similar to that of 1973 was always likely and probably inevitable. Between 1925 and 1980 world energy demand, measured in thermal units, had risen sixfold for two main reasons. Firstly, world population had increased in that period by four billion. Secondly per capita energy consumption had risen threefold despite a slowing down in the process in the 1970s. The latter factor is generally considered to be the more powerful of the two with the rise in energy consumption in the home, in industry and in transport.

Certain regions of the world have consumed the lion's share of world energy supplies. North America in 1980 consumed 30 per cent of world energy while its population comprised only 6 per cent of the world total. Western Europe consumed 18 per cent of world energy while its population comprised only 9 per cent of the world total.

Important changes in the relative importance of the different fuels also contributed to an unstable world energy situation. As recently as 1950 coal formed 56 per cent of total supply compared to 28 per cent for oil and 9 per cent for gas. By 1980 coal supplied only 30 per cent of world energy compared to 45 per cent for oil and 18 per cent for gas. Several factors explain this shift in supply patterns. New sources of oil had been found in the Middle East; oil was easier to transport than coal, by pipeline and tanker, it was a more efficient fuel per tonne than coal and was less of a pollutant. As a consequence many railways, factories, power stations and shipping lines switched to oil from coal, especially as economies of scale (the use of bigger pipelines, tankers and refineries) made it cheaper. The same factors applied even more to gas.

These changes in the world energy situation meant that some regions of the world became very dependent on imported energy and therefore vulnerable. Whereas in 1925 most regions of the world had been roughly self-sufficient in energy, by the time of the 1973 oil crisis Japan produced only 8 per cent of its energy needs, North America 83 per cent and Northern Europe only 37 per cent. The problem has since been compounded by stagnation in the growth of energy supplies in some regions. Up to 1973 the biggest source of supply additional to Middle East resources was the rising production of oil and natural gas in North America. This had been supplemented by African oil and North Sea gas. Since 1973 production of oil and natural gas in North America has fallen considerably while coal production in Europe, which had been falling prior to 1973, has remained constant. Both these developments may be attributed to physical exhaustion of existing reserves and the high cost and lengthy time span involved in developing new sources within those areas. Oil production in developing countries outside the Middle East and gas production outside Europe and North America have increased very little since 1973.

The Community Perspective

By 1973 crude oil was providing Western Europe with 61 per cent of its energy needs with most European oil imports coming from the Middle East. In 1973 Western Europe imported 429 million tonnes of oil from the Middle East, 67 per cent of total oil imports and around 35 per cent of total energy consumption. For the decade prior to 1973 the cost of oil had declined steadily in real terms through competition and economies of scale, while the amount consumed had risen threefold.

European governments and industry had assumed that there would be a steady growth in worldwide oil consumption of about 7 per cent a year until at least 1985 and it was also assumed that the Middle East would provide much of the increase in supply needed. Then in 1973 came the Yom Kippur War during which the Arab states imposed oil embargoes and began to comprehend the potential power given to them by their oil resources. The embargoes were significant; for the first time oil had been used as a political weapon and the governments of Japan, the United States and Western Europe were made to realise how dependent upon Middle East oil they had become and how difficult it would be in the short and medium terms to secure adequate alternative supplies. Now the power to control the rate of production of OPEC's (Organisation of Petroleum Exporting Countries) oil resources and the price at which they were sold passed into the hands of OPEC governments. As a result the price for crude oil quadrupled in 1973–74 and doubled again in 1979.

The oil crisis of 1973 focused attention on the longer term problem of a basic inadequacy in energy supplies generally as existing fossil fuel reserves were depleted to the level where further extraction would be uneconomic. Ironically European coal production was declining in 1973, partly as a deliberate policy, and oil production was small. Consequently Western Europe relied on large imports of fuels. The production of primary fuels and energy in the EEC had reached 365 million tonnes by 1973 while other Western European countries produced the equivalent of 66 million tonnes, making a total of 431 million tonnes. But the consumption of energy was 973 million tonnes in the EEC and 182 million tonnes in the rest of Western Europe so that energy production was 37.5 per cent and 36.2 per cent of consumption in those two areas.

Only the contributions from The Netherlands and Britain promised to mitigate this gloomy prospect. The discovery by the Shell/Esso joint com-

Table 8. Self Sufficiency in Energy in Western Europe 1973

	EEC	Rest of Western Europe	All Western Europe
Coal %	90.0	61.2	87.6
Oil %	2.0	4.3	2.4
Gas %	96.6	47.6	94.9
Overall %	37.5	36.2	37.3
Total production (million tonnes)	365.0	66.0	431.0

pany NAM of the huge Groningen gas field in north-east Holland with reserves of 2,100 billion cubic metres, equivalent to 1,764 million tonnes of oil, changed the gas supply pattern in Western Europe dramatically. Gas sales from this field in 1973 were equivalent to 50 million tonnes of oil. The British were even better placed. Gas production in the southern sector of the British North Sea was well under way by the end of 1973 with the oil companies Amoco, Phillips, Esso and Shell selling all production to the British Gas Corporation, a monopoly buyer by law. But in addition Britain had huge reserves of coal at Selby and the Vale of Belvoir which could be expected to last for 300 years at present rates of consumption. The most promising element was, however, British North Sea Oil. By 1978 production was satisfying more than half of domestic requirements and by the early 1980s was furnishing a surplus for export.

The Slow Evolution of a Community Energy Policy 1957–80

It was significant that the first important reaction to the events of 1973–74 by European governments was the creation of the International Energy Agency in November 1974. This body which aimed to reduce the dependence on oil supplies and work towards a more stable oil market was not set up by the Community but by the Organisation for Economic Co-operation and Development (OECD). The oil crisis had in the words of Robert A. Black, 'stripped away the mask of pretence that had surrounded Community energy policy and demonstrated the Community's inability to deal with a "manifest crisis". It drove the Nine into confusion.' The episode was indeed symbolic; the path towards a coherent Community energy policy has been slow and painful.

The concept of a common energy policy is embodied in all the three treaties establishing the Community. The Treaty of Paris establishing the ECSC gave the High Authority considerable powers of intervention to create a common market in coal, maintain orderly supply and low prices, remove any trade restrictions and to promote modernisation and improved wages and conditions for the workforce. Over the years it has helped the coal industries of the Community to re-employ their labour force in more viable operations.

The Treaty of Rome setting up the Atomic Energy Community—EURATOM—aimed to develop the civilian use of nuclear energy at a time when the Suez Canal crisis (1956) had cast doubts on the reliability of Middle Eastern oil. EURATOM was to pool together the member states' research and development in nuclear reactors and fuels. It was, however, politically premature as its founders did not perceive the future of oil. After the merging of the three Communities, EURATOM'S administrative functions were handled by Directorate-General XVII (Energy).

The other Treaty of Rome setting up the EEC did not specifically mention a common energy policy but Articles 100, 101 and 102 are relevant since they provide for the approximation of laws in the member states to complete the common market. Mention must also be made of Article 235 which enables the implementing of policies not covered in the treaty if they are needed 'in the course of the operation of the Common Market'. There was no explicit reference to a common energy policy because the founding fathers assumed that atomic energy and coal, as provided for in the other treaties, would supply Community needs. Consequently the Commission was given no specific authority for energy and was limited to carrying out actions permitted by the Council.

Early attempts by the executives of the three Communities to co-ordinate energy policy proved abortive. The first significant move was the 1964 'Protocol on energy problems' which gave priority to cheap supplies of oil and authorised a Community system of state aids for coal. The merger of the three executives in 1967 created the first comprehensive energy directorate in the Commission which in 1968 presented 'First Guidelines for a Community Energy Policy'. It proposed the establishment of a common energy market and the achievement of cheap and stable supplies. The Commission did not expect this common policy to be created at once but rather over time by such measures as the gradual reduction of the discrepancies in grants and taxes between the member states.

The following years saw little in the way of development towards a common energy policy, though energy supply was coming to be recognised as a world problem just as the enlargement of the Community was imminent. In 1972 the 1968 Guidelines were brought up to date by two studies which recommended the reduction of Community dependence on oil imports from the forecast 65 per cent by 1985 to 40 per cent and the need for the stockpiling of oil to be extended from 65 to 90 days as from January 1975.

These and other suggestions were overtaken by the oil crisis of October 1973. The Copenhagen Summit of December 1973 was almost totally absorbed by this one issue and completely failed to generate a united Community stance. It took six more months for the Commission to come up with its 'Towards a New Energy Policy Strategy'. This assumed for the first time that hydrocarbon prices would tend to rise, a trend which as late as 1972 had appeared unlikely. The consequences of this assumption, in the Commission's judgment, were that the demand for oil would slow down and give good prospects for the development of nuclear energy, natural gas and coal. It envisaged that the decline of coal should be arrested and Community production of coal maintained at 250 million tonnes with subsidies for coal production and stockpiling. Only in September 1974 did the Council adopt this strategy which in any case was not really new but simply readjusted the 1968 Guidelines in the light of revised national forecasts of consumption. There was, as Robert Black points out, no translation of general principles into specific policies. The events of 1973 did not influence the Nine towards a common energy policy; rather they resulted in a marked loss of interest by the Nine in using the Community arena to safeguard their energy requirements. The member states, especially Britain and France, preferred to go their own way, seeking bilateral arrangements with oil producers. At the Energy Committee meeting in November 1975 the Commissioner responsible for energy, Henri Simonet, condemned the Nine for their half-hearted efforts to show the flexibility required for the creation of a Community energy policy. Perhaps he had the British particularly in mind because in December 1975 the Conference on International Economic Co-operation was to be held and all of the member states save Britain wanted to establish a common Community position for the conference. The anticipated status of Britain as an oil producer in its own right led James Callaghan, the British Foreign Secretary, to insist on a separate seat on the assumption that British interests could not be properly represented in a Community position weighted in favour of consumer concerns. Only after a bitter row was a compromise found.

Given Simonet's disappointment, it was predictable that in its 'First Report on the Achievement of the Community Energy Policy Objectives for 1985' the Commission in January 1976 drew attention to the lack of determination by member states to reduce their dependence on imported energy. The Commission consequently proposed certain actions to the Council and Parliament of which the following were approved: minimum insurance stocks of coal and oil for 90 days, encouragement for oil exploration north of 60° latitude, control of natural gas imports and exports, aid for coking coal and measures to conserve energy. Emphasis was to be placed on the role of electricity and in particular electricity supplied by nuclear power stations.

This still left a number of areas in which progress was needed. These included the Community co-ordination of nuclear power station construction, the establishment of Community centres for the storage of radioactive waste and materials, the establishment of an insurance stock of uranium (because of dependence on American supplies), a legal requirement for coal to be used in all fossil-fuelled power stations and the development of the fast breeder reactor. The Commission's 'Second Report on the Achievement of Community Energy Policy Objectives for 1985' in September 1977 showed that the expansion of the Community's indigenous energy resources was less than that predicted in 1975. Delays in the construction of nuclear power stations had reduced the forecast of installed nuclear power in 1985 to below half of the original estimate.

Community Energy Policy in the 1980s

Objectives of the Common Energy Policy

As seen in the above summary, Community energy policy has been a thing of bits and pieces rather than a coherent whole. Nevertheless it was still sorely needed as the 1980s began. The Community was the world's largest single oil importer with over half its supplies coming from three countries—

Saudi Arabia, Libya and Nigeria. Oil still accounted for 51 per cent of Europe's energy consumption in 1981, compared to 61 per cent in 1973.

By 1980 a somewhat more coherent energy package had been pieced together, based on the 1974 objectives for implementation by 1990. It called for conservation programmes and a cut in oil consumption to around 40 per cent of total energy consumption. Solid fuels and nuclear energy were to supply 70 to 75 per cent of electricity generated. To reduce the dependence on oil, gas consumption which was fulfilling about 18 per cent of energy needs was to be maintained by doubling imports. Between 1980 and the year 2000, coal consumption was to be increased from 314 million tonnes (about 21 per cent of needs) to 500 million tonnes of which half was to be imported. The use of renewable energy resources such as solar energy was to be encouraged though this was seen as a slow development. Finally the use of nuclear power was to be stimulated for two reasons. It would vary the sources of energy supply and was believed to be of great potential for industrial productivity; a kilo of uranium could generate as much electricity as 10 tonnes of oil (and as much as 600 tonnes when fastbreeder reactors came into full use) for a third of the price. It was the Commission's aim to increase the share of nuclear power in electricity generating from 16 per cent to about 38 per cent in 1990.

The Chief Fields of Action

These were ambitious objectives indeed and the Commission in 1982 pointed to five fields of action in which some limited progress had been made and which should be regarded as priorities for the future: (1) investment; (2) prices and taxation; (3) research and development; (4) stabilisation of the market; (5) external relations.

(1) It is clear that the Community needs to diversify its energy supplies and ensure more rational use of energy so that European goods can remain competitive. It is equally clear that this requires a massive and sustained investment. So far such an investment effort has not been achieved. In the early 1980s energy investment in the Ten was stagnant at about 1.6 per cent of gross national product (GNP) and was not expected by the Commission to exceed 2.2 per cent by 1990. Major competitors were achieving a better track record. The United States was aiming at energy investment of 4 per cent and Japan at 3 per cent or more of GNP.

European investment could be even lower than forecast for a number of reasons. Coal and nuclear investment, for example the Vale of Belvoir coal resources, are often slowed down by legitimate public concern about safety and potential environmental damage. Investment in energy has its own peculiar difficulties: uncertainty about long-term price changes for different forms of energy, the long span of time needed for returns on investment and often a basic lack of knowledge about the nature of different energy sources. The recent slump combined with a period of high interest rates has not been conducive to investment in energy, either public or private.

The Community's investment record has been modest. It has contributed to the financing of nuclear power stations, plants for the production and transport of hydrocarbons, the modernisation of coal mines, the conversion to coal of oil-burning plants and a range of energy conservation projects mainly in industry. In 1981 loans to the energy sector from the ECSC, EURATOM, the EIB and the new Community lending and borrowing instrument (NCI) reached about 1,900 million ECU. But much more investment than this was needed, particularly in the development of nuclear power, the encouragement of the coal industry, the exploration of Europe's gas resources and the rationalisation of energy use.

One exciting investment to which the Community has contributed is the Central Electricity Generating Board scheme at Dinorwic in Wales. This provides essential reserves for the United Kingdom grid. If there is excess demand for electricity it releases water which is later pumped back to the upper reservoir in off-peak periods. It has received £150 million in Community loans, probably more than any other Community project.

(2) As energy accounts for a substantial share of industrial production costs, its price has influenced industrial competitivity between the member states and third countries. The Commission has wanted to identify any measures that influence prices artificially and if possible reduce price differences between member states so that there are no significant cost differences. In other words it is aiming at a genuine common market for energy in which prices do not vary from one country to another more than is justified by local advantages or transport costs. But energy prices have often been highly influenced by differences in member states' pricing policies. Prices are sometimes deliberately kept below or above economic levels by member governments either generally or for a specific group of consumers. Taxation also has a significant effect on prices paid by the final consumer, especially in the oil sector. What the Commission is seeking here is a gradual alignment of national tax systems in order to limit distortions in competition because different tax levels create different energy costs from one country to another. In addition to causing unfair competition, they can discourage people from saving energy or substituting other fuels for oil.

Two recent examples of the contradictory needs of member states in pricing policy have been provided by the Dutch and the British. The British pricing of North Sea oil has disgruntled other Community countries as North Sea oil exports have been priced only slightly below the equivalent of Libyan or Algerian crudes and well ahead of the restrained Saudi Arabian price. In fact British moves fitted in with the need to conserve oil as the Conservative government has reduced the gap between oil and other energy prices since 1979.

The Dutch had antagonised their partners for the opposite reason. Low-priced fuel to Dutch farmers had, in the view of the other member states, given them a competitive advantage. In this respect, a major step was taken in December 1981 when agreement was reached on energy pricing throughout the Community, ensuring that energy prices were not to be kept at an artificially low level and providing users with adequate access to information on prices and on methods used to determine prices and tariffs.

(3) One essential route to the solution of the Community's energy problems is through research in the development of new methods of using ex-

isting energy sources and the discovery of new energy sources themselves. The Community could play an important role here in carrying out projects that are too costly or too large scale for one member state to carry out alone. It could also avoid any waste of resources caused by duplication of effort and ensure that any research results are widely diffused.

In 1981 overall Community funds for industrial research and developments projects in the energy sector totalled 334 million ECUs, a sum which represented some 10 per cent of total public aid to energy research in Europe. This finance has helped to co-ordinate a large proportion of European research. A major example of research initiated at Community level is a joint undertaking under the EURATOM Treaty and financed to the extent of 80 per cent by the Community, 10 per cent by Britain and 10 per cent by the other participants. It is called the Joint European Torus (JET) which is a machine essential in the development of new energy sources based on the fusion of light atoms. The basic materials for this new form of energy are deuterium and lithium which are not radioactive. Several advantages have been claimed for such a project. Firstly its energy potential. It has been estimated that the amount of energy generated by the fusion of one gramme of the deuterium–lithium mixture is equal to that produced by the internal combustion of over 10,000 litres of petrol. Secondly the independence that it would give Europe, whose domestic energy resources are currently very low, with over half its requirements having to be imported. Deuterium can be found in large quantities in sea water. Lithium which is abundant in the earth's crust produces tritium and helium when bombarded with neutrons. Since fusion produces neutrons, the core of the fusion reactor simply has to be covered with a 'blanket' of lithium to renew the required quantities of tritium. Thirdly the safety factor. The only radioactive element used is tritium and this is produced inside the reactor and does not therefore have to be transported. The 'ashes' from the fusion reaction are not radioactive like those produced by fission. Finally, the quantity of fuel in the reactor is sufficiently small to limit the impact of any accident.

JET was formally established in June 1978 and its members include EURATOM, the member countries of the Community, Sweden and Switzerland. While the construction phase is scheduled to end in mid-1983, the operating stage of JET will last for five to seven years. Consideration at Community level is already being given to the next step with the first exploratory studies for NET (Next European Torus).

The European Commission set up a Fusion Review Panel in November 1980 to evaluate the importance of fusion as an energy source for the Community. In its June 1981 report, the group recommended that the JET projected be implemented as fully as possible and that a fusion technology programme centred round NET should be launched. The European Commission based the new programme which will be implemented during 1982–86 on these recommendations. This programme, with a Community financial contribution of 620 million ECU will in part replace and in part extend the 1979–83 programme worth 385 million ECU.

The JET project was an enterprising one but its establishment demonstrates the problems of initiating research at a Community level. A commitment to build the machine was delayed until October 1977 by disagreements among member states as to the appropriate site. Both the British and the West German governments insisted upon their own respective sites though in the end Culham in Oxfordshire was chosen.

Yet once again, as the Commission admitted in 1982, more was needed to be done. Much more spending was required in a number of sectors—energy conservation, nuclear fusion, nuclear fission (particularly problems of storage and disposal of radioactive wastes) and the more efficient and environmentally sound use of coal. In the period after 1979 most energy programmes including nuclear energy were slowed down or indefinitely postponed in all countries in the Community with the exception of France.

What was needed was a programme on the lines suggested by Viscount Davignon in 1982. In his view the current plans for energy investment of some 100 billion ECU up to 1990 were inadequate and the money spent on them should be nearly doubled. As such spending could create 300,000 jobs or more in the construction and electrical industries, his programme was relevant to two of the chief challenges facing the Community in the 1980s.

(4) The 1973 Arab–Israeli war and the subsequent embargo demonstrated how easily oil supplies to the West could be interrupted. Similarly in 1979 the overthrow of the Shah's regime in Iran triggered off further sharp rises in the price of oil, showing how a limited and temporary reduction in supplies, or even the mere threat of such a reduction, could provoke oil price rises unrelated to the real state of the market.

A few Community measures have been taken to avoid such instability in price or supply of oil. A system of fuel stocks for power stations, equivalent to 30 days' consumption now operates. For general oil consumption, there is another compulsory stocking system for oil, equivalent to 90 days' consumption.

Again, it has to be stated that this area of energy policy is still in an embryonic state. Similar stocking safeguard measures need to be carried out in the coal and gas sectors and plans arranged for reduction in consumption in times of crisis. The Commission is planning action here for the future.

But market stability can only be achieved with continuity of energy supplies, in particular continuity of oil supplies. There is at present no real Community supply policy and it seems unlikely to evolve. As far as coal is concerned, Britain and West Germany would benefit from a more developed policy of subsidising coal output on a Community basis but France and Belgium would benefit only a little and Italy, Holland and Denmark not at all. Yet stimulating coal production would reduce the Community's oil imports directly. Oil import reductions could also be achieved by allowing low price coal from the United States, South Africa and Australia to enter Europe in times of energy crisis. In the early 1980s though, the recession had caused a surplus of coal stocks rather than a shortage.

Oil supplies remain the major uncertainty and the only major domestic source of Community oil is Britain. Once oil is extracted, the United Kingdom is limited by the Rome Treaty in its competence to limit exports. Article 34 states that 'quantitative restrictions on exports and all measures having equivalent effect shall be prohibited between member states'. However, Britain has sovereign rights over its section of the Continental Shelf and is free to determine the optimum rate at which its oil reserves are extracted or depleted.

Both France and Germany would like to see a commitment by the British to step up North Sea oil production if and when the Community faces new shortages. It is hard to envisage a situation in which any British government, Labour or Conservative, would give such a commitment, short of major concessions over other aspects of British membership. Britain is committed to sharing oil with countries of the International Energy Agency only if world supply falls short of consumption by 7 per cent. In 1979 the German Chancellor, Helmut Schmidt, suggested at the Dublin summit that, for oil, rules similar to those of Article 59 of the Coal and Steel Treaty should apply. If this had been agreed, then the Council of Ministers and the Commission would have had the right to set consumption levels and production programmes. In fact the issue resulted in British politicians as wide apart as Tony Benn and Margaret Thatcher actually in a state of broad agreement! Both Labour and Conservative governments have insisted that Britain must remain in full control of oil found in the country or in the area of the offshore continental shelf. As a result the British have disappointed their Community partners over both the price and supply of oil.

One way of encouraging more oil exploration at a Community level would be to set a minimum support price. The International Energy Agency was able to agree on this in 1976 but within the Community the subject has caused bitter arguments between Britain and the other countries. The British were naturally in favour of such a scheme but the other countries, in the absence of any British commitment over supplies, were unwilling to underwrite such a proposal. In the context of rising oil prices, the concept of a minimum support price may seem irrelevant but oil prices at times have fallen in real terms in the years since 1973. Certainly the issue created much ill-feeling in the Community.

(5) In view of the difficulties in creating a common energy policy between the Ten, the Commission's call for a united front in the Community's energy dealings with the rest of the world has sounded optimistic indeed. However, a united stand would ensure a more balanced dialogue with the worlds' exporters and importers of energy.

Some agreements have been achieved. In the nuclear sector the Community has concluded agreements with its major suppliers of uranium—Australia, Canada and the United States—to ensure non-discrimination between users. In the gas sector, the Ten have agreed to consult before major contracts are drawn up with external gas suppliers like Algeria, Norway and Russia. A similar arrangement exists over coal imports from countries like the United States. The problems of the non-energy producing Third World countries have not been entirely forgotten. The Community and its member states have made some contributions to the development of energy resources in the Third World. In 1980 total European subsidies and loans in this field amounted to over 700 million ECU.

The outstanding international agreement over energy has been the Tokyo

Summit of June 1979, a summit of the main oil importing countries. At the heart of this meeting was a wish to control American oil imports. Whereas between 1973 and 1978 Community net oil imports had declined from more than 500 million tonnes to 472 million tonnes, net oil imports by the United States increased by over 42 per cent from 287 to 409 million tonnes. At the Tokyo Summit the United States, Japan and the Community agreed to limit their oil imports until 1985 to given quantitative targets. The question arose of dividing the amount allowed to the Community between the individual member states. This was a difficult task but the need to make the United States adhere to the agreement forced the Community countries to reach a compromise by September 1979. A major factor assisting agreement was the prospect of increased British oil production making Britain a net exporter of oil. This would allow the other Community members to import more oil within the agreed overall ceiling.

Such steps require to be built on in the future. The impact of the United States on the world oil market has been highly negative and needs to be controlled. More should be done to encourage European companies to invest in developing countries and more public aid should be given to assist the development of energy in the Third World. Finally the Community must work at its most obvious task—good relations with the major exporters of oil.

Conclusion

Superficially some progress had been made towards solving the Community's energy problems by the 1980s. The development of alternative energy sources, linked with energy-saving measures and a fall-off in demand due to the recession had reduced the Community's net oil imports from 573 million tonnes in 1973 to 420 million tonnes in 1980. One of the main factors behind this improvement has been North Sea oil; British North Sea oil production rose from 12 million tonnes in 1976 to 80 million tonnes in 1980 with a projected rise to 89 million tonnes in 1982 and at least 95 million tonnes in 1985.

The other major factors concern coal and gas. Both Britain and West Germany have been investing heavily in their coal industries and have been substituting coal for oil. The West Germans, for example, have planned to increase the coal used in power stations from 33 million tonnes in 1980 to 45 million tonnes in 1990. Gas reserves held in Britain and Holland should last until the end of the century.

Yet in truth the underlying energy position leaves no room for complacency. Even if oil imports were cut after 1973, the total oil bill rose from 10,000 million ECU in 1973 to 76,000 million ECU in 1980. Unless there is further substitution of other fuels for oil, there is a risk that a revival in economic activity will stimulate an increase in demand for oil. The Community's balance of payments forced into deficit largely by oil imports could deteriorate still further. Already the strengthening of the dollar—the currency in which oil prices are expressed—has added to the oil bill. If world economic activity revives, then other oil importing countries will increase their demand, thus enabling the oil exporting countries

Table 9. EEC Energy Trends

	(*million tons oil equivalent*) 1980 (*unless stated*)	1985	1990
Coal:			
Production	(1979) 149.2	149/152	151/157
Lignite and peat	(1979) 31.0	35	39
Net imports*	45.0	60/57	93/89
Demand*	219.0	244	283/285
Oil:			
Production	90.0	108/147	84/123
Net imports	423.5	467/441	465/455
Demand (inland)	485.0	542/554	514/542
Natural gas:			
Production	129.0	127/128	115/122
Net imports	41.0	84	124/114
Demand	170.0	211/212	239/236
Nuclear:			
Production	37.2	97	160
Net imports	—	—	—
Consumption	42.8	—	—
Hydro and Geothermal:			
Production	(1979) 12.1	13	14
Net imports (electricity)	1.2	1	1
Demand (primary electricity etc.)	(1979) 52.6	115	189/187
Others (new sources):			
Production	(1979) 1.8	4	14/12
Total			
Consumption (gross inland)	931.9	1,112/1,125	1,225/1,250

* All solid fuels.

Source: EEC Commission.

to increase oil prices sharply yet again. Meanwhile some Community energy targets are not being met. For 1985 the expected contribution of nuclear energy is less than half the level (17 per cent of energy consumption) envisaged in the 1974 Resolution.

The Community has seemed at times so at odds over energy issues that the question must be asked whether it has a common energy policy at all. Disagreements over appropriate solutions have been met at all levels of Community operation. Several examples of national disagreements have already been given in this chapter. In addition conflicts within the Commission itself have proved a further complication; in particular clashes between Directorate I (External Affairs) and Directorate XVII (Energy) have blocked progress on some issues, for example the conduct of the dialogue with the producer countries.

Energy policy cannot be isolated from other Community policies. The financial burdens of developing new sources of energy are made worse by the heavy social costs of rationalising coal production. Energy issues conflict with competition policy; the member states have explicitly prevented the inclusion of hydrocarbons in the Community competition policy with the result that different national policies distort intra-Community trade. The increased concern for environmental issues (see chapter 11) since 1970 constitutes yet another complication for energy policy. Enlargement of the Community will add further difficulties for decision-making by bringing in other countries with different interests.

If a common policy means a combination of a clear vision of the future, a set of principles and the means to carry out objectives laid down, then Europe does not have an energy policy. Much of the power for the planning and implementing of energy policy still remains with the member states. Yet the Community does need an energy policy for a number of reasons. Negative integration (a common market in oil) cannot be gained without positive integration (effective oil-sharing). Community security of energy supplies can be furthered only by a united front which promotes increased bargaining strength. Lastly, it may be suggested that if the vision of the future Community is an ever closer union between the peoples of Europe, then the combining of national and Community interests in the field of energy is essential.

Finally, the global context cannot be over-stressed. In 30 years time the world's population will have grown to 12 billion, according to the most recent estimates. World energy needs will be three times what they are today. Therefore, for its own long-term economic survival, the Community needs to act together on energy issues.

Further Reading

Coffey, P., (ed.), *The Economic Policies of the Common Market,* chapter 8, Macmillan, London, 1979.

El Agraa, A. M., *The Economics of the European Community*, chapter 14, Philip Allan, Deddington, 1980.

Swann, D., *The Economics of the Common Market*, chapter 6, Penguin, Harmondsworth, 1978.

Articles

'European Energy Problems', *European Trends*, February 1980.

Questions

(1) Critically examine the underlying causes of the Community's energy problems.

(2) Why has a Community Energy Policy been slow to evolve?

(3) What are the advantages and disadvantages of a Community project like JET?

10
Financial and Fiscal Affairs

A The Community Budget

Keeping the Budget in Perspective

The Community's budget has been increasingly in the public eye in recent years and yet it is a grey area not fully understood by Community citizens. It forms an extra tier on top of the local, regional and national levels of public finance which have gradually evolved in the member states. This requires new forms of financial adjustment in the handling of an ever-growing volume of funds. Such forms of adjustment, for example the precise contributions of the individual member states, are customary procedures in federal states like West Germany but most Community countries are centrally constituted states where such practices are unknown. As a consequence, Community finances have seemed strange and unfamiliar to many citizens.

The Community budget for 1981 (for the first year with ten member states including Greece) was worth some 20 billion ECU (£11 billion). Such an amount may look enormous but it is a modest sum when put into perspective. It is in fact far too small to be useful as an instrument of fiscal policy or as a means of altering the distribution of income between rich and poor in a Community of 270 million people. In 1981 the Community budget represented only 0.9 per cent of the member states' joint Gross Domestic Product. By contrast the national budgets of the member states accounted for 710 billion ECU, 32 per cent of the Community's Gross Domestic Product. The Community's budget was equal to only 2.7 per cent of national spending.

Nevertheless the Community finances have increasingly been a target for criticism in a period of financial constraints, the chief charge being that it has been a major cause of rising public expenditure.

The charge has in fact little real substance but has been easy to make, given that the size of the Community budget has risen steadily over the years as Table 10 demonstrates.

The Community's Taxing Powers

The Community has no bottomless purse because its taxing powers are

Table 10. The Community Budget 1973–82

Year	Units	Payments	Percentage increase from previous year
1973	UA	4,245,282,000	
1974	UA	5,079,465,000	19
1975	UA	5,825,283,000	14
1976	UA	8,470,609,000	45
1977	UA	9,586,994,000	13
1978	EUA	12,362,654,000	29
1979	EUA	14,446,993,000	17
1980	EUA	16,182,497,000	12
1981	ECU	20,331,000,000	19
1982	ECU	21,984,000,000	12

rather limited. Under Article 201 of the Rome Treaty, the EEC was to be financed mainly by contributions from member states in a fixed agreed proportion. The Commission was, however, instructed to study the conditions under which these contributions 'may be replaced by other resources available to the Community itself, in particular by revenue accruing from the common customs tariff when finally introduced'. After long and difficult negotiations the results of the ensuing Commission study were incorporated in a decision of April 1970 which provided for the replacement of financial contributions by member states by the Community's 'own resources'. This was to be achieved by a process of gradual transition between 1971 and 1978.

As a consequence of the 1970 decision these Community 'own resources' now consist of four parts:

(a) Customs duties are the duties levied on imports from outside the Community. They are collected by member states under the Community tariff and passed on to the Commission which refunds the cost of collection.

(b) Agricultural levies are charged on agricultural products imported from non-member countries. They are chiefly designed to offset the differences between the usually higher Community price and the price at which the products are supplied, i.e. the world price.

(c) Sugar levies are charged on the production of sugar and isoglucose (a sugar derived from corn starch) to pay at least part of the cost of market support of these products. Expenditure on the sugar market in 1981 amounted to 740 million ECU and the revenue from the sugar levy offset this by 571 million ECU.

The first three 'own resources' are suspect as reliable or adequate sources of revenue. The volume of customs duties has tended to dwindle as those duties have been progressively reduced through agreements with non-member countries. The Kennedy Round of the General Agreement on Tariffs and Trade (GATT) resulted in the Community reducing tariffs by 30 per cent from 1967. The Tokyo Round will mean further tariff reductions of 33 per cent on average between 1980 and 1987. The same process results from the Community's agreements with Third World countries, for example the two Lomé Conventions. Growing imports and rising prices barely compensate for such reductions in Community customs duties.

Agricultural levies reflect the difference between the Community price for a given product and its price on the world market, so that import prices are brought up to the Community level. Agricultural prices, however, are not fixed at a higher level in the Community for the purpose of raising revenue. The yield from agricultural levies depends on trends in Community and world food prices. Occasionally world food prices have been higher than Community food prices (1974–75) and it therefore follows that the revenue from this source is unpredictable.

(d) Given the built-in unreliability of the first three sources of revenue, an additional source was needed and the Community agreed in 1970 to create an additional source of finance by claiming a share of Value Added Tax from member states. VAT has become the Community's biggest source of revenue, providing 54 per cent in 1981. Under the Community's 1977 directive, VAT systems were harmonised in the member states. This does not mean that the rates charged are the same (Britain's VAT rate is 15 per cent compared to Denmark's 22 per cent) but that the value of taxable goods and services is assessed in the same way in each country. Member states have thus agreed to assign to the Community's own resources a rate not exceeding 1 per cent of a uniform basis of assessment of Value Added Tax. This is a ceiling which can only be exceeded if the member states agree to amend the decision of April 1970 and if the amendment is ratified by the national parliaments.

The 1 per cent ceiling is probably an inadequate rate and financial pundits were predicting in 1982 that Community spending would soar above this ceiling in 1983 or 1984. Possibly, as A. J. Brown has argued, VAT is in

Table 11. Community Sources of Revenue 1980–81

	1980	1981
Size of budget (million ECU)	16,182	20,331
of which (%):		
Customs duties	37.0	32.5
Agricultural levies	9.3	9.8
Sugar levies	3.1	2.9
Value Added Tax	44.7	53.9
Total own resources	94.1	99.1
Other revenue	5.9	0.9
	100.0	100.0

any case a complicated tax unsuited to a Community in which some states have stronger traditions of tax evasion than tax collection.

Community Expenditure

The Community revenue is spent mainly on five policies.

(a) The CAP swallows up two thirds of Community funds, mostly on price support for commodities where the Community's degree of self-sufficiency is high. It is in milk and dairy products that the operation of the price support system has been most expensive. These absorbed about one quarter of the whole budget in the years between 1977 and 1982. In most years considerable extra expenditure has been incurred by 'monetary compensation amounts'—payments made to offset discrepancies in the cost of agricultural products from different countries in the Community. These discrepancies arise from changes in the green rates (see chapter 4). Expenditure on 'guidance', i.e. structural changes in agriculture, has generally run at only 10 per cent of agricultural expenditure and in 1982 was only 5 per cent.

(b) There is significant expenditure through the Regional Development Fund. In 1981 the Community spent 2 billion ECU under this Fund on grants and subsidised loans for industry and infrastructure projects in Europe's depressed regions. This sum amounted to 10 per cent of total Community spending in 1981.

(c) Under the Social Fund just over 690 million ECU (4 per cent of the Budget) were spent in 1981 on projects for retraining, rehousing, education and other social measures such as help to Britain's Youth Opportunities Programme.

(d) About 313 million ECU (2 per cent of the Budget) was spent in 1981 on research, energy, industry and transport, mainly on scientific research projects like the Joint European Torus (JET) at Culham. The European Coal and Steel Community spent 162 million ECU of this sum.

Table 12. Community Budgetary Expenditure 1982

	1982 (million ECU)
Administration	1,103
Social Fund	1,022
Regional Fund	1,293
UK Refund	1,654
Industry, Transport, Energy and Research	436
Development Aid	817
Agriculture	14,532
Other	1,127
Total	21,984

(e) Development aid reached just over a billion ECU (5 per cent of the Budget) in 1981. Such aid was mainly directed at the 63 African, Caribbean and Pacific (ACP) countries that have signed the Lomé Convention.

The remaining 13 per cent of Community expenditure is accounted for by administration costs, repayments and reserves.

The Budgetary Procedure

Under pressure from the European Parliament, the budgetary procedure has been considerably revised in recent years.

Before 1st July each year the institutions draw up estimates of their expenditure in the next financial year (1st January to 31st December). The Commission then consolidates these estimates into a preliminary draft budget which it places before the Council of Ministers before 1st September if possible. The Council consults other concerned institutions whenever it intends to modify the draft budget, acting by qualified majority (see chapter 3). Its next action is to forward the now established draft budget to the European Parliament by 5th October.

The Parliament has the right to amend the draft budget as regards non-compulsory expenditure and can propose modifications to compulsory expenditure to the Council. If within 45 days of the draft budget being placed before it, Parliament proposes changes, the draft budget, with the proposed modifications, is returned to the Council.

If within 15 days the Council accepts the changes proposed by the Parliament, the budget is finally adopted. If the Council revises the Parliament's suggested changes, the draft budget is again forwarded to the Parliament with a report on the Council's deliberations. Within 15 days the Parliament acts by a majority of its members on its response to the Council's modifications to its amendments. Normally it must vote by 19th December on whether to accept or reject the entire budget. Only once, in 1979, has the Parliament rejected the budget. However, the whole budgetary procedure seems likely to become more fraught as time goes on as the Parliament attempts to gain more real control over Community expenditure. Its increasingly combative mood was seen in December 1982 when it voted against the rebate due to Britain as a way of trying to force the Council to tackle the question of permanent reform of Community finances.

The Chief Budgetary Problems

It is clear that two problems bedevil Community budgetary issues—the size of revenue and the question of equitability.

Though Community revenue has expanded because of inflation and economic growth at about 10 to 12 per cent in the years 1980 to 1982, expenditure has grown even more quickly. Farm spending, the Community's prodigal son, grew at more than 20 per cent a year between 1977 and 1981. As a result the budget soared towards its permitted ceiling and in 1982 there was a gap of 975 million ECU between planned spending and the forecast revenue available. If farm spending were to increase still further, then the Community's revenue would be exhausted.

Such an event would come as no surprise. For some years it has been realised that the moment is approaching when the Community's increases in expenditure will no longer be covered by increases in its own resources. The MacDougall Report of 1977 and a Commission Memorandum to the Council in 1978 ('Financing the Budget') both warned of an impending budgetary crisis.

The relatively small size of the Budget means that it has at present only a small impact on the European economy, with the exception of agriculture. Even in the agricultural sector the expenditure does not seem to result in diminishing welfare differences between the rich and poor regions of the Community; in fact the reverse situation applies. By the same token, the Budget does little to stimulate economic activity in either particular member states or in the European economy as a whole and there is an urgent need for the Community to expand its spending on research, energy, industry and transport beyond the present pathetic 2 per cent of resources. This whole question will become even more critical when Spain and Portugal make their demands on Community revenue from the mid-1980s.

The second major problem—the inequitable burden that the Budget places on Britain—is also discussed in chapter 16. The Budget is so structured at present as to make Britain a net contributor to the Budget. The net contributions and net receipts of member states are calculated as the difference between their gross contributions to, and gross receipts from, those parts of Budget expenditure which the Commission is able to 'allocate' between member states. A member state whose contributions to the allocated Budget exceed the amounts of Community expenditure received by its residents is said to be a net contributor to the Budget. A member state whose residents receive more from the Budget than its contributions is said to be a net recipient.

Two member states—Britain and West Germany—consistently tend to be net contributors while the other eight tend to be net recipients. This pattern reflects the budgetary impact of the CAP which accounts for about two-thirds of allocated budget expenditure. The result is that member states whose share of Community agricultural production or surpluses exceeds their share of Community GDP or who are large producers of Mediterranean produce are likely to obtain net receipts from the budget while West Germany and Britain whose share of Community GDP exceeds their share of Community agricultural production or surpluses, are likely to make net contributions. However, whereas it is arguably not unreasonable for West Germany, one of the richest members of the Community, to make such contributions, it is manifestly unreasonable for Britain to do so when she is the poorest member (per capita income) of the Community bar Ireland, Italy and Greece. The table below shows the projected net contributions and receipts from the allocated budget before Mrs Thatcher's 1980 budget deal (see chapter 16).

Britain's partners often argue that net contributions and receipts are irrelevant concepts that have no place in the Community. The Community has, they insist, certain policies in areas such as agriculture, and these

Table 13. Net Contributors (−) and recipients (+)

	million ECU		
	1979	1980	1981
Denmark	+380	+327	+285
Germany	−1,430	−1,526	−1,750
France	−78	+431	+597
The Netherlands	+288	+454	+191
Belgium/Luxembourg	+610	+439	+568
United Kingdom	−849	−1,512	−1,422
Italy	+534	+737	+778
Ireland	+545	+650	+586
Greece	—	—	+167

policies transfer resources from Community consumers and taxpayers to Community producers and other beneficiaries. The fact that they also transfer resources from some member states to others is incidental and unimportant.

Such arguments do not convince British people because net transfers represent flows of real money from the citizens of some countries to the citizens of others. The scale and the direction of these transfers serve to increase the differences in prosperity between the member states. Yet the Community is supposed to be committed to economic convergence between member states and the pattern of net transfers should bear some relationship to relative prosperity.

The French also produce a further argument—that the net contributions are an avoidable problem, for which the net contributor countries have only themselves to blame. If such countries would import less from non-Community countries or increase their agricultural production, so the French argue, their net budget contributions would rapidly disappear.

However, this line of argument ignores the Community's commitment to open trade in Article 110 of the Rome Treaty and even if Britain were to reduce her agricultural imports from outside the Community, this would in fact not make much difference to Britain's net financial position. The idea that Britain could solve her Budget problems by increasing agricultural output is neither realistic nor sensible. To eliminate the UK's budgetary losses would require an increase in agricultural production of about one third, followed by annual increases in production in line with the Community average. Even if this were possible the Community as a whole would be harmed owing to the steep rise in the cost of disposing of surplus agricultural production.

There is only one real solution—reform of the Community budget itself.

Reform of the Community Budget

Britain has been virtually alone in claiming that the Community Budget should be re-designed so as to distribute resources towards the poor. For this reason the Commission over the years has failed to propose radical changes in the way the Community raised or spent revenue. However, in 1981 and 1982 Christopher Tugendhat, the Budget commissioner, set out a number of possible options which could both enlarge the Community's revenue and cure the problem of Britain's excess contributions. In July 1982 Mr Tugendhat put forward five main proposals:

(i) An increase in the 1 per cent limit on Value Added Tax to perhaps 1.5 per cent. This would appear to be the easiest solution at first sight but any increase in the Community share of member states' VAT would have to be ratified by the national parliaments and the idea could well be blocked. Nevertheless if the Community budget were to be solved by an increase in VAT, this source of revenue would dwarf the revenue raised by customs duties and agricultural levies. As a result the Community tax burden would be distributed more nearly in proportion to private consumption, a development that would help Britain.

(ii) A tax related to each country's Gross Domestic Product. This was not a new idea; a Commission study group in 1974 suggested that the Community should control 10 per cent or more of member state's total public expenditure or at least 4 to 5 per cent of their GDP. Again, such a leap forward in Community powers would seem likely to foment much national opposition though it is an equitable solution as member states would contribute in accordance with their relative wealth.

(iii) A tax on imported energy, especially oil, a solution that would favour Britain as a member state nearly self-sufficient in energy.

(iv) Levies on tobacco, alcohol and petrol. Such levies would raise the most revenue from the richer member states and again this would favour Britain.

(v) More co-responsibility levies such as those imposed on surplus-producing dairy farmers. If the practice of co-responsibility levies were to develop along with the gradual alignment of Community food prices with those prevailing on the world market, then the cost of the CAP could be contained because the cost of disposing of surpluses would be reduced to manageable proportions. In the path of this solution lies the formidable farming lobby but in 1982 it was at least mildly encouraging that Mr Tugendhat's fellow commissioners, though opposed to an increase in VAT, approved the idea of more general use of co-responsibility levies. Excess spending on farm subsidies is the main reason why Britain has to pay such a high budget contribution.

B Progress Towards Monetary Union

The Potential Value of Monetary Union

Although the Treaty of Rome does not specifically state that European monetary union should be established, the founding fathers foresaw the Community evolving into a fully-fledged common market with the complete monetary and economic integration of its members.

Such monetary integration could have both political and economic advantages. It would be a powerful impulse towards real political unity as the peoples of the member states shared over time a common economic experience. Also, if the EEC were to adopt a common unit of account (a Europa?) it would certainly become a major world currency, able to complete with the dollar on equal terms. The existence of one currency (or even fixed exchange rates between the currencies of member states) would encourage trade, cause capital to move to where it was most productively rewarded and would ensure that labour moved to where the highest rewards prevailed.

Further compelling reasons for European Monetary Union (EMU) were set out in a report to the Council of Ministers in 1970 by Luxembourg's prime minister, Pierre Werner. Community economic development had highlighted the different levels of growth and stability between member states. Without effective harmonisation of economic policies, Werner insisted, there would be growing tensions within the Community. The Werner Report went on to spell out the major elements of EMU which might ward off the growth of such tensions. They were indeed ambitious objectives and included the total convertibility of Community currencies, centralisation of monetary and credit policy, a common currency, a unified capital market, Community-fixed budgets and Community-fixed decisions over regional and other policies.

Progress towards EMU in the 1970s, however, was slow and limited mainly to attempts at control of exchange rate fluctuations, including the 1979 creation of the European Monetary System (EMS).

The Background to the European Monetary System

In the early years of the Community, little interest in the idea of monetary union existed. Since 1945 the free world had successfully created a system of fixed but adjustable exchange rates, a system which rested on the international agreements reached at Bretton Woods in the United States in 1944. The International Monetary Fund (IMF) was set up to support this system, the foundation of which was the overwhelming economic importance of the United States in the post-war world.

The United States was ready at that time to accept that the dollar should be the main reserve currency of the system with its value strictly tied to the value of gold, to assist the reconstruction of other countries through generous Marshall Aid and to make it possible for the central banks of other countries to rebuild their reserves of dollars. The United States was able to perform such a role because it had large gold reserves, few foreign debts, was much less dependent on foreign trade than its trading partners and had a strong competitve advantage in many products, especially high technology products. As the economies of other industrial countries expanded in the 1950s and 1960s they required greatly increased reserves of dollars which came increasingly to be supplied by the United States as credit.

Such domination by the almighty dollar was resented, particularly by the French. In February 1965 de Gaulle at a famous press conference eulogised the various qualities of gold, in particular the quality that it 'has no nationality'. Ironically, American economic domination was already coming to an end by 1965 as the strength of American industry declined relative to the rest of the industrialized world. Along with relative industrial decline came a weakening of the dollar as an automatically reliable currency. However, the Bretton Woods system of fixed exchange rates survived until 1971. In that years President Nixon tried to inflate the American economy with a package of measures which caused international speculation against the dollar. The free market gold price rose sharply and several countries began to demand conversion of their surplus dollars into gold at the offical price. The Federal Reserve Bank which held only $10 billion of gold reserves against debts of $50 billion in other countries' currencies could not cope and was forced to suspend convertibility in August 1971. The dollar now became free to float, mainly in a downward direction.

The decline of the dollar was not the only cause of a breakdown in currency stability in this period. Towards 1968 came rising unemployment and an acceleration in inflation which started to rise from the annual rates of between 3 and 4 per cent of earlier years to rise steadily into double figures, with wide differences from country to country. The first serious crisis came in France in the wake of the 1968 'French Revolution' and though a devaluation of the French franc was avoided in 1968, it became inevitable in 1969 along with a revaluation of the German mark.

These two developments seriously disrupted the Community and prompted the introduction of monetary compensation amounts (see chapter 4). They also prompted much discussion in 1969 and 1970 on possible solutions to the new situation of currency instability. At the Hague summit meeting in December 1969 the Heads of State agreed in principle to the creation of an economic and monetary union and that work should begin on methods of implementing it.

Two schools of thought emerged on how to approach the issue—the monetarists (mainly comprising the French, Belgians and the Commission) and the economists (the Germans and Dutch). The monetarists wanted immediate implementation of fixed exchange rates within the Community, with strict controls over capital mobility. Co-ordination and harmonisation of member states' economic policies should, in their view, be introduced later. A major French motive here was that the immediate adoption of fixed exchange rates would eliminate the new problem of MCAs.

On the 'economist' side, the leading protagonist was Dr Schiller, the West German Finance Minister, who produced a plan for Monetary, Economic and Financial Co-operation. He wanted more or less immediate introduction of the co-ordination and harmonisation of economic policies to be followed quickly by complete freedom of capital mobility. Only then, in his view, should fixed exchange rates leading to a single European currency be introduced. What worried the Germans was that an early freezing of exchange rates could lead to heavy inflation in West Germany and an underpricing of her industrial commodities. They also argued that permanent fixing of exchange rates would force the weaker members to manage their economies by high interest rates and a pruning of government spending, both of which would be deflationary and result in higher unemployment.

The West German methods, with hindsight, do seem more realistic. Until the economic policies of member states are co-ordinated, the introduction of fixed exchange rates will create probems. For example, if a country with higher inflation than its competitors is precluded from devaluing its currency, then it is likely to experience an adverse balance of payments for which the only remaining remedy is deflation—and rising unemployment.

Faced with this diversity of view, the Council of Ministers set up a group led by Pierre Werner, the prime minister of Luxembourg, to examine the problem. The Werner Report which encapsulated the group's findings, was a compromise between the position of the monetarists and that of the 'economists'. It proposed the achievement by 1980 of an economic and monetary union by stages but was specific only about the first stage from 1971 to 1973. It did not follow the wishes of the monetarists who wanted fixed exchange rates immediately but it proposed a compromise scheme in the shape of a reduction of the margin of fluctuation around the central parities when a Community currency was exchanged for another. Here lay the origins of what became known as 'the Snake in the tunnel'.

Two crises in 1971 accelerated the adoption of the first stage of the Werner Report. In May speculation caused by expectations of a revalued German mark forced the closure of the foreign exchange markets in West Germany, The Netherlands and Belgium as speculators sought to buy marks. More seriously in August, the deteriorating American balance of payments forced President Nixon to announce a package of measures which included the suspension of convertibility of the American dollar for gold. The old order that had existed since 1945 had well and truly ended.

Some degree of stability was restored in December 1971 by the Washington (Smithsonian Institute) agreement which allowed exchange rates more room to fluctuate than they had under the Bretton Woods rules. After a new set of exchange rates was agreed, including a devaluation of the dollar, currencies were free to move within a band of 2.25 per cent on either side of their dollar parity. As a result, European currencies could move against each other by 9 per cent because if one currency was 2.25 per cent above its dollar parity and another 2.25 per cent below, the gap between the two was 4.5 per cent. If they were in reversed positions, they would open up a 4.5 per cent gap the other way.

Many European governments thought that this 9 per cent swing was too large a permitted fluctuation. Therefore at the Basle agreement of 1972, narrower limits were set for Europe's currencies. The Six, plus the three countries about to join the Community (Britain, Denmark and Ireland), agreed to allow their currencies to move against each other by a maximum of only 2.25 per cent. This band was to be maintained within the 4.5 per cent limits allowed against the dollar. From this arrangement came the phrase, the 'snake in the tunnel'.

The 1972 snake had a brief and unhappy life. Exchange market pressure forced Britain and Ireland (whose pounds were still closely tied) to withdraw within six weeks. In 1973 Italy also withdrew. France withdrew in 1974, rejoined in 1975 and left again in 1976. The snake by then had become merely a West German group with small countries like Holland fixing their currencies against the mark.

Why did the snake fail? The Marjolin working group of 1974 pointed to three main factors—a lack of political will among member states, adverse events and an inadequate understanding of the nature of an economic and monetary union. The adverse events were the international monetary crisis that had continued since the late 1960s (especially the instability of the dollar) and the abrupt rise in oil prices in 1973. Member states had very mixed success in coping with the economic difficulties that resulted. Until 1972, at least in the Six, the disparities in inflation between European states had been kept within tolerable bounds, even though the inflation rate itself was becoming excessive. From 1973 on the differences in inflation rates became so large as to be incompatible with exchange rate stability. In the years 1971 to 1975, for example, Britain's average inflation rate was 13 per cent compared to West Germany's 6 per cent. If a member state with a higher inflation rate than average found itself with a balance of payments problem, it would then need to devalue its currency.

The situation deteriorated further between 1976 and 1978 as both inflation and unemployment in the Community rose and exchange rates floated, often in a highly volatile way. Clearly a new initiative was needed.

The Birth of the European Monetary System 1978–79

The Commission proposed new measures in the Jenkins Report of 1977 which stressed the need for stronger co-ordination of short-term economic policies, measures to complete the common market and an overall strategy on industrial redeployment. Following the Commission's initiative, the European Council, mainly at the prompting of Helmut Schmidt and Giscard d'Estaing agreed to devise 'a scheme for the creation of closer monetary co-operation leading to a zone of monetary stability in Europe'. The principle was agreed at the Bremen summit of July 1978 and the Brussels summit of December 1978 the European Council adopted a resolution on the introduction of a European Monetary System and related questions. Eight member states agreed to participate but Britain declined to enter the system which began operation in March 1979.

The European Monetary System (EMS) is a highly complex system composed of fixed but adjustable exchange rates, an intervention system, a new kind of money and large credit facilities. Its novel features are:

(a) The creation of a European currency unit (ECU), the value and composition of which are defined in terms of a basket of Community currencies, weighted according to each country's GNP and volume of intra-European trade. The value of the ECU was identical with that of the former European unit of account (EUA). The composition of the basket can be reviewed every five years or whenever the weight factors of one currency change by 25 per cent. The initial composition of the ECU is shown in table 14.

The Greek drachma is scheduled to become part of the ECU by 1985. By 1982 the weight of the German mark rose to 35.48 per cent as a result of its upvaluing in June 1982.

The ECU has become part of the international reserves of the European central banks. They obtain ECUs in return for depositing 20 per cent of their holdings of gold and dollars with the European Monetary Co-opera-

Table 14. Composition of the ECU

	Quantity of each currency in ECU basket	Weighting in terms of total (%)
West Germany	0.828 marks	33.36
France	1.150 francs	19.70
United Kingdom	8.850 pence	13.60
The Netherlands	0.286 guilder	10.40
Italy	109.000 lire	9.40
Belgium	3.660 francs	9.20
Denmark	0.217 krone	2.81
Ireland	0.760 pence	1.14
Luxembourg	0.140 francs	0.35

tion Fund (EMCF) which is sometimes known as FECOM from its French initials. Central banks also use the ECU to denominate their debts and credits with each other and each currency's central rates in the EMS is defined in ECUs. The ECU is also being used increasingly in commercial transactions. Companies that wish to minimise the risk of fluctuating exchange rates find a currency basket like the ECU a more stable way to borrow or put a price on export contracts and hold bank deposits.

(b) A two pronged approach to stabilising exchange rates by use of a parity grid and a divergence indicator. Participating Community currencies are assigned a central rate expressed as units of currency per ECU. The 1982 ECU central rates are shown in table 15.

Table 15. ECU Central Rates 1982

	%
Belgian and Luxembourg francs	44.70
German mark	2.32
Dutch guilder	2.67
Danish krone	6.20
Italian lira	1,305.13
Irish pound	0.69
British Sterling (February)	0.56
French francs	6.20

From these central rates can be derived a parity grid, showing the bilateral central rate between any pair of participating currencies. Bilateral intervention limits are calculated by applying margins of plus or minus 2.25 per cent (6 per cent for the Italian lira) to these central rates. When two currencies reach their maximum permitted divergence from the bilateral central rate, their central banks are required to intervene in the market for foreign exchange to prevent any further divergence. If, for example, the French franc falls to its 2.25 per cent floor against the German mark, the Bank of France sells marks while the German Bundesbank buys francs.

This method of defending currencies is similar to the arrangements in the old snake. To avoid too many interventions by central banks, the EMS is equipped with an early-warning system known as the divergence indicator and nicknamed the rattlesnake. Each EMS has a divergence threshold set at three quarters of the maximum permitted difference between its actual ECU rate and its ECU central rate. Once a country's ECU rate diverges by three quarters of its permitted difference from its central rate, the government of that country should take remedial action. If the currency is weak, then interest rates may have to be raised, taxes increased and government spending reduced. If the currency is strong, then the reverse of these policies will obtain. A government which fails to apply remedial action should explain its reasons for its non-action to other governments and central banks.

In addition to these novel features there exist credit mechanisms to enable central banks to defend par rates more easily. As stated above, member states, including Britain, have pooled 20 per cent of their gold and currency reserves in the EMCF in exchange for ECUs which can be used for settling up to 50 per cent of debts arising from intervention in Community currencies. If, in the hypothetical case cited above, the Bank of France needs to borrow German marks from the Bundesbank to finance its intervention, its debt will be calculated in ECUs and repaid in them.

The new system may be said to be more realistic than the snake in at least three ways. It allows margins of fluctuation wider than the norm to countries which are experiencing economic difficulties, for example Italy, with the divergence threshold signalling the stage at which it may be useful to take joint action before the problems become too acute. The second major advantage of the EMS is that it imposes remedial responsibility on a country with an appreciating currency as well as on country with a depreciating currency. Under the snake, action to restore the balance between the two currencies had been the exclusive responsibility of the country with a depreciating currency. The third improvement on the snake lies in the large increases in resources available for intervention in support of the system. With the previous system the funds available in 1974 amounted to about 3 billion dollars; the funds now available for intervention are roughly ten times this amount and more in line with the scale of potential speculation.

However, the EMS was very unlucky in its date of birth. It was launched only two months before the second steep rise of oil prices in 1979, a rise that precipitated more inflation and unemployment. Therefore it was not surprising that as currencies exceeded their divergence indicators, governments had no alternative but to alter their central rates. These alterations occurred reasonably smoothly, albeit accompanied by tough bargaining among Community finance ministers. For example the German mark was upvalued by 2 per cent in September 1979, by 5.5 per cent in October 1981 and by 4.25 per cent in June 1982 against all other European currencies. In contrast, the French franc was devalued by 3 per cent in October 1981 and by 5.75 per cent in June 1982. The West Germans have felt that there have been too frequent parity changes and insist that the EMS rules are intended to impose more discipline on governments.

The EMS has succeeded in reducing short-term fluctuations among its members at a time when other currencies have gyrated alarmingly. But this is only a small part of what was envisaged by the 1970 Werner Report which with hindsight can be seen as astonishingly optimistic. The EMS rules on exchange rate discipline are supposed to be a first step towards convergence, i.e. adoption of similar economic policies by member governments so that their inflation rates and economic performance will converge. There seems little sign that this will happen in the near future. The same may be said of other EMS targets. No date has been set for the establishment of a European Monetary Fund to replace the EMCF. The architects of EMS had hoped that such a fund would be able to issue ECUs against national currencies and intervene against currencies like the yen and the dollar on behalf of all Community members. Even further off is the establishment of irrevocable rates of exchange. If this were achieved, the Community, in the words of Denis Swann, 'would in effect have a common currency, since any one member state currency could always be freely guaranteed to exchange at a known rate into each of the other currencies. The way would be paved for a common currency which psychologically would be more attractive to "Europeans".' Such visions of monetary union must lie far in the future because the political will for such momentous developments does not exist. Member states are not yet ready to surrender their sovereignty over their own economic and monetary policies.

Britain and the European Monetary System

When the EMS was formed in 1979, the then Labour government was sceptical about the long-term aims of the new system, preferring to see it as a first step towards the restoration of monetary stability rather than as a move towards economic and monetary union with the Community. It was also more concerned with reforming the CAP and solving Britain's budgetary problems before entering the EMS. The government perhaps felt that such a move anyway would not be popular in the Labour Party generally.

The Conservative government, elected in May 1979, though apparently more committed to the Community, effectively continued the same policy as Labour between 1979 and 1982. It did agree to pool 20 per cent of its gold and dollar reserves with the EMCF in return for ECUs as a gesture towards Europe but was in no hurry to link sterling to the EMS. To the Thatcher government, already set on tight monetary policies, the EMS, with its central role as an external instrument of economic discipline, seemed irrelevant. The left-wing or 'wets' in the Conservative party have since campaigned for British entry into the EMS 'without delay'.

Certainly there are arguments for and against British entry into the EMS. Sterling has been volatile since 1977, its considerable fluctuations caused by Britain's trade performance, high British interest rates and Britain's new position as a petro-currency. Therefore to join in a system where sterling has a fixed parity would not be easy and would limit the government's freedom of manoeuvre in formulating economic policy.

Against this, Britain could make a demonstration of the genuineness of her European intentions by joining the EMS. Membership could also have advantages for British business which has been displeased by the fluctuations in interest rates and exchange rates in recent years. In 1981 Douglas McWilliams, head of the CBI's industrial trends and forecasting department commented that the number of businessmen complaining about the fluctuations of sterling was rising.

Such fluctuations do create uncertainty for businessmen whether or not they are exporters. A fall in the pound creates inflationary pressures and catches out companies that have run down their stocks of imports because they will have to pay more sterling to replace them, especially if the commodities are priced in dollars at a time when the dollar is strong. In 1981 ICI lost heavily when the pound's international value fell because the firm's export sales were mainly in European currencies which changed little against the pound while its imports were chiefly in dollars which had risen 25 per cent against the pound.

Conversely there are problems when the pound appreciates; a rising pound makes British exports less competitive abroad yet exporters are expected to plan ahead, win orders and hope that an appreciating pound will not wipe out their profits and markets. When the pound rose 30 per cent against the French franc between 1979 and 1981, the French market for some British exporters like British Leyland became virtually untenable.

Joining a fixed exchange rate system like the EMS would not remove all the risks; many other factors influence British competitiveness such as the speed of innovation and domestic inflation compared to foreign inflation. Nor would joining the EMS make the pound stable against the dollar but Britain now relies on the United States for only 25 per cent of her trade compared with 46 per cent in the case of the Community. Therefore a British accession to the EMS would help the business decisions of many British entrepreneurs.

Further Reading

Cipolla, C. P., *Fontana Economic History of Europe: The Twentieth Century*, chapter 11, Collins, London, 1978.
Strasser, D., *The Finances of Europe*, HMSO, London, 1981.
Wallace, H., *Budgetary Politics: The Finances of the European Communities*, Allen and Unwin, London, 1980.

Articles

'The Background to the EMS', *European Trends*, February 1979.
'The EMS', *European Trends*, May 1980.

Questions

(1) Why is there a Community budgetary problem?
(2) How can Community budgetary problems be solved?
(3) What novel features did the EMS contain at its inception in 1979?
(4) What are the arguments for and against British membership of the EMS?

11
The Consumer and the Environment

Why a Community Consumer Policy?

Several arguments may be put forward to justify the need for a consumer protection programme at a Community level. Firstly it fits in with the basic objectives of building Europe. The European treaties impose on the Community the responsibility of promoting economic and social progress and therefore the improvement of the quality of life of its citizens. This in turn implies the protection of health, safety and the economic interests of the consumer.

Such a general aim leads in practice to a second argument: the need to complement the work of national governments in areas where consumer interests are affected. Member governments interfere on a considerable scale in establishing technical standards and one of their main motives is to protect the public against physical harm and deception. For example the need for government surveillance in the field of drugs and medicines is indisputable after the tragic case of the thalidomide children. In addition standards have to be established over flavouring, colouring and other additives in food, and safety levels in electrical equipment. But also the consumer must not be exploited through deceit or through lack of information. However, national legal provisions are so divergent that the Community has a role in harmonising national regulations so that a sound general level of consumer protection is achieved.

If the diverse national standards were not harmonised the consumer would suffer in other ways—over choice or price. To the extent that standards differ between member states, they constitute a non-tariff barrier. This means that either the goods cannot be exported (in which case the consumer loses a wide choice) or if they are exported they have to be adapted to the standards of the country to which they are being exported. The latter alternative will mean that economies of large-scale production in the form of long runs of a standardised product are to some extent lost with less possibility of lower prices for the consumer. If the goods are not exported, competition is reduced in that particular national market, a factor which may also influence prices adversely as far as the consumer is concerned.

The Origins of the Consumer and Environment Programmes

Several clauses in the Rome Treaties have a bearing on consumer interests.

The need to harmonise standards was recognised in Articles 100 to 102 on the harmonisation of laws. The consumer also benefited from the removal of tariff barriers which led to more vigorous competition among manufacturers. Competition helped keep prices down and gave the consumer a greater choice of goods.

However, at the time the Rome Treaty was being drafted in 1957, the consumer was not regarded by the Six as a likely cause for political concern. As a result, consumers are mentioned only twice in the Treaty. Article 38 refers to the need for food supplies to reach consumers at a reasonable price as an aim of the Common Agricultural Policy. The two major articles concerning competition, Articles 85 and 86, require that the consumer receives a fair share of any benefit which may result from certain authorised agreements and they outlaw restrictive practices or abuse of a dominant market position which may harm the consumer's interests. Though it may be argued that the competition rules have given some protection to the consumer, it is doubtful whether the level of food prices has been reasonable as far as the consumer is concerned. The CAP has ensured relative stability of prices and security of supply at a time when the growth of the world's population has threatened recurrent food shortages. A part, at least, of the so-called 'mountains' represents a sensible food reserve. However, the consumer has normally paid for food at prices well above the world level.

In the first 15 years of the Community, then, the main benefit that the consumer derived from the common market was from the competition generated by the removal of some non-tariff barriers and the free exchange of goods and services. By 1972 a new interest in the consumer was evident at the October summit meeting in Paris. Three new member states—the United Kingdom, Ireland and Denmark—were about to accede to the Community and it was known that public opinion in these countries was lukewarm about membership. It was felt by both the Commission and the existing member governments that the current Community image needed improving. The Commission's concern for harmonisation had led to a rather legalistic approach which seemed to threaten the ordinary citizen's way of life by imposing on him 'eurobread' or 'eurobeer'. It was therefore seen as desirable to promote a new and fairer image of a Community with a human face, a Community where the citizen could feel that his interests were being taken into account.

Accordingly, the Heads of Government at the Paris Summit stated that 'economic expansion is not an end in itself; it should result in an improvement in the quality of life as well as in standards of living'. They specifically called for measures which would give a greater degree of consumer protection and in 1973 the Commission's Environment and Consumer Protection Service was established.

The Environment Policy from 1973

The Council of Ministers in July 1973 adopted an initial two-year programme of environmental action to be commenced immediately. The programme which was drawn up and adopted in accordance with the July deadline set by the Paris Summit of October 1972 had been forwarded by the Commission to the Council of Ministers in April. The Environmental ministers at French insistence approved the programme only so long as certain provisions came within the competence of the individual member states.

Among the principles laid down in the Community environment policy were the following:

(a) The best protection of the environment consists in preventing at source the creation of pollution or nuisances rather than subsequently trying to counteract their effects.

(b) All exploitation of resources and the natural environment causing significant damage to the ecological balance must be banned.

(c) The cost of preventing and abolishing nuisances must be born by the polluter.

(d) The Community and its member states must take into account in their environment policy the interests of the developing countries and must in particular examine any repercussions of the measures contemplated under that policy on the economic development of such countries and on trade with them, with a view to reducing adverse consequences as far as possible.

(e) For each different class of pollution, the level of action (local, regional, national, Community, international) best suited to the type of pollution should be sought.

(f) Environment policies should be harmonised in the Community and national programmes on the basis of a long-term plan.

The First Programme on the Environment lasted from 1973 to 1976 with some 40 Commission proposals being accepted by the Council. Three types of project were specified in this programme: (1) projects aiming at reducing and preventing pollution and nuisances; (2) projects intended to improve the environment and the quality of life; and (3) Community or member-state action in the international organisations dealing with environmental questions. In 1977 a Second Programme on the Environment was adopted to cover developments up to 1981 by which year some 50 directives had been adopted.

The two programmes gained only limited success with some failures, for example, the thwarting of proposals for air quality. Nevertheless some success was achieved in the areas of water pollution, energy production, waste disposal and noise. For water, a number of directives were adopted laying down quality objectives for various uses of water as well as an important directive on the discharge of dangerous substances into the aquatic environment. The most popular measure in the years up to 1981 was probably the Council directive of April 1979 on the conservation of birds.

The Programmes paid special attention to industrial activities in which the manufacturing processes involved the introduction of pollutants or nuisances into the environment. A list of priority industries was drawn up and proposals submitted for certain industries. Draft directives was submitted to the Council to limit the amount of mercury discharged into the waters of the Community. A proposal for a directive which would require national planning procedures to involve assessment of environmental impact in specified cases was being examined in Council working groups.

By 1982 further progress had been made with the Community adopting a directive ٫o control the discharge of cadmium, a highly toxic substance. By January 1983 all member states were to have started controlling industrial wastes containing cadmium.

The First Consumer Protection Programme

The Commission's preliminary programme for a consumer protection and information policy was adopted by the Council in April 1975. Legal justification for measures implemented was to be found in Article 100 (approximation of laws) and Article 235 (the catch-all clause which allows for any additional action needed). The programme summed up consumer interests in terms of five basic rights: (1) the right to protection of health and safety; (2) the right to protection of legal and economic interests; (3) the right to information and education; (4) the right of redress; and (5) the right of representation.

The overwhelming emphasis of the First Consumer Programme was on the right to protection of health and safety. Some of the progress on this front pre-dated the establishment of the Environment and Consumer Protection Service and involved five of the major Directorates: D–G III (for industrial affairs and the internal market), D–G IV (competition policy), D–G V (employment and social affairs including health), D–G VI (agriculture) and D–G XI (environment and consumers' protection).

On the industrial side, a series of directives had by 1981 established common standards in such areas as the lighting of motor cycles, the adequate fitting of such lighting, the sound level and exhaust system of motorcycles, the classification and labelling of dangerous substances with special attention to benzine and solvents and safety standards against radiation dangers. Even if some of these measures were primarily designed to eliminate non-tariff barriers (see chapter 8) they were nevertheless of direct benefit to consumer health and safety.

The harmonisation of national legislations relating to food standards had preoccupied the Commission since the early 1960s. A major part of the Industrial Directorate's work related to the use of additives in food. Directives relating to anti-oxidants, colourings, preservatives and emulsifiers were adopted and regularly updated both as regards permissible use and the establishment of purity criteria. Other so-called 'horizontal' measures (measures applicable to a range of individual foodstuffs) included directives on dietetic foods and materials in contact with food, particularly vinyl chloride monomer (VCM). Some vertical proposals (measures relating to a single product or group) were approved—for cocoa and chocolate, fruit juices, preserved milk, honey, sugar, jams and marmalades, natural mineral waters and coffee and chicory extracts. Sometimes as in the cases of the level of erucic acid in rapeseed and the use of VCM for wrapping food the directives were adopted speedily and forcefully. On other occasions, as on the question of the use of saccharin and other artificial sweeteners, the Council decided only to issue a recommendation.

A number of aspects of the Agriculture Directorate affected the consumer's health and safety: risk to public health in the processing and distribution of all types of meat, including livestock slaughtering; risks from certain animal diseases; dangers from the use of veterinary medicines and feed additives; and the use of pesticides. In 1972 a directive laid down standards for abattoirs and was followed in 1977 by one dealing with health problems connected with the trade in meat products. Financial aid from the Community was given to help the eradication of bovine tuberculosis and brucellosis.

Special mention should be made of consumer protection in the areas of cosmetics and pharmaceuticals. A 1976 directive brought in regulations over the composition, labelling and packaging of beauty products. It involved also the banning of some 360 substances. Similarly several directives controlled the norms relating to the use of colouring matters in and the marketing of medicines.

The protection against health and safety hazards was the main preoccupation of the 1975 programme and the achievements were not inconsiderable. Much less was achieved in promoting the other four rights. Little was done to safeguard the economic interests of the consumer. In the early 1970s some directives were passed to harmonise national legislation on travel insurance and vehicle insurance and during the life of the first Consumer Protection Programme the Commission proposed harmonisation in the fields of insurance contracts and legal expenses. It also presented in these years proposals to the Council for directives on doorstep selling (1977), misleading and unfair advertising (1978), liability for defective products (1976) and consumer credit (1979). None of these measures, with the exception of insurance, was fully approved in the period up to 1981.

Nothing at all concrete was done to improve the consumer's right to the redress of his or her grievances but some progress was made in the field of consumer information and education. To make a more rational choice the purchaser of goods and services needed to be better informed as to the essential characteristics of the product, its quality, quantity, energy consumption and price among other considerations. The work of the Industrial Directorate helped in this regard by harmonisation measures relating to the size range of prepacked food (including cans and bottles), unit pricing and the labelling and description of foodstuffs. In the general area of information a Council decision was adopted which enabled detailed statistics of accidents in the home involving products to be collected. A proposed decision on the rapid exchange of information between member states on dangers which might suddenly arise from the use of consumer goods was held up in the European Parliament.

Finally a start was made, and no more, on the consumer's fifth right—the right of representation. By 1980 the voice of the consumer could be heard in a number of the Community forums. Consumer problems were the subject of debates in the European Parliament and the Economic and Social Committee, a body where the consumers were represented. In addition the Commission had been able to consult the Consumer Consultative Committee since 1973 on all preliminary drafts of legislation affecting consumers. The Consumer Consultative Committee was composed of 25 members: three from the European Consumer Bureau (BEUC), three from the European Family Committee (COFACE), three from the European Consumer Co-operatives (EURO–COOP), six from the European Trade Union Council and ten appointed on an individual basis.

The Second Consumer Programme 1981

A proposal for a second Consumer Programme due to follow on the five year preliminary programme from May 1980 was first submitted by the Commission to the Council in June 1979. Agreement was only reached in the Council in May 1981 but in view of the fact that many measures arising out of the First Programme were still in the legislative pipeline, the year's delay was hardly significant. Indeed the Second Programme merely aimed to 'continue and intensify the measures taken'; in other words it consisted largely of a restatement of the objectives of its predecessor with some elaboration of the original proposals. Like the First Programme, it was based on the five basic rights of the consumer established by the Council in 1975.

Consumer health and safety remained a major preoccupation of the Second Programme and a whole battery of new measures was envisaged in this field. In the food area new legistlation was proposed on flavourings, extraction solvents, starches, sulphur dioxide and sulphites and on materials in contact with food such as plastics, regenerated cellulose film and ceramics. Vertical directives were to include those on edible caseine and caseinates, soft drinks, quick and deep frozen foods and baby foods. Consumer protection through harmonised rules on public and animal health were to be promoted in amended legislation on trade in fresh meat and in new rules on trade in minced meat and in poultry. In the controversial area of the use of hormones in livestock production, the Council agreed in 1981 that the sale of stilbenes (aromatic hydrocarbons) and other substances should be prohibited. Certain other substances were to be used by veterinary surgeons only for therapeutic purposes. In 1981 also the Council agreed to attempt early implementation of provisions on the use of certain hormonal substances such as growth promoters and on the difficult problem of detecting their residues in meat. In this field the problem was not only technical but political; the Council had to decide how far governments should bear the cost of inspection and analysis. As the level of government help varied from one member state to another, competition in the area of veterinary services could be distorted.

Public health was to be further safeguarded by measures to control the presence in animal feedingstuffs of certain undesirable substances and the level of use of various pre-mixtures and bio-proteins. The detection of pesticide residues in foodstuffs and animal feeds was also to be dealt with by appropriate legislation.

The Commission was committed to examine measures taken by member states to limit the consumption of tobacco and alcohol. If any distortions were found in the market for these goods, it was resolved to present proposals dealing with their advertising as well as consumer education and information in relation to them. As far as cosmetics were concerned, the Commission intended to draw up lists of authorised substances, including anti-oxidants, hair dyes, preservatives and ultraviolet filters.

Other safety risks on which the Commission intended to legislate included the inflammability of textiles and the use of fire-proofing substances or colouring matters which were sometimes dangerous to health. A draft directive on toys had been prepared by 1981 and was to be complemented by more detailed texts on the prevention of poisoning, fire and electrocution through faulty toys. Further work was to be done to safeguard the consumer against toxic substances with particular emphasis on the safety problems of cleaning products, paints, varnishes, adhesives and other potentially dangerous preparations used in the home. Finally the Commission was hoping to develop its work on the safety of motor vehicle components and other manufactures. Already 20 directives governed the safety of cars and trucks over aspects such as shock resistance and pollution. The safety of other manufactured products in terms of inflammability was regarded as particularly urgent, especially in furniture and products used for fitting out and covering buildings.

Useful progress in the field of health and safety had been made during the First Programme. The record had been less impressive in the protection of the economic interests of the consumer and therefore the 1981 Programme gave this aspect particular emphasis. The need for progress was seen in four main fields. (1) The consumer was to be protected against unfair sales practices and terms of contract and extortionate credit terms. (2) He was to be protected against the consequences of defective products and deficient services. (3) He was to be protected against misleading promotion and advertising of goods and services and inadequate or inaccurate labelling of goods. (4) He was to be entitled to reliable after-sales service and spares.

Proposals on these areas had been presented by the Commission to the Council during the life of the First Consumer Programme but they had been slowed down by wide divergencies in national outlook. However, the growth of the service industries, the share they took of the household budget and their position in the economy as a whole (employing half the working population) led the Commission to believe that the position of the consumer needed to be strengthened, the more so since the quality of services was more difficult to compare objectively than the quality of goods. As a result price comparisons were more difficult and the transparency of competition reduced. The public sector posed a particular problem here; a wide range of services like gas, water and electricity were supplied by public services which were usually in a position of monopoly and therefore the consumer was unable to negotiate tariffs or change the supplier. The Economic and Social Committee showed particular interest in the clauses of the Programme referring to the public utilities and hoped that consumers could be more effectively represented in decisions where their interests were affected.

Proposals over the remaining three consumer rights were more modest. Recognising the limited scope for Community action in the sphere of the right to redress, the Commission committed itself in the 1981 Programme to 'continue to study the procedures and channels for obtaining legal remedy which exist in the member states, particularly with regard to the right of consumer associations to institute legal proceedings, the simplification of court procedures and the admissibility of proceedings by consumers against public undertakings administered according to commercial criteria'. When the study is completed, it will be published so that consumers are aware of the procedures and means of recourse available to them to deal with manufacturers, traders and public services. The Economic and Social Committee had wanted rather more than this, recommending that the Commission should encourage the setting up of legal advice centres and conciliation and arbitration bodies.

As regards consumer information and education, the Commission undertook in the 1981 Programme to encourage improved dissemination of information on labels and packages of particular goods so that the consumer could use them correctly. A typical example in this respect was information on the energy consumption of household electrical appliances. The Commission also hoped to organise consultation between consumers' representatives and suppliers of goods and services in order to promote voluntary labelling and other sources of information. Co-operation between testing bodies was to be encouraged and increased transparency of the market was to be promoted by ensuring wider publication of comparative tests so that the consumer was kept informed about the quality and price of goods and their value as regards conditions of warranty and after sales service. The Economic and Social Committee also emphasised the need to inform particular groups of consumers such as the aged and the handicapped. Finally the Commission hoped to examine ways of developing consumer education both for the young and adults. A European network of pilot schools had already been formed but it was envisaged that television courses and study-holidays for the staff of consumer organisations could also be implemented.

The Commission stressed in its Programme that the promotion of consumers' interests (the right to be heard) was important on grounds of democratic principle. It also pointed out that in the age of mass markets, the voice of the isolated consumer had little chance of being heard and therefore consumer organisations needed to be developed so as to re-establish a balance between consumers and producers. Therefore in the 1981 Programme the Commission undertook to draw up a report on the current situation relating to consumer representation at a Community and national level. It promised to strive towards increased representation of consumers on the Community specialist consultative committees and national organisations. It hoped to encourage consultation between the various European consumer organisations, to increase aid to them and to improve the training of their staff.

The Commission also undertook to take consumer interests into account in implementing the Common Agricultural Policy. Consumers had been represented on the consultative committees for each main agricultural product since the 1960s but their views had been overshadowed by the farming lobby. Pressure from the European Consumer Bureau (BEUC) succeeded in persuading the Commission to permit it formally to submit to the Commissioner for agriculture and senior officials of D–G VI the consumer viewpoint on the Commission's annual farm price proposals. This provided in theory some counterweight to the privileged access to the Commission enjoyed by the farming organisation (COPA). In practice, of course, other interests have louder voices than the consumer in the Council of Agricultural Ministers.

Obstacles to an Effective Consumer Policy

Many factors seem likely to continue to obstruct the evolution of an effective Community consumer policy. Widely divergent national viewpoints make the adoption of such policies a very slow business indeed. Those member states with extensive existing consumer protection legislation tend to see Community initiatives as unnecessary. Four member countries—Denmark, Germany, The Netherlands and the United Kingdom—have laws which recognise the consumer's five basic rights and are in many respects ahead of the aims set by the Second Programme. Their representatives have little incentive to spend time and money on improvements in consumer's rights in countries like Ireland, Italy or Greece. Member states with little existing legislation tend to regard Community initiatives as undesirably radical and expensive.

National viewpoints necessarily complicate the decision-making process when issues that are already complex are being considered. Take for example the issue of advertising. The Commission would allow the concept of fairness to admit competitive advertising; certain member governments have taken an opposite view. Opinions also differ as to whether all advertising or only that enjoying wide diffusion, especially that crossing national boundaries through the medium of television, should come within the scope of a Community directive. Nor has there been agreement as to whether mandatory controls should be established or whether only voluntary codes of conduct are necessary. Both the Commission and BEUC have stressed that codes, however acceptable in themselves, need to be backed by a legal framework. For advertising, the Commission has therefore suggested some kind of office of fair trading to enforce advertising codes, a kind of birch in the cupboard. On the other hand some consumer organisations have pointed to the difficulty of imposing the same standards in all member countries when in some cases the standards would be most difficult to achieve. They have therefore suggested the setting of certain minimum standards in advertising with national governments having the option to apply more rigorous standards if they so wish.

But there are constraints on decisive action arising from the Community's administrative process itself. Firstly its bad reputation has hindered action. Its officials have certainly in the past approached the task of harmonisation in an excessively legalistic way so much so that harmonisation became a perjorative term connected with plots to force the ordinary citizen to abandon a genuine national way of life. To counter this the then President of the Commission, Roy Jenkins, announced at an unofficial commissioners' meeting in 1978 that harmonisation would be limited strictly to a minimum of cases where there was a definite obstacle to the free movement of goods and services. As a result, a number of draft directives relating to consumer protection were abandoned. These were mainly vertical proposals, most of them dating from 1970 or earlier. Some of the proposals like those for beer, bread, ices, pasta and mayonnaise were abandoned for ever while others were to be revised.

More important than the unpopularity of harmonisation in slowing down the development of consumer protection have been institutional constraints. As explained earlier, responsibility for initiating measures has been divided between five of the Directorates-General, a serious weakness because there has been relatively little co-ordination between Directorates covering similar or related policies.

Even if this were not the case, the process of turning a proposal into a firm directive is a long and involved affair. The proposal has first to be drafted after due consultation with national governments, individually and through committees of experts, and with the private interests concerned. Where aspects of public health or safety are involved, the Commission will often have to begin by obtaining scientific advice from independent national committees of which there are a bewildering variety—for pharmaceuticals, foodstuffs, animal feed and many technical matters concerning cosmetics, aerosols and toxic waste. When this has been done the Commission has to consult the relevant advisory or consultative committee on which there is usually some form of consumer representation. These advisory committees include those for food, toxicity and all agricultural products. Finally the Consumer Consultative Committee itself must be approached for its views.

To reconcile the views of the various parties and at the same time to promote the Community interest is obviously difficult. Further delay is caused by the practice of obtaining the opinions of the European Parliament and the Economic and Social Committee. Usually considerable areas of disagreement remain when the proposal at long last finally arrives for consideration by the Council of Ministers. As the working groups seldom meet more than once a month, a proposal will rarely become a directive in less than two years. Even when a directive has been agreed, its application may be equally slow. In most cases member countries are given several years in which to adapt their legislation to the standards laid down in the directive.

Other institutional drawbacks concern the Economic and Social Committee, the Parliament and the Council of Ministers. Many of the members of ESC have expertise in consumer affairs and can submit opinions to the Council but their views can be ignored. Much was hoped from the elected Parliament but so far it has proved obstructive rather than helpful. The Parliament's Legal Affairs Committee held up for months its opinion on the product liability and consumer credit directives on the grounds that they were perhaps incompatible with the Rome Treaty. Similarly the Parliament's Committee on the Environment, Public Health and Consumer Protection expressed unfavourable views on the Commission proposal for a system of rapid exchange of information about dangerous goods between member states. At Council level, the absence of a regularly constituted group of ministers specifically responsible for consumer affairs is a major handicap. Consumer affairs are usually added to the agenda of meetings of the foreign affairs ministers and are given relatively little support compared to agriculture or even energy or transport.

Finally consumer affairs in the Community context suffer from a lack of resources. The Directorate-General for Consumer Affairs (D–G XI) has fewer than a dozen top civil servants and is severely understaffed for the task of implementing the Second Programme. It has little cash to finance necessary aspects of the Programme such as the commissioning of studies, the promotion of research and product testing and the dispensing of information to the consumer. The 1981 Budget only provided just over one million ECU for the work of D–G XI compared to a budget of over 12 billion ECU for agriculture.

Given the above obstacles, it can be seen that though the consumer lobby has in recent years established a more effective presence in Community affairs, its power is very limited. It may also be argued that the methods of D–G XI are not in any case the appropriate ones for protecting the consumer. In place of the laborious attempts to harmonise national laws should come greater implementation of the rules of competition and free circulation which in practice more effectively protect consumer interests. A good example of the consumer's choice being extended by firm application of the competition rules was the 'Cassis de Dijon' case of 1979. The European Court overruled a German Federal Court's ruling that the export of the liqueur Cassis de Dijon from France to West Germany was inadmissible on the grounds that its alcoholic content was inferior to the minimum laid down for liqueurs in West Germany. The European Court stressed that there should be free movements within the Community of any goods whose production was legal in the country of origin unless such goods were prohibited in the country of destination on grounds of public health or of being misleadingly labelled. The Cassis de Dijon judgment set an important precedent which could widen the consumers' choice without their health or safety being put at risk.

Further Reading

Twitchett, C. C., (ed.), *Harmonisation in the EEC*, Macmillan, London, 1981.

Articles
'Consumer Protection', *European Trends*, August 1981.

Questions

(1) Why does the Community need a Consumer Policy?
(2) What has the Community done to protect the environment?
(3) What are the five basic consumer rights?
(4) Outline the main objectives of the 1981 Consumer Programme.
(5) What are the implications of the Cassis de Dijon case?

12
Transport Policy

The Need for a Community Transport Policy

At a general level, policy-making for transport, whether at national or Community level, has three major objectives. Firstly it should contribute to economic growth and prosperity by providing an efficient service to industry, commerce and agriculture. Secondly it should meet social needs by securing the mobility of the work force and the general public, particularly by providing public transport for people who cannot travel by car. Thirdly it should control the harmful effects of transport in terms of danger to people and damage to the environment.

However, transport costs are also an important factor in influencing the level of intra-Community trade because they form a considerable proportion of the cost of many articles. As an example of this may be cited the cost of stone in West Germany where in the 1950s 50 per cent was added to the producer price by railway freight charges. Like tariffs, transport costs can be an obstacle to free trade in goods and both have the effect of protecting the local producer from the competition of outside producers. Therefore since the Community has as a chief objective the increase of inter-state trade, it is crucial that there should be a cheap and integrated Community transport system.

Community supervision is necessary for a second reason. Transport has been subject to state intervention in all the member countries. Often transport costs have been consciously managed by member governments so as to help exports and inhibit imports. Such manipulation is a blow at the concept of the free movement of goods as enshrined in Article 3 of the Rome Treaty.

Transport in the Treaty of Rome

Transport is one of the four spheres (along with commerce, agriculture and competition) in which the adoption of a common policy is an aim of the Community as set out in Article 3 of the Rome Treaty. However, until 1974 the Commission's field of action was limited under Articles 74 to 84 of the Treaty and Article 70 of the European Coal and Steel Community Treaty (the Treaty of Paris) to rail, road and inland waterways. Only in 1974 did the Court of Justice rule that the Treaty provisions could be extended to include sea and air transport.

Articles 74 to 84 of the Treaty of Rome laid down that the Council of Ministers would establish a joint transport policy and common rules for international transport within or through the Community, covering road, rail and inland water transport. The Council were to decide the conditions under which transport undertakings of one member country would be permitted to operate in another. The decisions were to be taken unanimously initially and by a qualified majority thereafter, but unanimity would still be required whenever the Council's decisions involved principles of transport policy and might seriously injure the standard of living and employment in certain areas. The Treaty stated that all freight rates which discriminated as to the national origins or destination of the goods transported should eventually be suppressed. Similarly all special rates or privileges granted by a member country for the purpose of helping or protecting specific undertakings or industries should also be phased out, unless specially authorised by the Commission.

It is clear from these terms that the founding fathers wanted a transport policy which would contribute to the development of a freer and more competitive market in goods and services, as well as to the implementing of a free market in transport itself. In fact their hopes that the Rome Treaty would be the basis for a wider ranging policy implementing such freer markets were to be disappointed. The Commission's subsequent work led to controls on entry, prices and the harmonisation of conditions of operation which were restrictive rather than liberalising.

The Slow Evolution of the Common Transport Policy

The clauses in the Rome Treaty referring to transport had not been very helpful beyond specific injunctions on discrimination in transport matters but the Treaty did give the Commission powers to make proposals for a fuller transport policy. The Commission duly presented its first proposals on this issue in April 1961 in the Schaus Memorandum, named after Lambert Schaus the first Transport Commissioner. The Memorandum emphasised the general Community objective of a freer and more competitive market but it also identified several characteristics of the transport sector such as the high degree of public intervention and unstable prices. In the view of the Commission these aspects of transport hindered the normal play of competition and therefore, as the Memorandum stressed, 'action must be based on removing the special aspects or on neutralising their effect where they continue to exist'. Given the highly regulated nature of transport within the Community this was a controversial proposition. But it did augur an interventionist approach to transport policy by the Commission.

Having digested the implications of the Schaus Memorandum, the Council of Ministers asked the Commission in February 1962 to present detailed proposals for a common transport policy by May 1962. The Commission submitted its Action Programme in June 1962. It was based on the principles of: (1) equality of treatment; (2) financial independence; (3) freedom of action for transport enterprises; (4) free choice by the user of the means of transport; and (5) co-ordination of investment. The Commission's proposals for intra-Community traffic aimed at bringing into line the regulations of member states over admission to the market so as to end discrimination on grounds of nationality. The Commission also proposed that the present bilateral quotas would be gradually replaced by a Community quota open to carriers in the Six; this was to be phased in by 1969. A system of scales of charges was to be introduced; until 1964 member states would apply their own rates but from 1966 national systems would be harmonised so that by 1969 there would be a common system of tariffs for transport throughout the Community. Finally, various harmonisation measures for transport taxation were proposed—on fuel, modes of transport and vehicles.

Not until June 1965 did the Council of Ministers reach agreement on these proposals. A framework for a Community transport system to regulate competition in all sectors would be implemented by the introduction of fixed rates in two stages. During the first stage from 1966 to 1969 the Community regulations would only apply to commercial transport between member countries. Upper and lower tariff limits would be published for certain classes of road and rail traffic though agreements outside these rates could be made under certain circumstances if the details were published. In the second stage from 1969 to 1972 the tariff limits would be extended to certain categories of national as well as international traffic so that by 1970 most of the rail and road traffic in the Community would be covered by a system of rate control, though a more flexible system would apply to waterborne traffic.

The decision to produce a framework did not lead to rapid implementation as a virtual standstill now occurred on discussions between the Transport Ministers. Only in July 1968 did they adopt five regulations as a basis for a common transport policy. (1) All agreements which adversely affected transport competition in the Community, such as price-fixing or market sharing, were to be abolished. (2) Hitherto lorries from one Community country had only been able to operate in other Community countries under special licences derived from bilateral agreements. 1,200 Community licences would now be available up to 1971 to enable their holders to operate goods traffic between member countries. (3) From 1969 goods vehicles would be allowed to take 50 litres of fuel in their tanks duty-free into any Community state. (4) Detailed working conditions in intra-Community road transport were laid down. These conditions governed both goods and passenger transport and concerned rest periods and the maximum hours of driving allowed in a day or week. The new regulations would not prejudice more favourable agreements reached within the transport industry or by national government action. The regulations would apply from 1969. (5) The appropriate authorities would publish fixed maximum and minimum freight charges for intra-Community road transport with the maximum permitted spread 23 per cent below the ceiling level. Goods were to be transported freely within these rate limits though there could be exceptions made for some private contracts. To ensure that this regulation was complied with, a special committee made up of representatives from the member states and the Commission would supervise its operation.

In 1969 the Community took further steps towards establishing a common policy by adopting more regulations. The Council agreed on a common definition of the obligations that governments could impose on road, rail and inland waterway transport in return for subsidies. Public service obligations were only to be maintained to the extent that they were necessary to provide adequate transport services. Regulations on how subsidies should be paid were agreed, including the provisions of cheaper services for certain groups like the armed forces or the large family. Common rules were established for the standardisation of railway accounts to ensure that the pattern of subsidies paid to railways was the same in all member states. The accounts should reveal all payments made and which lines were uneconomic.

By the 1970s some progress towards a common transport policy had been achieved but there was a feeling of dissatisfaction with certain interventionist aspects of the policy. With the enlargement of the Community imminent and new personnel in charge of the Transport Directorate (D–G VII), there was the opportunity for a shift in the direction of transport policy. Therefore in 1973 the Commission sent to the Council a new set of proposals entitled 'Common Transport Policy: Objectives and Programme'. This consultative document suggested action to improve consultation between member states and the Commission on major projects of transport infrastructure, the harmonisation of social legislation affecting inland waterways and road haulage and proposals for capacity control in the road haulage sector to replace in the long-run the system of quotas agreed in 1968 though with increases in the Community quota for the time being. Certain harmonisation proposals were made including the standardisation of the weight and dimensions of commercial vehicles, and the standardisation of the national taxation systems relating to commercial vehicles. Other measures related to the railway financing by governments, a study of air transport, freedom of movement for transport operators, the mutual recognition of driving licences and roadworthiness tests and preliminary studies indicating the scope of Community action on ports and maritime transport.

However, the significant feature of the new communication was its unequivocal support for the free market economy 'as an effective means of allocating resources'. The Commission admitted that 'the common transport policy has not made striking progress in recent years' but in a sense it only had itself to blame. Some of its own measures such as the rate-bracket system were a clear contradiction of its professed belief in a truly free competitive system. What now seemed equally clear was that the Commission intended less interference in fixing transport tariffs and that in the future prices should gradually be allowed to find their own level in a more competitive environment.

With the Court of Justice ruling of April 1974 that the Treaty provisions could be extended to sea and air transport, hope was aroused that the common transport policy was about to develop strongly. But this was a false dawn. Divergent national viewpoints slowed down decision-making in the later 1970s, much to the Commission's exasperation. Even directives agreed many years before were not being implemented and the Commission was forced to threaten legal action against those member states who were deemed guilty of backsliding. A good example of the slow implementation of Community transport provisions was the delay over Regulation 543/69 on the harmonisation of working conditions for drivers. Member states have implemented this very tardily and its application in the new member states was postponed to 1976. The controversial proposals on technical standards concerning the weight and dimension of commercial vehicles caused deadlock until the 1980s.

The Achievements and Travails of the Common Transport Policy

The record of development in the Community's common transport policy is, to say the least, rather mixed. In this section it is intended to analyse five aspects of the policy: (a) the elimination of discrimination; (b) freedom of operation and licences for road haulage; (c) harmonisation measures; (d) prices; and (e) infrastructure.

The Elimination of Discrimination

One of the main objectives of the Schaus Memorandum of 1961 was the elimination of obstacles which transport might place in the way of the establishment of a Community common market. Such obstacles included discrimination on grounds of nationality (for example over price), un-justifiable state aids and barriers to frontier crossing of a physical, fiscal or technical nature. The year 1960 had already seen a Regulation relating to the prohibition of such discrimination. By the end of 1964 conscious national discrimination, for example in preferential tariffs, had been elim-inated. Since then the Commission has continued to monitor general sup-port tariffs where they have been allowed to continue under Article 80 of the Rome Treaty. In addition, the physical facilities for frontier crossing have been improved so that this area of the common transport policy is no longer at the forefront of debates even though frontier procedures require further improvement.

Freedom of Operation and Licences for Road Haulage

Originally the Commission had hoped for complete liberalisation in terms of freedom of entry to the transport market. In other words producers would have been able to carry their own products in their own vehicles anywhere in the Community with no member state being able to limit the number of foreign vehicles operating in its territory. Such a solution was unacceptable to the six member states, all of whom had been operating restrictive bilateral licensing systems which limited the number of licences available to foreign hauliers.

When in June 1965 the member states reached agreement on the organ-isation of the transport market, it was presumed that a common domestic licensing system would be introduced which represented a compromise between the various national systems. In June 1967 the Commission sub-mitted a draft regulation to the Council on entrance to national road haul-age markets and in 1971 stressed the need for creating 'a climate of healthy competition'. Whether the Community licence system as brought in by the

1968 agreement constitutes 'healthy competition' is debatable. 1,200 licences were authorised for issue until December 1971, enabling their holders to operate goods traffic between the member countries. The distribution of licences was: Belgium 161, France 286, Western Germany 286, Italy 194, Luxembourg 33, The Netherlands 240. A series of regulations extended the period beyond December 1971 and increased the number of licences from 1973 onwards.

However, the quota system suffered from two chief drawbacks. Firstly it was a complex process for the individual operator and indeed for the member states themselves. Hauliers who wished to gain a licence for short-distance work had to provide information on the services which they intended to operate and their anticipated receipts. They had to back up their statements with documentation, including statements from customers. Similar conditions applied to long-distance haulage but in this area each member state was to set an overall capacity limit for this area of transport.

The addition of the Community quota made the permit system more complicated as there were already other types of permit operating—bilateral permits which counted as a fixed amount against the Community quota including agreements negotiated independently between individual member states, and co-operation permits which enabled hauliers of different countries to make 'return-load' arrangements. The main cause for complaint was, however, not so much the complexity of the system but the shortage of permits available. In 1977 the Commission indicated that it would like to double the number of quotas for 1978. This would have meant the United Kingdom, for example, being allocated 544 quotas instead of 272. However, the Council refused to adopt such a radical policy and would only agree to a 20 per cent increase. As a result the United Kingdom quota rose only to 326. On the face of it it seems absurd that road transport in a supposedly free trade area should be hampered by such tight Community restrictions and there have been calls for the removal of all permits and quotas.

Harmonisation Measures

As resistance to free entry has been stubborn, the Commission has believed that harmonisation measures might help to create a fair and free competition in the transport market. For example it has affirmed that employment conditions should be similar all over the Community, otherwise one country's transport system or perhaps one type of transport might enjoy a competitive advantage.

The Commission has attempted to implement harmonisation in three areas—fiscal, social and technical. Not much has been achieved in terms of fiscal harmonisation. The Community standardised the conditions for free admission of fuel in tanks of vehicles engaged in intra-Community trade in 1968 but has not succeeded in resolving the problem of double taxation of road vehicles even though the Commission proposed as long ago as 1964 that vehicles should only be taxed in their country of registration. Very wide variations continue to exist between member states' taxation policies as they affect transport. Public transport has been zero-rated for VAT purposes in the United Kingdom, Denmark and Ireland. In Belgium, The Netherlands and Luxembourg a reduced rate of between 4 and 6 per cent has been charged, while in France and Germany publicly owned transport pays a reduced rate of VAT. Road tax has also continued to vary from one member state to another. In 1976 it ranged from over £90 for a car in Belgium to £15.75 in Luxembourg. Taxes on petrol and diesel fuel have also varied considerably.

The measures for fiscal harmonisation for rail transport were embodied in the 1969 regulations. These should have prevented undue subsidising of their railways by member governments but in practice the governments have subsidised their railway networks as and when they felt fit. The Commission failed to define precisely what may be classed as legitimate commercial aid to the railways for the existing regulations to control subsidies.

Harmonisation of social conditions in transport has enjoyed rather more success though not without considerable controversy. After several years of discussion and negotiation the Regulation of 1969 controlling the working conditions of road transport crews was fully adopted in 1977. The Regulation laid down the minimum age of drivers, stipulated that drivers of vehicles of over 20 tons loaded weight who travelled over 280 miles (450 kilometres) between rest periods must be accompanied by another driver from the beginning of the journey or be replaced by another driver after 280 miles. The maximum hours of driving permitted for drivers of all goods and passenger vehicles was fixed at eight hours a day (four hours at a stretch and 48 hours a week.)

The United Kingdom opposed this Regulation even though it was due to be implemented in full at the end of the transitional period (January 1978). The British arguments against the 1969 Regulation were several. The cost was estimated to be approximately £350 million per year for the road haulage industry and £100 million a year for the bus and coach industry. It was also pointed out that some longer distance bus and coach operators might have to close down and that some sectors of the transport industry (for example bus services operating a seven day week) would have their operations disrupted. Finally the British doubted whether the new rules were enforceable, given the difficulties experienced in other countries, and indeed whether they would be effective in promoting safety.

Once again, the British were out of step with their Community partners and wanted special arrangements for the United Kingdom. However, a three-year transition period from 1978 was all that could be obtained under Community law. During this period the requirements became progressively stricter. For example the limit on daily driving was nine and a half hours from December 1978 to June 1979, followed by nine hours until January 1981 when the eight hour limit was finally introduced.

A similar position arose over the tachograph, the on-board device which automatically records a vehicle's speed, the distance travelled, the time spent driving and the time of day. The Commission Regulation No. 1463 of 1970 required the installation of a tachograph in new goods vehicles of over 3.5 gross tonnes and in passenger vehicles with more than nine seats if not used on regular services. There were some exceptions to the rule, for example minibuses operating internally and most goods vehicles operating only within a 50 kilometre radius. However, all eligible vehicles were required by the Community to have the instrument fitted and operating by January 1978.

This requirement was not complied with by the British. The British Freight Transport Association was most alarmed and put the cost of installation and working of tachographs at £350 million a year. The Labour government of the day was not impressed either and the Secretary of State for Transport, William Rodgers gave the government view in January 1977 when he said: 'We would prefer not to see the tachograph in domestic use and we are not planning to move in that direction.' As a result of this inaction the Regulation was not enforced in Britain which as a result was in breach of Community law. In the summer of 1978 the Commission announced its intention of taking the British government to the European Court of Justice on the issue. In December 1978 the hearing took place and in January 1979 the Court found in favour of the Commission. The then British Labour government reluctantly accepted the court ruling but gave no firm date for actual compliance. The advent of a Conservative government in May 1979 meant that a new administration was left with the responsibility of implementing the relevant legislation.

Tachographs had first been used in a Community country in 1953 when the West German government introduced them into long-distance haulage at the request of the drivers' unions. In time opinion in most Continental countries came to regard tachographs as a useful mechanical safeguard against exploitation by unscrupulous employers who might order their drivers to work excessive hours over long distances. For the British the issue seemed to be more than a merely technical or social issue. The introduction of the tachograph, in the words of Carol Cosgrove Twitchett, 'raised the spectre of believed infringements of sovereignty and the threat of a foreign bureaucracy dictating to the British working man'.

One area of road harmonisation where agreement was more straightforward was roadworthiness tests. In December 1976 the Council of Ministers issued a directive on the approximation of laws relating to road worthiness for motor vehicles and their trailers. The directive applied to all commercial vehicles over 3.5 tonnes laden weight, all passenger vehicles having more than eight seats, taxis and ambulances. After 1st January, 1983 all these vehicles were to be subject to specified roadworthiness tests one year after the date when they were first used and annually thereafter. Annual certificates of roadworthiness were therefore to be compulsory and each member state was to recognise the certificates issued by other Community countries as equal in status to its own.

The harmonisation of technical standards has not presented undue problems in the fields of railway and waterway transport. Harmonisation of railway transport was already developing through the International Railways Union and the only contentious issue—the introduction of automatic coupling—was agreed by the European Conference of Ministers of Transport. In waterway transport, the working environment decided the technical characteristics of the craft used but some agreement was reached on common standards for the construction of new equipment.

It was road haulage that once again presented problems and once again in particular to the United Kingdom. Within the Community wide variations had existed in both the maximum permitted gross weights and axle weights of lorries. The maximum allowed in the United Kingdom was lower than in any other member state except Ireland. For example the maximum gross weight in the United Kingdom was 32 tonnes while in The Netherlands it was 50 tonnes. The British recognised that heavier lorries had advantages in terms of costs and productivity but were worried that raising the limits would adversely affect the roads and the environment.

The Community had in fact been striving for common standards in this field long before British entry. As early as 1963 the Commission had submitted to the Council its proposals limiting the maximum length, width, height, weight and axle weight for various categories of road vehicles. The Council quickly reached agreement on most issues except axle weights but delayed proceeding with a regulation covering the agreed matters in the hope that a comprehensive agreement could be reached. By the time that such an agreement between the Six appeared possible in 1972, it was clear that the three acceding countries, including the United Kingdom, wanted lower limits, for example no more than 10 tonnes per single axle. Open disagreement occurred before the Commission in 1976 produced a promising compromise proposal suggesting a gross weight limit of 40 tonnes with a 10 tonne axle limit. Another suggestion was that the current 38 tonne limit in West Germany and France should be adopted by the Community as a 'Euro-standard'. The axle weight was crucial though; it was as important a factor in road wear as the gross weight. One possibility, therefore, was to redesign lorries to give them an extra axle, thus redistributing the total weight. Then, it was believed, a 38 or 40 tonne lorry would have no worse effect on the environment than a 32 tonne lorry and the overall dimensions of all of them would be similar. Eventually after another period of debate, David Howell, the Conservative Transport Minister, was forced by his backbenchers to opt for the 38 tonne lorry in March 1982.

Prices

The 1961 Schaus Memorandum had proposed that transport rates (i.e. prices) should be both transparent (i.e. published) and controlled. The Commission believed that this was needed to prevent exploitation of a dominant position on the one hand or price and service instability through excessive competition on the other. The former situation would lead to high rates, the latter to ruinously low rates. From this emerged the concept of controlled rates with upper and lower limits, known as the bracket system.

The Council reached agreement on tariff brackets in 1965. During stage one which would last for three years from 1967, the rate bracket system would apply to international transport only. There would be two forms of rate-bracket system—compulsory and reference (advisory). International road and rail transport would be bound by the compulsory system but for international inland waterway traffic the reference system would apply to domestic transport as well (i.e. journeys of less than 50 kilometres).

Progress in implementing the system slowed down to a snail's pace. The Regulation of 1968 introduced a system of bracket tariffs but for international road haulage only. Even this limited application of the system ran into difficulties. Provision had been made in the 1968 arrangement for private contracts to be undertaken outside the published brackets but it was difficult to determine the conditions under which these should be allowed. The proper publication of rates also caused problems and in practice member states implemented the new rules in very different ways.

In the end the Commission, despite its original hope of a tariff bracket system for all traffic, seemed to give up in disgust! In 1975 it proposed the replacement of the compulsory tariff bracket by a purely advisory tariff system. In late 1977 the Council decided that the tariff system should continue to cover international road transport only but now the member states themselves would choose whether to employ the reference or compulsory bracket system. The new arrangement was to run for five years from 1978 as an experiment.

Thus tariff control has ceased to be an instrument of organisation of the national markets and has become merely a guideline. In some ways this was a relief to transport authorities because the administrative task of operating a tariff system was potentially immense. What will probably now happen over tariffs is that some of the original Six will continue to use the compulsory system while others, particularly the newer members will prefer the reference system only. Such variety hardly constitutes a common policy over pricing.

Infrastructure

In no field has Community transport policy so clearly failed as in infrastructure investment. The Commission had always intended some kind of infrastructure investment policy but its early attempts in the 1960s to develop such a policy were unacceptable to the member states. The only agreement was a rather bland Council of Ministers decision in February 1966 to adopt a consultation procedure which left the submission of projects to the discretion of the member states. The procedure did not operate effectively owing to the particularism of the member states and the inadequate consultation procedure itself which did not indicate what information should be provided or at what stage in the development of projects.

Therefore in 1973 the Commission Memorandum argued for increased attention to infrastructure policy. It continued the same theme in greater depth in a proposal of June 1976. It pointed out that economic integration within the Community had had a much greater effect on cross frontier traffic than on purely national traffic. In West Germany between 1957 and 1973, cross-frontier traffic had increased elevenfold, compared with a threefold increase in national traffic. Therefore if traffic was to flow smoothly, member states needed to improve their consultation procedures with each other and with the Commission so that infrastructure projects were planned with Community as well as national needs in mind. In the view of the Commission, it followed that the Community itself should take a financial stake in such projects, particularly those that were needed at Community level but which member states were reluctant to undertake on their own, owing to the cost.

The Commission's proposal suggested improvements in the consultation procedure agreed in 1966. It also suggested that the Community could help towards the cost of projects of Community interest which would be submitted by the member states. Four kinds of project were envisaged: those which would remove obstacles to Community traffic such as the inadequate railways of Northern Italy, those contributing to regional development, cross-frontier projects and technical improvements.

In 1978 the Transport Commissioner, Mr Richard Burke, added flesh to the 1976 proposal in a radical paper on transport policy. The paper proposed infrastructure investment of £20 billion in road, railway and canal projects. Top of the Commission's list of proposed projects were the Channel Tunnel, a bridge across the Messina Straits between Sicily and the Italian mainland, road and rail improvements in Ireland and better canal links between the Rhine and the Rhône to allow large cargo barges to sail between the North Sea and the Mediterranean. The Community would pay up to 20 per cent of the cost of such projects.

It would seem that it is in this area of infrastructure development that the best hope lies in making Community transport policy a meaningful entity. Given the funds and the political will, it could assist imaginative projects like the Channel Tunnel or the development of high-speed trains. Such projects would not only make a united Europe more of a reality but would materially assist the work of the Regional and Social Funds in reducing unemployment.

Sadly, the Channel Tunnel project has resolutely failed to take wing. Anglo-French discussions in 1974 and 1978 came to nothing and from 1979 the Conservative government viewed such costly schemes as a grave threat to its control of government spending. In September 1981 the new French President, François Mitterrand, gave strong backing to the concept of a Channel Tunnel while on a visit to London but Mrs Thatcher intimated that her government could not afford to invest public money in it. The British government's economic adviser Professor Alec Cairncross poured further cold water over the scheme in 1982 when he claimed in a report that the scheme would not be viable and that the money would be better spent on ferry and harbour facilities. It may well be that both Professor Cairncross and the government were taking too narrowly a commercial view of the project. Its political implications for Community integration were immense while in a number of ways it would assist overall transport strategy in the United Kingdom. It would reduce the need for a third London airport by taking away much of the West European traffic particularly from Paris and Brussels. The journey from London to Paris by rail would be reduced to under five hours with the advantage of being able to remain in one mode of transport throughout the journey. Finally a Channel Tunnel would give rail freight a boost, bringing it more into line with the proportion of total freight in other Community countries. This is desirable on energy grounds, as rail as a form of transport is more energy efficient than air or road.

Conclusion: Problems and Prospects

The difficulties of achieving a common transport policy have been immense. They have been aggravated since 1973 by the entry of new members, located on the periphery of the Community with very different transport structures. The transport sector of the United Kingdom exemplifies this problem. Integration of the United Kingdom into the Community's transport system has been made more difficult by the way in which transport policy has a bearing on policy in so many other sectors, by the involvement of large nationalised concerns as well as many small private operators, by the perennial economic crisis and by the relatively slow progress in social issues such as working conditions.

But in general the Community's transport policy has encountered opposition from national governments bent on retaining their autonomy, however recondite the matter in hand. Averaging out the axle weights of lorries to a Community standard might appear to the Commission to be merely a technical matter; to the British it appears a threat to the rural environment and to the French it threatens the interests of their leading lorry producers.

As a result there have been areas of transport where the Community has had little influence, in particular maritime and air transport. Yet these are important sectors which have faced serious problems in recent years. Competition from east European shipping has posed a serious threat to Community operators. The COMECON merchant fleet grew from 2.8 million tonnes in 1965 to 27.5 million tonnes in 1976. Most of this fleet was of recent construction and well equipped, undercutting the freight rates of western operators by 20 per cent. COMECON countries have established offices in the West to engage in freight traffic between western countries but western concerns have been prohibited from setting up business in COMECON states. The Community needs to develop a shipping policy so that its members can speak with one voice in all international bodies concerned with shipping and combine to meet the competition from COMECON operators.

Similarly air transport has faced severe difficulties in recent years. So far only the nucleus of a Community policy is visible. Only in 1976 did the Commission put forward a working paper outlining ideas on air transport to the administrations of the member states. The ideas included improvements in scheduled and unscheduled air services in the Community, application of the Rome Treaty competition rules to air transport and strengthened co-operation with international organisations especially the European Civil Aviation Conference (ECAC) and the International Civil Aviation Organisation (ICAO). This Commission initiative led to the Council of Ministers deciding in 1977 to set up a working party to work out which areas of air transport might benefit from Community intervention. The working party reported in 1978 after which the Commission published a memorandum in 1979 under the title 'Contribution of the European Communities to the development of air transport services'. Some of its proposals have been implemented, for example co-operation procedures with ECAC and ICAO, but the 1979 memorandum did come under heavy criticism from transport unions and other Community institutions. Nevertheless in 1980 the Council agreed that the Commission should look into another of the important issues raised in 1979—the question of air tariffs, but there is obviously a long way to go before an effective Community policy develops in this field.

Criticism has been levelled at Community transport policy for its rather negative concentration on issues like rates and harmonisation of technical details. As Stuart Holland has put it, 'the Community's transport policy has been so concerned with harmonising rear-view mirrors that it could not see where it was going'. The Transport Minister in the Labour government of the late 1970s, William Rodgers, normally a supporter of the Community, was so exasperated by the Community transport policy that he described it as 'preoccupied with trivia'. On the other hand, it has been difficult for the Community to move into more fulfilling spheres, given the equally negative attitude of member governments. Yet given the entry of Greece and the probable entry of Portugal and Spain in 1984, transport links require imaginative improvement. As usual, infrastructure development has been starved of cash in a Community context.

With these obstacles, it is difficult to believe that Community transport policy will make any great strides in the near future. Certainly the present Commissioner, Giorgios Kontogeorgis, who took over Transport in 1981, has not been able to build on the ideas put forward by Richard Burke. But then, as *The Economist* pointed out in 1981, the new transport commissioner has had his plate too full of fish, for which he is also responsible, to be able to ponder on infrastructure. Nigel Despicht's comments on the differences among the member states regarding transport policy in the 1950s and 1960s still hold good today: 'like a pilgrim, the common transport policy wends its way from the sins of the member states to the fulfilment of the Community's task through the vale of tears of EEC institutional procedures'. Indeed the Commission virtually admitted its own failure in 1979 when it stated that its approach to working out a common transport policy had become increasingly pragmatic. A fully fledged common transport policy remains a remote goal.

Further Reading

Coffey, P., (ed.), *The Economic Policies of the Common Market,* chapter 6, Macmillan, London, 1979.

El Agraa, A. M., *The Economics of the European Community*, chapter 8, Philip Allan, Deddington, 1980.

Swann, D., *The Economics of the Common Market,* chapter 6, Penguin, Harmondsworth, 1978.

Questions

(1) Does the Community need a Common Transport Policy?

(2) Has the Common Transport Policy any achievements to its credit?

(3) Over which transport issues was Britain in disagreement with her Community partners between 1973 and 1983?

(4) What are the arguments for and against the Channel Tunnel?

13
The Community and the External World

The Wide Scope of the Community's External Relations

Foreign trade accounts for an average 24 per cent of the GDP of the ten Community countries, reaching as much as 57 per cent in Ireland and even at the other end of the scale comprising 18 per cent in France and Greece. The Ten's foreign trade is largely dealt with as a joint Community matter, though each member state naturally tries to maximise its own trade. Fifty per cent of trade is between Community countries and is not normally subject to customs duties or quantitative restrictions. The remaining 50 per cent which is trade with the rest of the world is subject to a customs tariff barrier which is common to all member countries as an obligatory part of an internal customs union (CET). External trade is a Community matter with the Commission having the power to negotiate international trade agreements which fix the customs duties and quotas. The Community has consequently emerged on the world scene as an entity in its own right, one of the world's largest trading partners with a 22 per cent share of world trade compared to 15 per cent for the United States and 9 per cent for Japan.

However, the Community's influence on the world scene is not only commercial but political as well. More than 100 countries now have diplomatic relations with the Community as a body. The Community has observer status at the United Nations, participates in the Western 'summits' with the United States and Japan and has negotiated at numerous international conferences on issues concerning trade (GATT) and development (UNCTAD). It contributes to the development of the Third World through its aid programmes and as discussed in chapter 2 it has begun to evolve a common foreign policy so that a united stand can be taken on specific issues such as the Palestinian problem and Afghanistan.

Supporters of the Community would argue that the development of its external relations contribute to securing Europe's economic future and to the reducing of world tension. The Community has normally played a positive role in trade liberalisation, a natural position in view of the fact that it imports about 90 per cent of its raw materials. By assisting Third World development, the Community helps to assure new outlets for its industries whilst diminishing the risk of conflict which could result from the continuance of current inequalities. Negotiations conducted under the Community umbrella gives the individual member states more political clout in a world dominated by the superpowers. Critics of the Community still assert that though it may be an economic giant it is still a political pygmy. They argue, in addition, that it is by its very nature protectionist. However, its record in trade is relatively liberal. The average Community customs tariff for industrial goods is one of the lowest in the world and should fall from 9 to 7.5 per cent by 1988 as a result of the Tokyo Round negotiations conducted between 1973 and 1979 within the framework of GATT. Other reciprocal duty reductions had already been negotiated in the Dillon Round (1960–61) and the Kennedy Round (1963–67). The Community is admittedly more protectionist over agricultural products but it is still a major importer of food. It buys 27 per cent of all world food exports and in contrast to the United States has a trading deficit which reached 9 billion ECU in 1980. Generalised preferences permit all Third World countries to export finished and semi-finished goods to the Community without paying duties though quantitative restrictions are applied to sensitive products like textiles. Tariff reductions have also been agreed for numerous agricultural products.

Table 16. Community Trade in 1980*

	Nine's imports			Nine's exports		
	Million ECU	As % of foreign trade	1980 index (if 1958 = 100)	Million ECU	As % of foreign trade	1980 index (if 1958 = 100)
Other W. European countries	62,656	23.1	1,488	75,664	33.7	1,368
Eastern Europe	19,621	7.2	1,911	16,375	7.3	1,854
Other developed countries	71,445	26.3	946	43,314	19.3	765
of which: USA	44,250	16.3	1,120	26,564	11.8	1,013
Japan	12,462	4.6	5,171	4,569	2.0	2,308
Developing countries	114,562	42.2	1,075	83,388	37.2	883
of which: OPEC	67,218	24.8	1,751	36,618	16.3	1,392
Total extra-Community trade	271,552	100.0	1,148	224,446	100.0	1,016

*The Community of Nine before the accession of Greece on the 1st January, 1981.
Source: Eurostat.

Relations with other European Countries

In 1973 the Community formed a free trade zone with EFTA (European Free Trade Association). The countries of EFTA comprised Portugal, Switzerland, Austria, Sweden, Norway, Iceland and Finland and together with the Community embraced 300 million consumers. Customs duties and restrictions on industrial trade were abolished and some reciprocal concessions were agreed over agriculture. Special arrangements were made for Iceland, given its large fish exports and Portugal, given its low level of development, has been granted aid from the EIB worth 655 ECU since 1974. Trade between EFTA and the Community represents 21 per cent of Community trade (more than the US share) and about 53 per cent of EFTA countries' share. Co-operation between the two groups is expected to continue in the fields of research, the environment, fisheries, steel and transport.

Naturally relations have been less smooth with countries in the Soviet orbit. Despite a series of meetings held since 1974 between Community representatives and those of COMECON (the Soviet bloc Council for Mutual Economic Assistance) with the aim of establishing closer economic links, few significant results have been achieved. COMECON does not have the same power in the trade field as the Community and both sides still refuse to recognise fully the status of the other.

Individual countries from Eastern Europe have sought closer economic relations with the Community. When in 1974 the Community proposed to each of the East European countries the opening up of trade negotiations, the only state to respond to the offer was Rumania which in 1980 signed an agreement to set up a committee with the Community to discuss trade questions. Rumania also benefits from generalised preferences and has concluded with the Community a non-preferential agreement on trade in industrial goods. Following the Afghanistan crisis, a new co-operation agreement which replaced one which had expired in 1978 was signed with Yugoslavia in 1980. Describing the country as 'non-aligned', 'developing', 'Mediterranean' and 'European', this was the most comprehensive treaty ever adopted by the Community for a state in any or all of the above categories and is the reason why Yugoslavia may be envisaged as a future member of the Community. The commercial arrangements give free access to Community markets for 70 per cent of Yugoslavia's industrial goods, together with credit facilities for projects of mutual interest. Despite these terms, Yugoslavia's high inflation reduced the country's ability to compete in West European markets and her trade with the Community contracted between 1979 and 1981.

Economic links with Eastern Europe seem likely to persist despite political tensions. The proposed Trans-Siberian pipeline which is to lead Soviet gas to Western Europe has already led to the signing of several contracts for gas supplies, equipment purchases and the provision of finance notably with France, despite American opposition. The Community foreign ministers also decided to send aid mainly in the form of food and medicine to Poland. Finally, because of mounting surpluses and scarce storage space, the Commission in recent years has significantly increased its sales of subsidised farm products to the Soviet Union. Such sales were interrupted somewhat by an embargo after Soviet Russia's invasion of Afghanistan; they were however resumed in the autumn of 1982.

The Community and its Chief Commercial Rivals; The United States and Japan

By 1980–81, the Commission had become increasingly disturbed by worrying trends in the Community's international trade, in particular the growing trade deficit of over 30 billion ECU in 1979 and 45 billion ECU in 1980. Oil price rises since 1973 were a major factor in this growing trade deficit; in 1980 the Community had a trade deficit of 30 billion ECU (two-thirds of the Community's total trade deficit) with the oil exporting countries. Nevertheless the trend towards large trade deficits had been established before 1973; only once since 1968 (in 1972) had the Community experienced an overall trade surplus.

The other major factor explaining this trend was the huge Community trade deficit with Japan and the United States, a deficit which in 1980 amounted to 25 billion ECU. In 1979 it had been hoped that the Tokyo Round Multilateral Trade Negotiations under the General Agreement on Tariffs and Trade would ease this deficit through cuts of some 30 per cent in average industrial tariffs to be phased in between 1979 and 1987. At that time the Commission was pleased that any progress had been made at all in a period of recession when trade wars were prophesied. 'The main thing is that they happened,' said one Community trade official who seemed to believe that protectionist pressures had been held in check. Nevertheless the Community's relations with both the United States and Japan have given cause for concern in the early 1980s.

Since the establishment of the Community in 1957, trade with the United States has grown rapidly and in each year the United States has had a surplus with the Community, often a substantial one. In 1976, for example, the deficit was 8 billion ECU. One reason for this is the higher level of American protection. The Community tariff is more uniform and few items have a high level of protection. In the late 1970s only 13 per cent of Community industrial tariffs exceeded 10 per cent and less than 25 per cent exceeded 15 per cent. On the other hand, nearly 40 per cent of American industrial tariffs exceeded 10 per cent and nearly 25 per cent exceeded 15 per cent.

Until recently the United States and the Community managed to maintain reasonably cordial trade relations because American and Community officials regularly consulted each other to ensure that each side understood any moves intended by the other. Thus the imposition of restrictions on American exports of polyester to Britain and an anti-dumping duty on polyester into the Community as a whole caused no initial friction. Both had been preceded by intensive consultations and the Americans told the Community privately that they accepted the measures as justified. Similarly disputes over steel were initially resolved in a conciliatory fashion.

However in 1980–81 both the steel and textile industries again strained relations. The Americans claimed that Community steel was being dumped into the United States and imposed countervailing duties, an action against which the Industry Commissioner, Davignon, protested vigorously. Community exports of steel to the United States began to contract rapidly, falling from 7.5 million tonnes in 1979 to 5.4 million tonnes in 1980. Similarly the American dual pricing of oil and gas has given a price advantage to a wide range of industries of which synthetic fibres has been the most contentious because of the depressed state of the European textile industry (see chapter 8).

But it is agricultural issues that are the chief threat to good United

States–Community relations. The Community still has a large deficit on agricultural trading—over $34 billion in 1979—but most of the deficit consists of cattlefeed and tropical commodities. In other sectors such as dairy products, sugar, beef and cereals the Community has become a major exporter. In fact it is now the world's largest dairy exporter, number two in the sugar trade and in 1982 its likely export of beef was 600,000 tonnes. This rapid expansion impinged on markets long held by Australia and Argentina. The Americans were particularly worried about cereals because by 1982 the Community was exporting 8 million tonnes of wheat and flour a year. The rest of the world agreed not to challenge the Community's policy during the 1979 Tokyo Round negotiations on condition that the EEC did not use export subsidies to expand beyond its existing markets. This is now clearly happening and Americans are anxious to keep the Community out of their traditional markets, notably the Soviet Union, a market which they lost temporarily during the post-Afghanistan grain embargo.

At a time when American farmers have been going bankrupt at a rate unseen since the 1930s, the American farming lobby has criticised the whole Community philosophy of subsidised food exports. But they are also worried by certain recent developments in the Common Agricultural Policy. Having raised farm prices by 9 per cent in 1981, the Community planned to raise them by 10.7 per cent in 1982. The effect of this would be to encourage surplus food production even more, leading to more dumping on world markets. In the eyes of three million hard-pressed American farmers, the decision was criminal on two counts. First, the price increases took place at a time when world food prices had fallen by 20 per cent and second the dumping would be done in world markets which the Americans were used to regarding as their own.

In 1982 the Americans were even more outraged by another piece of Commission protectionism. It was planned to impose controls on American exports of gluten, a yellow grey powder which extracted from maize flour is used as a high-protein animal feed. The gluten which had been sold to British and Dutch farmers at prices below home-grown cereals was worth over £300 million a year to American farmers. The Reagan administration threatened that if controls were imposed, then the United States would retaliate.

Not that the American stand on its alleged free trade principles was entirely convincing. The Reagan administration had also been protectionist in, for example, its limiting of imports of Japanese cars. It had also been trying to dispose of its own butter and grain mountain, surplus stocks of which were subsidised and sold to the Communist world. As Poul Dalsager, the Community farm commissioner, pointed out, American farmers had a worldwide export surplus of £13,000 million in 1981—a third of which was with the Community. As the Community's subsidies were approved in the 1979 Tokyo Round, it was unlikely that they would be scrapped to please the Americans.

Nevertheless such incidents, trivial in themselves, were significant. The protectionist surge in America threatened to create a trade war. In 1982 a Pennsylvanian senator John Heinz proposed a bill authorising the President to strike back at trade barriers without consulting GATT or using its procedures. Such tendencies worried the Community and in February 1982 Gaston Thorn in a speech to the European Parliament stressed that the deterioration of relations with the United States was the Commission's main concern. He warned: 'Our differences could escalate into something much more serious than the present trade dispute, which has been exacerbated by the economic crisis and by domestic problems. We get the impression that Europe and the United States are beginning to doubt and hence distrust each other.'

Rightly Gaston Thorn also pointed out that the Community's differences with the United States were not only commercial. The Reagan government had taken a much less sympathetic and less positive stand over the problems of North–South relations. Also American economic and monetary policies with their accent on high interest rates had imposed burdens on the entire Western economy.

Relations between the Community and the United States reached a new nadir in the autumn of 1982 when in November the British condemned American support of a United Nations resolution calling for renewed Anglo-Argentinian talks over the Falklands. Shortly before this, new and swingeing American duties on Community exports of steel to the United States had only been avoided, literally at the eleventh hour, by the Community agreeing to reduce such exports.

Another serious issue clouding United States–Community relations was the attempt of the Reagan administration to forbid Community subsidiaries of American companies, or Community companies operating under licence from American companies, supplying equipment for the Soviet Siberia to Western Europe pipeline. Such interference provoked a sharp response from Community member governments; even Mr Reagan's staunchest ally Mrs Thatcher pronounced that she was hurt by such insensitive American behaviour. Community governments with companies affected by American action compelled them to fulfil their contracts with Russia even though it led to American retaliation in the way of fines. The British government, for example, enforced the fulfilment of contracts for delivery of turbines by John Brown Engineering in Scotland.

American attempts to stop European firms contributing to the construction of the Soviet gas pipeline were particularly resented by Europeans at a time when President Reagan had fully resumed exports of food to Soviet Russia after a period of some interruption following the Afghanistan crisis. In 1982 Reagan's offer of 23 million tonnes of grain to Russia represented the largest flow of food between two countries that had ever been recorded. The Americans argued that the sale of grain used up Soviet cash which might otherwise be used for weaponry whereas the pipeline contract gave the Soviet Union a chance to earn money which could then be used to develop weapons; in addition Western Europe would become dangerously dependent on Soviet gas supplies. Such arguments were unconvincing to Community countries like Britain with depressed steel and engineering sectors and at the end of 1982 the Reagan administration began to compromise on the matter.

American protectionism and productivity have long concerned Europeans; the Japanese commercial rivalry is of more recent development. European fear of Japanese competition was well depicted in a *Sunday*

Times cartoon of February 1982. The cartoon showed Japan in the form of a Samurai warrior using heavy cannon to bombard a crumbling fortress Europe with cars, motor bikes and all manner of electrical goods. The Europeans were right to be apprehensive. Japan had undergone two medium-term investment cycles since the end of the Second World War and was in the middle of a third cycle by the early 1980s. The first of these had concentrated on the expansion of basic and heavy industries. The second concentrated on improvements in the production of consumer durables like cars. The third cycle aimed at the development of the high technology sectors such as computers. During Japan's immediate post-war reconstruction, government intervention had been universal throughout industry. In the 1950s a series of national plans was implemented in which government, especially the Ministry for International Trade and Development (MITI), still retained an important though reduced role in devising policies. Through emphasis on technical innovation, penetration of well-defined target markets and a combination of value in terms of price and quality of product, Japanese industry became extremely competitive.

The success of the Japanese economy was striking. Between 1948 and 1958, Japan increased its share of world exports sixfold from 0.5 to 3 per cent and by 1970 it had more than doubled it again to 7.2 per cent. Between 1970 and 1980, Japan's share of world exports remained at over 7 per cent despite the greater part taken in that trade by oil, whereas the Community share of world trade declined in the same period. Japan's GDP was only one third of Britain's in 1950; by 1969 it had overtaken Britain, France and West Germany. Japan's present GDP is roughly equal to West Germany and Italy combined.

No doubt much of Japan's competitive edge is due to factors that should be applauded—hard work, intelligent innovation and sound marketing. However, the European Commission has pointed to specific difficulties in the Community's trading with Japan: (1) the nature of Japanese exports to the Community; (2) the difficulties faced by Community exporters to the Japanese market.

(1) The Japanese have shown some willingness to listen to complaints from the United States where their sales have been huge but they argue that there is no real problem in Europe because their exports to the Community are less than 3 per cent of Community imports, less than the Soviet bloc's sales. The European reply would be that it is not the volume of exports that is crucial but the Japanese 'laser-beam' approach with concentration on a few highly critical markets—car, motor-bikes, consumer electronics and numerically controlled machine tools. A recent article by Booz, Allen and Hamilton (Outlook No. 4) has shown how consistent and systematic this competitive strategy of Japanese companies has been. Its effect has been devastating on key areas of European industry.

Machine tools provide an excellent example of this. Production in Japan's machine tool industry increased 2.9 times and exports 4.3 times between 1975 and 1981. While West German and American manufacturers emphasised the development of large machine tools for use in high precision industries such as aerospace, the Japanese concentrated on small multipurpose machines which were labour-saving but could also be used by smaller firms. The quality which separated Japanese machine tools from those of their rivals was numerical control. By 1982 half the machine tools being produced by Japanese firms featured numerical control and the biggest manufacturer in Japan of all types of machine tools, Fujitsu Fanuc, supplied half of the world market for NC machine tools. The Japanese had exploited this American invention before their competitors and highly competitive pricing helped Japanese firms by 1981 to account for 50 per cent of the American and French markets for numerically controlled lathes and 33 per cent of the West German market.

(2) If Europeans could counter these trends by increasing exports to Japan, the trade problems between Japan and the Community would be reduced but such is not the case. An exporter attempting to break into the Japanese market faces a whole host of technical or administrative restrictions on a wide range of products such as footwear, food, pharmaceutical and agro-chemical products, medical supplies and cars. These barriers to trade in the words of the February *Sunday Times* article are 'an ulcer-inducing nightmare for exporters to Japan'. Processed food is covered by a maze of regulations. Imported canned fruit, for example, must show on the tin how many pieces of fruit are inside. A similar picture has emerged over cars. When in 1981 Mitsuo Okada, president of Okada Motors in northern Japan, tried to import two Mercedes cars, he was told by the customs that they could not be imported because their first-aid kits and fire extinguishers did not comply with government drug laws and high pressure gas control regulations. The officials refused even to open the first-aid kit to see for themselves that there were no drugs inside.

This sort of petty frustration has formed an effective barrier to trade whereby the Japanese have protected their home market. Hardly surprisingly Japan has over the years built up massive trade surpluses. Japan imports an abnormally low percentage of manufactured products compared with the Community and the United States. In 1980 only 22 per cent of total Japanese imports were manufactures compared with 44 per cent in the Community. In 1980 also European exports to Japan actually declined.

By 1982 Japan's overall trade surplus was estimated to be $30 billion. The United States had been one casualty; American official estimates put the trade deficit with Japan in 1981 at $18 billion and in 1982 at $25 billion. The Community had been the other chief casualty; in 1979 the Community's trade deficit with Japan was $7 billion, in 1980 it reached $11 billion and for the first ten months of 1981 was almost $9 billion. There was no easy solution for this problem as the simple answer of a protectionist approach against Japan carried its own dangers. It would lead to the Japanese market being closed to Community produce but more seriously competition with Japan would intensify on other world markets which could result, in many sectors, in an erosion of the Community's share of world exports. European industry could become the victim of such a policy since in many advanced technology sectors, European manufacturers might be unable to fill the gap in production equipment adequately. If that happened, the United States, well equipped in engineering and electronics, would benefit. Finally, Europeans have been nervous about breaking the rules to which they are committed under GATT because it could trigger off a major world trade war in which Europe would be most injured. It is often overlooked that the major European countries depend on exports far more than do the Japanese. Nearly a quarter of British and German output is exported compared to 13 per cent of Japanese production.

Given these considerations, it was to be expected that the European Community's response to the Japanese problem was indecisive and unco-ordinated, a sign of internal divisions. As a result, the individual member states resorted to their own solutions and those that broke the rules did best. Italy kept the Japanese quota of cars down to 2,000 a year, France allowed them 3 per cent of the market with more to follow only if the Japanese buy more French cars. The British imposed a so-called 'voluntary restraint' to hold the Japanese to around 11 per cent of the market. By contrast the pro free trade Germans saw Japanese sales of cars in Germany multiply fourfold between 1979 and 1981 to take 10 per cent of the market.

In late 1981 the Europeans tried actively to work out a satisfactory position over the problem of Japanese trading relations with the Community. The problem was the subject of Commission-sponsored talks in Tokyo and also of a GATT meeting. In January 1982 further discussions took place between the Community and Japan and also at a high level meeting between the United States, Japan, the Community and Canada. The Japanese minister of international trade and industry, Mr Shimataro Abe, promised that Japan would take 'drastic' action to open its internal market to foreign imports by removing non-tariff barriers after the high level talks at Key Biscayne. Specifically, the Japanese committed themselves to loosening the controversial testing and control procedures on 67 catego-ries of imports, among them drugs and cosmetics as well as accelerating the tariff cuts agreed in the 1980 Tokyo Round of trade talks. A new ombudsman office was created with the ponderous title of 'Headquarters for promotion of settlement of grievance related to the openness of the Japanese market'. The outraged Mitsuo Okada was the first Japanese person to take a complaint to this office!

The Community response was one of scepticism. The chief negotiator for the Commission, Sir Roy Denman, had heard such promises before and regarded the concessions as mere gestures by the 'wily' Japanese. The Japanese promises to accelerate tariff cuts on a seemingly impressive range of 1,653 items was seen as a typically hollow concession. While the Japanese claimed that it would bring the average tariffs down from 15.6 to 6.7 per cent, the Europeans believed that the total effect only added up to a 0.5 per cent cut in average tariffs. The tax on whisky was to drop by between 8 and 11 yen on bottles of Scotch that were priced at 5,000 to 8,000 yen. The tariff on biscuits went down from 30 to 28 per cent. In any case the greater problem was not so much tariff levels as the non-tariff barriers.

In 1982 it seemed likely that, unless further agreements at a Community level were reached with Japan, the individual member states themselves would take further action to stem the flow of Japanese imports as Com-munity unemployment rose above 10 million. Even if Japanese markets were opened up to imports, the basic problem would still remain; Japan had become an industrial juggernaut which was already extending its domination of several crucial existing industries to all the vital industries of the future. But Community patience was running out and in March 1982 the Council of Ministers decided to take its case against Japan to GATT and in April it made strong pleas for easier access to the Japanese home market. President Mitterrand also visited Japan to hammer home Community unease at the trade imbalance and won the epithet 'helicopter salesman' for his pains from Japanese newspapers. Another European official felt that Japanese concessions on import restrictions were cynical tactics made with the May Versailles Summit in mind. He described the concessions as 'tossing Oxo cubes off the sledge to satisfy the wolves'. Small wonder that the French soon found means of retaliation; not only were Japanese cars restricted to 3 per cent of the French market but Japanese video equipment exported to France had to go to Poitiers in west central France for processing by a very small team of customs men, a necessarily lengthy procedure.

The Community and the Developing World

The CANCUN summit meeting in Mexico in October 1981 highlighted once again the demand of the developing countries for a new economic order. While their pleas to the industrial north did not fall entirely on deaf ears, little concrete seemed likely to emerge in the near future. Nevertheless the European Commission has stressed that the Community has a central role to play in North–South affairs. In a communication to the Council of Ministers in May 1980, it argued that 'the Community must demonstrate the political importance it attaches to the relaunching of the North–South dialogue and must translate into practical terms the direct participation of its political leaders in the process of discussions between industrialised and developing countries. It is to the Community that the latter are looking for an initiative; it is the Community that is already the best placed interlocuteur of the developing countries within the United Nations, and lastly it is the Community that has been able to indicate the path of change in its relations with the developing countries at a regional level.' The reference to the Community indicating 'the path of change' was a reference to its complex set of aid and trade agreements with various blocs of Third World countries. At the top of this pyramid of agreements is the Lomé Convention which the Community has applauded as 'a pioneering model of co-operation between equal partners'.

The Lomé Conventions

During the 1950s and 1960s the majority of the colonies belonging to European powers became independent states. This process of decolonisation coincided with the birth of the European Community and great importance was attached to its relations with the newly independent developing countries of the Third World. With the enlargement of the Community in 1973, relations with the Third World assumed a greater importance as a result of Britain's close ties with the developing countries of the Commonwealth.

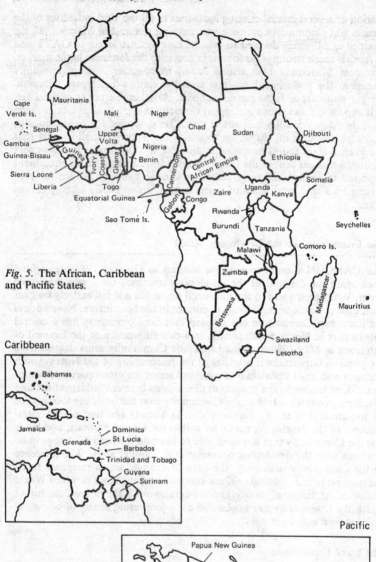

Fig. 5. The African, Caribbean and Pacific States.

Cape Verde Is.
Senegal
Gambia
Guinea-Bissau
Sierra Leone
Liberia
Guinea
Ivory Coast
Ghana
Togo
Benin
Equatorial Guinea
Sao Tomé Is.
Mauritania
Mali
Niger
Upper Volta
Nigeria
Cameroon
Chad
Central African Empire
Gabon
Congo
Zaire
Sudan
Ethiopia
Uganda
Kenya
Somalia
Djibouti
Rwanda
Burundi
Tanzania
Seychelles
Malawi
Zambia
Comoro Is.
Madagascar
Mauritius
Botswana
Swaziland
Lesotho

Caribbean

Bahamas
Jamaica
Dominica
St Lucia
Grenada
Barbados
Trinidad and Tobago
Guyana
Surinam

Pacific

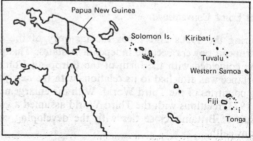

Papua New Guinea
Solomon Is.
Kiribati
Tuvalu
Western Samoa
Fiji
Tonga

Community motives were several. To some extent it felt a moral responsibility to nurture the developing countries but two rather more basic motives were probably stronger. The Community had become the world's chief importer of raw materials, depending upon the developing countries for more than 55 per cent of its raw materials. In most cases neither North America nor Australia could fill the gap if these supplies were cut off. In view of this dependence on the Third World, the attempts by the Soviet Union to exert greater political influence in the poorer regions of the world were disturbing. Finally, certain French motives should be mentioned. The French wished to retain a special relationship with their former colonies in Africa and insisted that the Community should help to shoulder the financial burdens involved. In the days of de Gaulle, the French government was particularly attached to Africa because of its burning belief in France's global role both politically and culturally. The former French colonies represented a huge area where French was the official language. It was important that these countries should not remain impoverished economic backwaters overshadowed by English-speaking Nigeria!

Such considerations soon led to agreements between the Community and a number of Third World countries. A first five-year Association Convention was signed at Yaoundé in Cameroon in 1963 and a second also at Yaoundé in 1969 with 19 African states. The agreements provided ultimately for free trade areas between them while allowing the Associated states to apply fiscal duties and tariffs to protect their infant industries. The second European Development Fund (EDF) operated during the course of Yaoundé 1 and the third EDF during Yaoundé 2. 730 million EUA in aid were given during the life of Yaoundé 1 and 900 million EUA during the life of Yaoundé 2. In addition the Community lent the Associated countries 271 million EUA through the EIB between 1963 and 1975. Complementary to the Yaoundé Conventions was the Arusha Convention, signed at Arusha in Tanzania between the Community and Kenya, Tanzania and Uganda. It was in operation from 1971 to 1975 when it was superseded by the Lomé Convention.

The Yaoundé Conventions were a useful start but in the early 1970s there arose a realisation in international bodies like the United Nations that world economic stability would not be achieved while the prevailing inequalities existed, that is to say, the wide and indeed growing disparity between the rich North and the poor South. The negotiations for a new Convention, the Lomé Convention, in 1974–75 mirrored this concern and influenced the Community in favour of a commitment to the countries of Africa, the Caribbean and the Pacific (ACP), a commitment which at least paid lip service to the notions of justice and equality. The rapid increase in the price of Third World commodities—coffee and sugar as well as oil— also encouraged the Europeans to make trade concessions to ACP demands. Not that the ACP countries spoke with a united voice in these negotiations; there were significant differences between them which militated against a coherent unity in their negotiations with the Community. The Caribbean, Indian and Pacific states tended to fear African domination in their counsels; the eight Caribbean states enjoyed relatively high living standards and were less dependent on the Community as a trading partner than the other ACP states. As a result they were suspicious of any measures that might compromise their links with North America. The seven ACP countries from the Pacific showed little awareness of the need for solidarity, perhaps because of their geographical remoteness from Europe. Though African states dominated the ACP group, particularly Nigeria with its oil wealth and population of 80 million, they were themselves divided between the desperately poor like Mali and the relatively modernised like Kenya. For the poor countries, their aid from the Community was the crucial consideration; for the richer African countries trading conditions was more important than aid.

Given such divisions, it was commendable that the ACP group did achieve some measure of unity and extract some concessions from the Community. The first Lomé Convention was signed at Lomé in Togo in February 1975 between the Community and 46 ACP states. It came fully into force in April 1976 and expired in March 1980. The Convention was a treaty designed 'to establish a new model for relations between developed and developing states, compatible with the aspirations of the international community towards a more just and balanced economic order'. By the end of 1979, 12 more states had acceded to the ACP group.

The Lomé Convention was seen as an enormous step forward in Community–Third World relations and at the outset it involved over 500 million people. Various common institutions were created to assist the smooth working of the Convention—a joint Council of Ministers, a Committee of Ambassadors, a Consultative Assembly and a small Secretariat established in Brussels and financed by the Community: with the Community absorbing 50 per cent of ACP exports and providing 42 per cent of their imports, trade co-operation was a major feature of the agreement. Under the terms of the Convention, the ACP countries were not required to give preferential treatment to imports from the Community but practically all ACP goods (99.2 per cent in 1978) had free access to Community markets.

The really novel clause was Stabilisation of Export Earnings (STABEX). Where an ACP country found that its earnings from the export of one of the products covered by the scheme fell below its average earnings, it could obtain help from the European Development Fund to meet the difference. The Community set aside 375 million EUA for STABEX, divided into five annual instalments of 75 million EUA. In general this took the form of interest-free loans but for the 24 poorest ACP countries, aid was given in the form of grants. The aim of STABEX was to help those ACP countries which were heavily dependent on one or a handful of commodities and whose export earnings were at the mercy of sudden market fluctuations or, in the case of agricultural products, a disastrous climatic year. For any one of the products to be taken into consideration it had to represent at least 7.5 per cent of the value of total exports in the preceding year though this percentage was reduced to 2.5 per cent for the poorest ACP states. In order to be eligible for aid, actual earnings from exports to the Community of a given product had to be less than the average of the corresponding earnings over the four preceding years by at least 7.5 per cent in normal cases or at least 2.5 per cent in the case of the poorest countries.

The third main area of the agreement was over financial aid and technical co-operation. The aim was to contribute to the economic and social development of the ACP states. Special attention was paid to the needs of the least developed countries with a special allocation of 150 million EUA set aside for ACP states having to cope with natural disasters. The Community originally allocated 3,390 million EUA for financial aid under Lomé 1. This was increased by 56 million EUA to take account of new members of the Convention. The two Community institutions which were responsible for allocating the aid were the fourth European Development Fund and the EIB. The EDF was financed not from the Community's budget but through direct contributions from the member states. It was the EDF's function to distribute 3,056 million EUA of aid. The EIB was allocated 390 million EUA to finance ACP projects in industry, mining and tourism through loans.

The first Lomé Convention was signed at a time of relative optimism but by October 1979 when a second Lomé Convention was signed for a five-year period, dating from March 1980, the atmosphere had changed. The first Lomé Convention had disappointed the ACP countries in a number of ways; their exports to the Community had not advanced greatly and their former favourable trade balance with the Community had deteriorated. Community investment in ACP countries had declined in real terms and the Community had soured relations in 1978 when it refused to exempt the ACP group from the textile trade restrictions under the Multi-Fibre Arrangement. However, the renegotiations came at a difficult time for the Community which in 1978–79 was facing rising unemployment, inflation, the launching of EMS, the first direct elections to the European Parliament and enlargement. Therefore, whereas the ACP group hoped for genuine developments on Lomé 1, the Community attitude was well summed up by Herr Genscher, then president of the Council of Ministers, when he remarked in July 1978 that 'the negotiations will not deal with sweeping changes or renovation but with adjustments and improvements'. Arduous sessions resulted and the temper of the ACP group was not improved by a suggestion by the British foreign secretary David Owen that the agreement should be suspended by either side in the event of the violation of human rights.

Lomé 2 did contain some improvements on Lomé 1. The STABEX scheme was extended. It had originally covered 25 agricultural products plus iron ores; eight new agricultural products had been added during the life of Lomé 1 and the number of commodities in the scheme was now raised to 44. The dependence threshold was brought down from 7.5 to 6.5 per cent as was the trigger threshold (the drop in export earnings in relation to the average for the same product over the preceding four years). In both cases the threshold for the poorest countries was reduced from 2.5 to 2 per cent. Other improvements in STABEX included increased financial resources (550 million EUA for the period 1980–85 as against 283 million EUA during Lomé 1). STABEX aid in the form of grants was now to apply to 35 of the least developed countries instead of 24.

One of the criticisms made of the Lomé 1 STABEX scheme by the ACP group was that apart from iron ore it did not cover a large proportion of their export earnings: that accounted for by minerals. Under Lomé 2, therefore, a new scheme, called SYSMIN or MINEX, covered the main minerals exported by the ACP countries: copper, cobalt, phosphate, manganese, bauxite, tin and iron ore. ACP countries also wanted to include diamonds, uranium, chrome and graphite but these commodities were judged too 'sensitive' to be covered. The new system was similar to an accident insurance scheme backed by funding of 280 million EUA. As with STABEX, there was a dependence threshold; for the Community to provide assistance, the product in question must have accounted for at least 15 per cent of all export earnings over the preceding four years. The damage had to be significant, entailing a drop by 10 per cent in production or export earnings. Compensation would not be in the form of cash but in the financing of projects put forward by the ACP countries. Particular help was to be given to the development of mining in the form of technical assistance and finance.

As regards trade, the ACP countries had criticised Lomé 1 because the Community had continued to protect its own farmers against agricultural imports under the CAP regime. Under Lomé 2, these restrictions were eased on a number of products—a number of vegetables like Senegal tomatoes and more significantly on beef and veal. The quota for meat was increased and the levy on it cut by 90 per cent. A sum of 40 million EUA was provided to promote the trade of the ACP countries.

One of the most contentious issues was over the total volume of aid. The ACP countries hoped for 10,830 million EUA in aid to compensate for inflation and the increase in the population and number of countries in the group. However initially the Community could only offer 5,107 million EUA, a sum which was then increased by 10 per cent with an additional 85 million EUA to take account of Zimbabwe's subsequent accession. The total sum of 5,692 million EUA was a considerable increase over the sum of 3,466 million offered under Lomé 1. In addition the Community promised for the 1980–85 period at least 300 million EUA worth of food aid.

Significant though these improvements were, they fell far short of ACP expectations. As explained above, the ACP group had hoped for more aid but they felt strongly on a number of other issues as well. Though the partnership between the ACP and the Community was supposed to be one between equals, ACP countries believe that they remain less than equal in European eyes. Their belief in this regard was confirmed during the negotiations for Lomé 2 when, in the words of Carol Cosgrove Twitchett, 'the prolonged haggling over technical details and the generally grudging response to ACP requests embittered the atmosphere'. Consultation since 1975 has often become no more than the Community informing the ACP countries of what it is proposing to do. The decision on whether or not to finance aid is taken by Community institutions alone and the EIB and Directorate VIII which administers the EDP and the Community has always reserved the right to refuse aid. In the ACP view this is a fatal flaw in the concept of partnership and co-management, even though the ACP are represented at all stages of the decision-making except the EDP Committee. The problem was compounded by difficulties over organisation. Bureaucratic procedures have led to considerable time lags in the granting of aid, especially in the operation of STABEX where the regulations are very complicated.

The ACP countries have also stressed that the trade provisions, though nominally generous, have not been as substantial as would appear at first sight. More than 75 per cent of ACP exports to the Community would have entered the Community duty-free anyway because they were tropical primary products or scarce minerals like copper. Secondly the arrangements are liberal in respect of goods that the ACP are ill-placed to export, notably industrial goods which have duty free access but do not figure prominently in ACP exports. Where industrial products like textiles did threaten the European interests, restrictions were imposed. Similarly ACP exports of foodstuffs which competed with European agricultural products were only partially exempt from levies; in 1977 some 11 per cent of ACP exports of foodstuffs were subject to CAP. ·

As a result of these and other shortcomings the Lomé Conventions have only scratched the surface of the overall problem of ACP development. Although it was proclaimed as a model for relations with the Third World, it has not been replicated by the Community with other developing countries nor by other industrialised countries. Nevertheless the Community contribution to ACP development remains a highly positive one, particularly in the harsh economic climate of the 1980s when neither the superpowers nor the Arab countries are likely to increase aid to the Third World.

It should be added that the Community is still trying to improve the relationship with the ACP countries. In December 1981 the ACP countries were not subject to the restrictions of the MFA which had been re-negotiated at Geneva. Other suppliers of textiles such as Hong Kong and South Korea remained so subject. Thus the West African states of the ACP now have a greater opportunity to export textiles to the Community though they will need to improve their competitive edge against European producers and other third countries.

However, the Commissioner for Development Aid, Mr Edgard Pisani, though enthusiastic in his wish to help the ACP countries, has faced formidable political obstacles. Community member states were reluctant to give more aid despite the fact that the STABEX scheme ran out of money by 1982; claims on the scheme for 1981 had amounted to four times the funds available and though the budget for the year was doubled, the Lomé countries gained only half of what they were entitled to under the system. The popularity of Lomé in Europe was further eroded by sugar fiddles. The EEC had agreed to pay its own high domestic price for 1.3 million tonnes of imported ACP sugar. Some ACP countries abused this concession, for example by buying sugar cheap on the world market and then selling it dear, as if it were their own produce, to the Community. As a result Community countries preferred to give bilateral aid which could be linked to purchases from the donor country. Some member states also felt that as the Lomé countries accounted for only 6 per cent of total Community trade, the Community would do better to direct its aid more towards other areas like the Middle East, South East Asia, the Indian subcontinent or even Latin America.

Mr Pisani himself felt that too much Community aid had been directed towards short-term immediate schemes for feeding the growing urban populations in the ACP countries. For the next Lomé Convention he hoped to concentrate even more aid on long-term rural development which would enable the ACP countries to feed themselves and would also check the drift to the towns, a drift that was reaching avalanche proportions in some ACP countries. Caught between reluctant Community member states and the ACP countries in a fighting mood, Mr Pisani's task in negotiating a third Lomé Convention from 1983 on looked formidable indeed!

Table 17. The 63 Members of the Lomé 2 Convention 1983

Antigua and Barbuda	Grenada	St Vincent-Grenadine
Bahamas	Guinea	Senegal
Barbados	Guinea-Bissau	Seychelles
Belize	Guyana	Sierra Leone
Benin	Ivory Coast	Solomon Islands
Botswana	Jamaica	Somalia
Burundi	Kenya	Sudan
Cameroon	Kiribati	Surinam
Cape Verde	Lesotho	Swaziland
Central African Republic	Liberia	Tanzania
Chad	Madagascar	Togo
Comoros	Malawi	Tonga
Congo	Mali	Trinidad and Tobago
Djibouti	Mauritania	Tuvalu
Dominica	Mauritius	Uganda
Equatorial Guinea	Niger	Upper Volta
Ethiopia	Nigeria	Vanuatu
Fiji	Papua New Guinea	Western Samoa
Gabon	Rwanda	Zaire
Gambia	St Lucia	Zambia
Ghana	São Tomé and Príncipe	Zimbabwe

Asia

Between 1974 and 1976 the Community concluded non-preferential co-operation agreements with the countries of the Indian sub-continent: Bangladesh, India, Pakistan and Sri Lanka. In addition the Community has conceded Indian sugar exports preferential treatment similar to those given to ACP countries. The generalised preferences given to other Third World countries have been extended to certain exports which are vital for Bangladesh (jute), India (jute and cocoa products) and Sri Lanka (cocoa products). The Community's Asian policy has developed recently. In 1978 a trade agreement was signed with China. In 1980 an economic and commercial co-operation agreement was signed with the countries of the Association of South-East Asian countries (ASEAN: Indonesia, Malaysia, Philippines, Singapore and Thailand). This agreement was also by way of being a demonstration of political solidarity.

Asia is, however, a poor relation in terms of Community aid received. The size of the aid programme has increased, reaching 138 million EUA in 1980 but it has always faced French and Italian opposition to assistance for ex-British colonies. The poor showing of South Asia in the Community's distribution of financial aid has been partly compensated by food aid. In 1980 Bangladesh was allocated 105,000 tonnes of cereals, making it the largest recipient while Pakistan and Sri Lanka were also in the top four. The bilateral aid programmes of the member states have also helped Asia as India has been the largest recipient of British and German aid.

The Southern Mediterranean and Near East

Though the Community likes to divide its southern Mediterranean partners into two groups, the Maghreb (Algeria, Morocco and Tunisia) and the Mashreq (Egypt, Jordan, Lebanon and Syria) it has in fact separate and different agreements with each state. The links first grew out of France's colonial past and existing trade patterns between member states and the Southern Mediterranean, but in 1972 the Community drew up a Mediterranean policy which recognised the strategic as well as the commercial importance of the region. The oil price rises of 1973 emphasised the need for closer links with the Arab world and in 1976 and 1977 all the Maghreb and Mashreq agreements were renegotiated. Together with the four Arab signatories of the Lomé Convention (Djibouti, Mauritania, Somalia and Sudan) the Community now has special links with 11 Arab states which include nearly three quarters of the Arab population.

The main characteristics of the new agreements compared to their predecessors were that Arab states were no longer required to give preferences for imports from the Community but they would continue to enjoy free access to the Community market for their industrial products, customs preferences for some of their agricultural produce and financial aid from the EIB which was to reach a total of 1,015 million ECU between 1981 and 1986. The aid on offer was not large compared to that available to the ACP countries but in addition to financial aid, some of the Southern Mediterranean states received Community food aid. In fact these states received the lion's share of all Community food aid (75 per cent of cereals, 86 per cent of butteroil and 78 per cent of dried skim milk). Egypt was a particularly favoured state and in 1980 was allocated 20 per cent of the cereals programme (100,000 tonnes). With nearly a million North African workers in the Community, the clauses on migrant labour in the Maghreb agreements were important. The Community undertook to guarantee the migrant workers minimum pay, pensions and health provisions identical to those enjoyed by Community citizens. In return the Maghreb governments agreed not to discriminate against Community citizens working in their countries.

The trade concessions by the Community were not as liberal as may first appear. The arrangements for the seven agreements were all different because the Community wished to discourage its trade partners from diversifying into new export lines that might cause problems for domestic European industry and agriculture. The agreements with the Maghreb states, for example, all contained restrictions on preferential treatment for motor vehicles in anticipation of these countries being able to export them in the future. Thus, the trade arrangements provided only limited opportunities for the Mediterranean states to develop their exports in the way which they would like. There were, in addition, important exceptions to their existing exports. For example, while Egyptian industrial exports had in general quite liberal treatment, the country's most important processed export, cotton textiles, was restricted.

Food Aid

Twenty years ago it was estimated that 300 million people were suffering from malnutrition; by the 1980s there were probably 500 million and the numbers seem likely to increase given the toll of wars, energy problems, soil erosion and drought.

With this grim background in mind, the Commission proposed in September and October 1981 a strategy of assistance to those countries most in need based on four types of operation. (1) The Commission wished the Community to allocate 40 million ECU (£24 million) in 1982 as part of an exceptional programme to buy 230,000 tonnes of cereals to help the 31 least developed countries. (2) It stressed the need to improve food policies by developing a more coherent food strategy from the various schemes in operation. (3) Some problems affecting food supply were not confined to one state but concern a whole region such as control of the tsetse fly. Here, the Commission proposed the creation of regional schemes rather than aid to individual countries. (4) One of the major complaints of developing countries is that their cash crops are fixed on world markets at prices which nowhere near compensate them for the increased prices of food, oil and manufactures which they need to import. The Commission suggested that an international food security reserve should be established to help such countries which could apply to it when international market trends led to excessive price rises in their imports.

Such proposals could usefully build on the Community's food aid record, the value of which was 550 million ECU from 1975 to 1980. To this Community aid must be added national governments' bilateral aid, and multilateral aid through other agencies such as the World Bank. When all aspects are taken into consideration, the Ten donate a larger percentage of their GNP in aid than do Japan and the United States. Between 1975 and 1980 total Community aid amounted to over 5 billion ECU.

Further Reading

Holland, S., *Uncommon Market, chapters 8 and 9,* Macmillan, London, 1980.
Stevens, C., *The EEC and the Third World*, Hodder and Stoughton, London, 1981.
Twitchett, C. C., *A Framework for Development: the EEC and the ACP*, Allen and Unwin, London, 1981.

Articles
February 1980. *European Trends*, 'The Second Lomé Convention'.
May 1981. *European Trends*, 'Japan's Trade with the EEC'.
November 1982. *European Trends*, 'Development Aid'.

Questions

(1) Why were the ACP states dissatisfied with the second Lomé Convention?
(2) Why has the Community been in dispute with Japan and the United States in the 1980s?
(3) Is the Community doing enough to help the Third World?

14
The Businessman's EEC

Introduction: The Importance of the Community Market for British Business

1980 saw Britain's overall visible trade with Western Europe move into surplus by over £700 million, with six Community countries among the ten top markets for British exporters. How much of that trade was due directly to Britain's membership of the Community is difficult to pin-point or quantify but certainly Community policies have helped to create a better trading environment. The abolition of tariffs between the member states was the first major contribution in this respect but in addition the harmonisation programme has developed which has aimed at aligning technical standards for manufactured goods, mainly in the field of engineering. British trade with Europe has been helped by the fact that an increasing number of component parts can be manufactured to one Community standard. This has particularly helped our export of goods like tractors and weighing machines. Once Community approval is given, then such goods can be sold anywhere within the Community without having to obtain the approval of the governments of the other nine members.

Some British firms have taken full advantage of what is Britain's fastest growing market. The Community is the largest export market for Rank Xerox and in 1979 its business with the Community was worth £268 million compared to £104 million in 1973, the year Britain joined the Common Market. Its photocopiers, typewriters, duplicators and word processors, specially designed for the continent, have all sold well, especially in West Germany. Exports to the Community from Rank Hovis McDougall have also increased impressively. In 1973 only a quarter of its exports went to Community countries; by 1981 this proportion had grown to a half. Other products which have sold well have been from the speciality end of the Sharwood range of goods like chutney and curry powder. British Aerospace has made many of its products—aircraft, guided weapons and space technology—in partnership with Community countries. Concorde was a joint venture with Aerospatiale of France and among its other co-products are the Jaguar with France and the Tornado with West Germany and Italy. Only by co-operation with other Community firms can European planemakers like British Aerospace compete with the major American manufacturers.

However, while some companies have taken the Community market seriously, others have neglected it, often by having only one Community expert in the organisation. With a population of 270 million people, the Community is after all the largest trading bloc in the world and it may be argued that it is odd for firms to have 50 salesmen operating in the United Kingdom for every one in other member states. To be successful in Europe, a company needs to produce competitive products backed by a good marketing organisation, reliable sources of information and a European awareness among its chief executives.

One should not exaggerate the importance of a detailed knowledge of Community law and policies. The Community perspective is only one factor among many in successful export management and Community issues do not normally impinge excessively on the average business. But as John Drew has stressed, companies need to be informed about Community developments for three reasons. (1) Information is needed about new technological standards or proposed business legislation directly affecting the company. It should be obtained as early as possible and ideally at the pipeline stage while there is still an opportunity of influencing the final form of the legislation. (2) Opportunities may occur for developing new products, processes or markets as a result of proposed new legislation. (3) Companies need to monitor the broad trends of European legislation because their international marketing and investment strategies will be affected by changes in Community law.

In this chapter it is proposed to outline under four headings the necessary steps that a firm should take when it wishes to commence or expand its operations in other Community countries: (a) sources of information and services; (b) breaking into the Community market and investment strategies; (c) the influencing of Community institutions; and (4) the development of a Community awareness in the company.

Sources of Information and Services

It is axiomatic that full knowledge of all the salient facts should assist firms to make more rational business decisions. There is no shortage of sources of information and advice on Community trading issues; indeed the opposite is the case and the following section is merely illustrative not exhaustive. The sources may conveniently be divided into two main areas: (a) Community sources; and (b) British government services for exporters.

Community Sources

The *Official Journal of the European Communities* needs to be carefully vetted by businessmen as it contains much important information on European trading opportunities, for example on public tender. Central and local authorities in the Community are required to publish calls for tender for public contracts of an estimated value of not less than one million EUA. Since 1978 public purchasing authorities in the Community are required to invite competitive bids from firms throughout the EEC on public supply contracts worth more than 200,000 EUA. Such calls for tender are published in special supplements of the *Official Journal of the European Communities* and may also include calls for tender from the ACP countries as well.

The United Kingdom Office of the Commission at 20 Kensington Palace Gardens in London offers general and specialised information about the work of the communities. The Commission has press and information offices in most European countries, including ones at 4 Cathedral Road, Cardiff and 7 Alva Street, Edinburgh. The Commission itself at 200 Rue de la Loi in Brussels can be contacted easily as the telephonists speak English, though it would be prudent for someone to find out the name of the official dealing with their particular problem first.

In certain cases the Commission might be worth consulting over the possibility of financial assistance from one of the Community funds. For example under Article 55 of the Treaty of Paris which set up the European Coal and Steel Community there are provisions for research grants. Financial aid may be granted to companies, research institutes or individuals who wish to carry out research of interest to the coalmining or iron and steel industries. Requests for such assistance should be addressed to the President of the Commission with details of the research project.

Another Commission service which might be worth exploiting is the Business Co-operation Centre which is sometimes referred to as the marriage bureau. It was set up in 1973 to encourage co-operation between firms in different member states wishing to increase competitiveness and respond to the opportunities opened up by access to the Community's markets. It also provides information on relevant national company law and Community provisions affecting co-operation. Any firm may use its services but its main function is to help small and medium-sized firms. The kind of co-operation that the Business Co-operation Centre tries to instigate between different companies is in the fields of research, joint buying and pooling of management knowledge and sales networks.

British Government Services for Exporters

The most valuable source of information for British businessmen wishing to strengthen their trading links with other Community countries is undoubtedly the Department of Trade and Industry which is mainly based at Export House, 50 Ludgate Hill in London. Its EEC Information Unit, however, is located at Millbank Tower, London and it can help businesses of all types and sizes by answering questions on Community membership and guiding them where necessary to more specialised information sources. It is a good and free service, has six lines and a competent staff who work hard to answer queries. Its telephone number is 01–211 7060.

However, many other sections of the Department of Trade and Industry may offer the information which the businessman is seeking. Its General Export Services Branch provides briefs to British businessmen on market prospects on the continent and gives assistance in finding an overseas agent. The aim is to ensure as far as possible that the service provided matches the ability of the firm to make effective use of it.

As West European trade amounted to almost 60 per cent of Britain's foreign trade by 1980, the Department of Trade decided in that year to carry out a reorganisation to cope with this development. The Western and General Division (WEG) was set up in June 1980 to deal with bilateral commercial relations with Western European governments. Thus if a businessman finds that Community or national law has given rise to difficulties or if he feels that he has been the victim of discrimination in his trade in Western Europe, WEG can make representations on his behalf to the government concerned. When requesting help of this kind, businessmen should give the fullest details possible.

The Department also offers an Export Intelligence Service. It is a computer-based service providing subscribers with a wide range of selective export information, including details of specific export opportunities, calls for tender, market reports, changes in tariffs or regulations and overseas agents seeking British contacts.

Within the Department of Trade and Industry, the BOTB (British Overseas Trade Board) provides a variety of services for the promotion of British exports. It can give financial assistance to groups of British firms wishing to invite overseas businessmen to Britain. BOTB's Director of Export Marketing Research can advise firms on how market research can help with a particular exporting problem. In approved cases he may offer financial assistance to the cost of export marketing research projects whether carried out by consultants or by in-house staff. BOTB organises group participation of British firms at overseas trade fairs, exhibitions and other displays.

In 1980 British Overseas Trade Board's Export to Europe Branch at the Department of Trade was set up to provide a single focus for the co-ordination of trade promotion in Western Europe and a single point of inquiry for all information about the national markets of Western Europe. The Export to Europe Branch works closely with BOTB's European trade committee and the regional offices. It provides general information and advice about the markets of Western Europe, including background economic information, details of trading patterns as well as specific information covering such matters as customs regulations, tariffs, taxes, and other legislation affecting British exporters.

All exporters should take note of the Market Entry Guarantee Scheme (MEGS). Its function is to help smaller- and medium-sized firms in manufacturing industry break into new overseas markets or mount new initiatives to capture an increased amount of business in an existing overseas market. It shares the risks involved. The BOTB also seeks out export opportunities in selected West European countries for British manufacturers of engineering components. It receives guidance from the European components group, a committee of businessmen and industrialists. The technical staff of the service visit buyers and engineers at European assembly plants and channel enquiries to appropriate suppliers in the United Kingdom. They try to bring potential suppliers and buyers into contact as quickly as possible.

The Commercial offices of the Department of Trade's Diplomatic Service can perform the valuable task of compiling reports for British firms on the quality or character of overseas companies. These reports assess the suitability of an overseas organisation or individual to act as a representative, agent or manufacture-under-licence partner for the British firm in question.

Finally, the Department of Industry's reference library, SMIL (Statistics and Market Intelligence Library) can save exporters time, money and research abroad. It contains an extensive range of published facts and figures, including trade statistics, business directories, market surveys and development plans from all over the world. SMIL has the most up-to-date collection of European trade statistics in the United Kingdom. The library, open to the public from 09.00 to 17.30 Monday to Friday, has good facilities for research and a document copying service.

Other government departments besides that of Trade and Industry also offer information and services. HM Customs and Excise, based at King's Beam House, Mark Lane in London will provide the essential information on VAT harmonisation and transit regulations. The Department of Transport located at 2 Marsham Street in London is useful for the rules relating to freight. The British Standards Institute should be approached by exporters on occasions when technical details require checking out. Her Majesty's Stationery Office (HMSO) whose headquarters are in Botolph Street, Norwich is a valuable source of Eurostat publications. It also publishes the *Official Journal of the European Communities*. The Department of Prices and Consumer Protection should be contacted for the regulations concerning the labelling, safety and packaging of goods. Finally all businessmen dealing overseas should take note of the Export Credits Guarantee Department. This separate government department which is responsible to the Secretary of State for Trade provides credit insurance for British exporters against non-payment risks, guarantees to banks for export finance and insurance against political risks on new overseas investments. Support is also available against cost-escalation on certain large capital goods contracts. Its address is Aldermanbury House, Aldermanbury in London. In 1980 it paid out over £290 million to British business for losses sustained overseas and over 12,000 British firms have taken insurance cover with it.

Let us take some hypothetical examples of firms from a number of sectors to see how they could exploit the services on offer. A firm which is intending to export engineering products to various Community countries is unsure of the national regulations and technical requirements involved. The firm would find that this information is available from Technical Help to Exporters (THE), a service established in 1966 by the British Standards Institute with government support. THE is geared specifically to supplying exporters with information on all aspects of overseas technical requirements to help British exporters gain the most favourable marketing situation for their products. It provides a translation service for technical documents and assists with specific engineering problems.

A cosmetics manufacturer wishing to export to other Community countries is worried about meeting Community labelling and packaging requirements. A cosmetics directive was in fact adopted by the Community in July 1976 and the full text of the provisions was published in the *Official Journal of the European Communities* in September 1976. The cosmetics manufacturer would learn from the text that cosmetic products marketed in the Community should be clearly marked with the name or style and the address or registered office of the manufacturer or the person responsible for marketing the product. The net contents, the expiry date for products with a stability of less than three years and the batch number of the manufacturer or the reference for identifying the goods must be shown. In addition, any particular precautions that need to be observed in use should appear on the container itself if possible or on an enclosed leaflet. Misleading information is, of course, prohibited.

Finally, take the position of a building firm which is trying to win a building contract in The Netherlands involving the use of local labour. The firm would be well advised to find out as much information as possible about employment conditions in that country. The CBI publishes annually a booklet called *Western European living costs* which sets out the likely cost of living in most West European countries. The Department of Industry's statistics and market intelligence library will have comparative statistics on consumer prices and the Department of Employment has information on wage rates by industry in The Netherlands. Further help for the prospective employer can be obtained by contacting the Dutch embassy in London. From these sources the employer would gain a comprehensive understanding of the employment scene in The Netherlands with regard to wage rates, prices, taxation and social security provisions.

Breaking into the Community Market and Investment Strategies

Once it has decided to develop its European operations, a company has to decide the best method of breaking into the Community market. Such a decision will depend on the type of product, the level of production, its financial situation and the state of readiness of its personnel.

The company will have several possibilities open to it. It could simply launch a sales policy from its home base or reach some agreement with agents, distributors or retailing networks in other Community countries. A third strategy would be to acquire an existing distribution system or establish a new one in the potential market.

Alternatively the company could move away from a purely home-based operation by merging with a local manufacturer who has a distribution network or by acquiring a majority holding in an existing manufacturing company which has distribution resources. The most spectacular and probably the most expensive course would be to set up a completely new factory in the Community countries concerned.

An early decision that has to be made is the scale of the initial operations, even if later the operation may develop significantly. The major problem for a company that has not previously made much effort in Community trading is that breaking into the Community market can be time-consuming, risky and expensive. Though some economic experts exhort businessmen to regard the Community as in some sense a home market, it is still in reality foreign territory beset by practical difficulties like the language barrier and the indirect barriers to trade. Thus many businessmen are tempted to make only a small initial investment but on the other hand it may be argued that the cost of a small operation is high whereas with a larger operation fixed costs, overheads and management time would, by being spread over a larger projected turnover, turn out cheaper in the long-run. Also in a time of inflation, some of the risk is reduced because in the event of the failure of the operation, sites could be resold or re-let at a profit.

Before plunging into the cold waters of European trade, the company must first ask some key *marketing* questions. It has to decide how large the total market is for its product in Western Europe in general and whether that market is a growing or a static one. It has to enquire how well the product sells in particular countries and even in particular regions and why. It must ascertain how the price of the product has moved over the last few years and how it is likely to move in the future. Finally, the strength of its competitiors in particular countries and regions has to be assessed. Much of this information can usually be gained from the Community and British government sources already mentioned earlier and this is a relatively inexpensive procedure. Nevertheless, it is apparently the case that many businesses do not yet use these services very efficiently and often pay more for advice from organisations which do have the sense to exploit such services.

Having decided what the specific business opportunities are in the market being considered, the company next requires to check on the potential for the *distribution* of the product. It needs to know what are the shipping facilities and their costs, the best port of entry and the availability of container services. Such issues will be linked with a consideration of the relative merits of road and rail facilities in the United Kingdom and in Western Europe.

It is essential that the company should analyse the *business climate* in the market under consideration. The company needs to forecast whether disposable incomes there are going to increase or decrease and also the future movement of exchange rates, a factor which could have a huge influence on the price of the company's product in the Community. The company accountants must have a shrewd grasp of the tax structure and future trends in this area. The question of labour relations is crucial and the company must be able to gauge the current and likely future trends in wages and salaries, the level of union power and the importance of employees' rights as regards social security payments, pensions, compensation and other benefits. Finally, if a new plant is to be built, the engineering and building costs compared to those in the United Kingdom need to be estimated.

Legal questions cannot be ignored. A fair amount of Community law impinges on business, for example the laws relating to fair competition, harmonisation of technical standards, equal pay provisions and company law. The national law of the countries in question requires firm understanding, for example the legal rights of shareholders. Impending changes in the law must be taken into consideration, especially as the European Community has many proposals in the pipeline in the field of company law and harmonisation of technical standards.

A company's entry into export marketing may be very temporary or marginal because the venture may fail, the cost written off and the affair forgotten. If, however, the initial venture succeeds, then the company has to decide whether to expand it into a really significant export operation, perhaps with manufacturing plant set up abroad. Such an investment decision will affect most sectors of the business concerned. For example the personnel manager, who is often not consulted in such decisions, will have the task of finding qualified personnel within the company or from outside to mount the expanded operation and if necessary arranging extra training for them.

One of the key points highlighted by the 1978 Betro Trust Report is the need for companies to concentrate on key markets. The United Kingdom exports to some 184 markets in the world. Of these, 100 take 4 per cent and 84 take 96 per cent of British exports. Obviously a company should direct its resources to its most profitable markets and cultivate several more which have growth potential because very few companies can profitably export to all the markets in the world. Many small companies could in fact improve their export performance by enlarging some markets and cutting out others.

John Drew suggests that there are several ways of looking at potential investment markets: by continents; country by country; regional areas; population centres and by language. For only a very few large companies is it worthwhile dividing the world into continents for the purpose of investment strategy. Very few companies are involved in all countries in several continents and even then continents are not economic entities. A country by country approach may be more useful but may pose problems if the best markets are so widely separated that exploitation of all of them is difficult. The regional approach is more promising especially for a company which can identify an area which really has something in common like the countries of the European Community.

Perhaps the most sensible approach is to look at markets with the chief criterion being the size of the population. If the company is investing in France, then it may well be that the main thrust of the company's efforts should be directed at the Paris area where there is a heavy concentration of the population including a large proportion of the richest people in France. The 'Golden Triangle' (i.e. N. France, the Low Countries, Denmark, Luxembourg and W. Germany) can also be viewed as a population centre. Over three-fifths of the Community population and its GNP are found in this comparatively small area which will be of particular interest to companies selling to or manufacturing for the mass consumer market.

Grouping countries by language or culture may be a valid approach where knowledge of the language is important. It is cost effective to train managerial staff in a language that can be used in a number of different countries. French, for example, is useful in Luxembourg, parts of Belgium and Switzerland, as well as in France and former French colonies.

Once a country has decided to invest in the Community in a big way but is still not sure in which country to begin, it can create a list of criteria on which to base its decision. A key factor is political stability because a country which is politically unstable is an investment risk. This should not normally bulk large in businessmen's thinking as far as the Community is concerned because all Community countries enjoy relatively high degrees of political stability, though a possible exception here would be Italy with its Southern problem.

Before a large investment operation is commenced, some further investment questions must be asked. The Company will look into the availability of investment incentives such as capital grants or assistance from regional funds. Government attitudes to nationalisation, mergers and acquisitions undertaken by foreign companies need to be gauged, especially in France where in 1981 a new Socialist government came to power and in Italy where the Communist party has at times been close to electoral victory. Finally, the company will wish to know how good are the banking facilities in the country in question in terms of bank charges, rates of interest and the availability of loans.

Influencing Community Institutions

This subject concerns many companies in the United Kingdom, even those which do not trade with companies in other member states. Community policies in a number of areas have direct effects within each member state and consequently upon the whole range of a company's domestic activities. As a result almost any firm in this country should have an interest in keeping informed about developments in Community policies and knowing how to influence them.

Some companies have ignored the Community almost completely and some have paid dearly for this neglect. Costly mistakes continue to be made by companies which have failed to appreciate that Community legislation can seriously affect their operations. As we have seen in chapter 5, heavier and heavier fines have been imposed for infringements of Community competition law and these fines can amount to as much as 10 per cent of annual turnover.

There are ten major channels through which an individual company can put over its point of view in a European context in the hope that favourable changes may take place: (a) national trade associations; (b) the British government; (c) the Commission; (d) the United Kingdom Representative in Brussels (UK Rep.); (e) foreign embassies; (f) the European Parliament; (g) the Economic and Social Committee; (h) European trade associations; (i) the Court of Justice; and (j) the media.

(a) National trade associations can perform a significant role in assisting their members, particularly smaller firms, to understand the implications of the development of Community policies. Though many are poor in terms of money or staff, some are powerful lobbies for the interests of their members, for example the Food and Drink Industries Council and the Society of Motor Manufacturers and Traders. Sometimes a company might not need to go any further than informing its trade association of its problem. The trade association will then investigate the problem thoroughly.

In addition to trade associations, there exist national employers' organisations such as the Confederation of British Industry (CBI), the British Institute of Management (BIM) and the Institute of Directors. The CBI is a particularly powerful organisation.

(b) In most sectors, any action taken by the Commission is subject to the final approval of the Council of Ministers since any one member state has the power to veto a proposal if vital national interests are deemed at stake. The Commission generally consults member governments as a matter of course throughout the evolution of a policy proposal. It therefore follows that if firms are concerned about possible or existing Community law they should in the first instance make their views known to government (normally through the Department of Trade and Industry) in order that these views may be taken into consideration by officials in discussion in Brussels.

In each government department there are a number of senior civil servants whose main function is responsibility for Community affairs. Businessmen can telephone, write or arrange meetings with these officials. The EEC information unit at the Department of Trade and Industry will often be able to solve a problem if it is merely one of information.

If government departments do not solve the problem, the lobbying of local members of parliament can be an effective way of influencing the Community. An MP has the power to ask questions and obtain an answer from the government department concerned and usually such pressure elicits a rapid response.

(c) The Commission itself can be approached directly and indeed it has indicated that it welcomes lobbying by industry as this can lead to an awareness of problems which might otherwise have slipped their notice. There may be situations where individual firms wish to contact the Commission but normally regular and established contacts, particularly those by bodies representing European-wide industry, carry more weight and are more likely to have established effective channels of communication. The Commission in fact usually expects and prefers a single contact for individual sectors but will consider any reasonable case from a single firm as well.

The offices of the Commission in the United Kingdom may be approached first rather than companies trying to contact Brussels. Commission officials based in the United Kingdom can then take the matter on from there. Normally, however, the Commission office in London will advise businessmen to take up the matter directly with the Commission.

Commission officials are in fact approachable. The first step for a company to take is to find out the names of the officials dealing with its particular problem. About three times a year the Commission produces a directory of its senior officials. It can be obtained from Commission sales agents in many countries as well as direct from the office for official publications at Boite Postale 1003, Luxembourg.

For businessmen in constant touch with the Commission, it would be worth obtaining an internal Commission telephone directory through a contact. The phone call can be as effective a way as any of obtaining a meeting with the officials able to help. Alternatively the Commission office in London can be asked whether they can arrange such a meeting. This is a sensible way if the nature of the enquiries necessitates meeting several officials or if the company does not know the names of the appropriate officials. Enquiries, particularly technical ones, should be put in writing to enable the officials to be better prepared for the meeting. The Commission official could be invited to visit the company in the United Kingdom to meet people from the industry. Such officials have good travel allowances and often readily accept such invitations.

(d) The United Kingdom Representative in Brussels (UK Rep.) may be another useful channel. Probably the best person to contact in his office is the first or second secretary who is likely to be the expert on a particular problem. He may also suggest people to contact in the Commission or elsewhere and will perhaps arrange a meeting with the UK Rep. counsellor responsible for the area of business in question.

(e) If a problem is connected with bilateral Community trade, the foreign embassies in London may be of some use. Each of Britain's Community partners has an embassy in London which has sections attached to it dealing with bilateral trade matters. Sometimes trading problems may be more open to solution by a national government than by the Commission. Contact with the appropriate embassy is relatively easy through a visit, phone call or letter.

(f) European members of parliament have seen their influence grow slowly over the years and should not be left out of the lobbying process. They can be contacted individually or through the parties to which they belong. Meetings with company representatives can usually be arranged in the member's constituency or in London. The European member of parliament is usually well informed about Community affairs and can ask both oral and written questions on behalf of the business concerned.

(g) As seen in chapter 3 the Economic and Social Committee (ECOSOC) has very limited power but its individual members can still on occasions give useful support to a company seeking a solution to Community-created business problems. As about one third of the Committee come from the world of business, they will normally be sympathetic to a company's difficulties. A list of members can be obtained from the Committee Secretariat.

(h) Companies can make their views known through well-established channels within Europe which are regularly consulted by the Commission. These are the European trade associations. Over the years the national trade associations in the Community and sometimes other European countries have developed close connections with each other. The Union des Industries de la Communauté Européenne (UNICE) brings together national confederations of employers' associations including the CBI and the Patronat of France. The directors of UNICE have regular meetings with the President of the Commission and other Commissioners and maintain close contacts with the individual directorates of the Commission. There are standing arrangements to consult UNICE, even though the Commission is under no statutory obligation to do so. The exchanges between the Commission and UNICE are two-way and UNICE can take the initiative in putting forward its views which may be based on a survey by one of its expert committees.

The permanent conference of the chambers of commerce and industry is composed of the national associations of chambers of commerce and industry within the Community. Like UNICE it is consulted by the Commission as a matter of course. The conference tries to influence the development of Community policies, formulate views and pass them on to the Commission and member governments. It holds regular conferences with the President and the individual commissioners.

At a sectoral level, a number of committees represent broad areas of activity such as the Permanent Committee for Agricultural and Food Industries (CIAA), the Committee of European Associations of Insurance Companies (CEA) and the Committee of Nationalised and Public Utilities (CEEP).

In addition to these broad organisations, there are organisations representing 40 more specific sectors. Approximately half of them are industrial and half commercial. Some of the most important such as COMETEXTIL, which represents the textile industries carry considerable weight with the Commission because they present a common view on behalf of a very fragmented industry. There are over 100 European federations covering particular product groups.

(i) If all the above means of tackling the problems fail to result in a solution, a company has the option of approaching the Court of Justice though it would be best to approach the Commission first. The Court of Justice can be petitioned by any country, company or individual on matters relating to Community law and it is obliged to respond to petitions.

(j) Finally, a company which has a problem which is newsworthy may find the media useful in giving publicity to its case.

The Development of a Community Awareness in the Company

In the view of some business commentators, British government departments have taken the European Community seriously since 1973 because Community law has implications for national legislation and vice-versa. As a result many civil servants have become closely involved in the work of the Community institutions and the Civil Service College runs courses for its personnel on the operation of the Community.

In contrast, managers in industry and commerce have often paid only lip service to the Community but in practice have not seriously pondered its significance for their organisation. Over time this has resulted in and will continue to result in lost opportunities. Some British companies do not put enough effort into developing European markets particularly at managerial level where more should be done to encourage senior staff to learn French or German and become aware of foreign cultures and foreign sensibilities. This will become an even more important issue as British trade with other Community countries increases and the British economy becomes ever more closely interdependent with those on the continent.

Therefore it is essential that companies with significant Community trading links should strive to create a European awareness among its staff. It will not be necessary or cost-effective to attempt to educate all the personnel to a high standard of awareness of the impact of the Community. Employees in general probably only need to know the company's views on how the Community will affect them and their jobs if the company extends its operations to other European countries. It might well be instructive for the workforce in general to be made aware of the higher living standards and greater productivity in many continental countries compared to the United Kingdom. An even greater impression might be created if staff in general were given the opportunity to inspect competing products.

First line managers such as foremen or charge hands need to have a similar briefing but also some explanation of Community legislation affecting industry, particularly aspects of the harmonisation of technical standards. Some companies have taken first line managers to visit continental countries where production is higher than in the United Kingdom.

A number of junior managers need to be singled out and their awareness of the importance of the Community strengthened. They should be encouraged to learn European languages thoroughly to a standard where they can converse fluently in the necessary technical jargon. Courses should be arranged for them on Community policies.

Middle managers who may well one day become top managers should also be familiar with Community policies and a foreign language. In addition certain individuals should become experts on a particular European country, if necessary by going on tours and studying in the country concerned.

Some specialists such as business planners or overseas marketing managers who are deeply involved in Community regulations will need to study European law more closely. In a large company, it could well be advisable to appoint a manager to specialise in Community aspects. Such a person could monitor Community developments and liaise with trade associations, government departments and the Commission. Ideally such a specialist would be fluent in languages, be able to make regular visits to government departments and Brussels and have the ear of senior management so that his expert advice is not wasted.

Senior managers need to be fully informed about the Community so that they can contribute sensibly to the creation of the company's European strategy. This can be achieved by the setting up of company seminars to which representatives from the Commission, civil servants from the Department of Trade and company staff whose work involves European business may be invited. To maintain an awareness of broad business strategy in the Community among senior management, such seminars should be repeated from time to time. Essential themes would be the workings of the Community institutions, Community policies affecting business, the business environment in the chief European markets and the company's business strategy towards the European Community.

Community developments need to be monitored by companies, especially directives on technical standards. Such information should come from the company's trade association but the Department of Trade and Industry publishes a free monthly supplement to its weekly journal *British Business* which contains the latest Community legislation. To ensure that this information is not neglected, it may well be worthwhile giving a senior manager overall responsibility for the supervision of the monitoring of Community legislation so that apparently insigificant developments are not ignored.

The company should have a reference section on the European Community. In addition to *British Business* it could include the *Bulletin of the European Community* which in its 11 issues a year gives a comprehensive account of the latest Community work. *The Economist* is a most useful journal. Each week it includes some treatment of European issues and its Intelligence Unit four times a year produces *European Trends* in which particular Community policies are analysed in some depth. *The Financial Times* always produces solid and reliable coverage of European news and both the CBI and the House of Lords Scrutiny Committee prepare excellent reports on Community policies and proposals affecting business.

In conclusion let it again be stressed that British business must continue to exploit the opportunities of a potential 'home' market of 270 million people. Some sectors have used the opportunities well as described earlier in this chapter. Others have patently failed to do so. In 1978 a report indicated that British car manufacturers had gained little from Community membership while European car firms had increased their share of the British market, a trend that has since continued. That British car manufacturers enjoyed cheaper costs than their rivals and still contrived to fail in Europe can be put down partly to low productivity but also to a lack of strategic planning for the European market.

Despite the harsh economic climate, there will still be new opportunities in the future for British business in the Community. Take, for example, financial services. The Community is slowly moving towards a common market in services, especially in air travel and insurance, and British financial institutions, including the insurance sector, are well placed to do well in this area.

Table 18. UK's Top Export Markets 1975–80

(a)

1976	£million	1978	£million
1 USA	2,454	1 USA	3,485
2 FR of Germany	1,856	2 FR of Germany	3,087
3 France	1,749	3 France	2,496
4 The Netherlands	1,512	4 The Netherlands	2,251
5 Republic of Ireland	1,236	5 Republic of Ireland	2,024
6 Belgium/Luxembourg	1,108	6 Belgium/Luxembourg	1,605

1977	£million	1979	£million
1 USA	3,065	1 FR of Germany	4,218
2 FR of Germany	2,514	2 USA	4,003
3 France	2,165	3 The Netherlands	3,061
4 The Netherlands	2,153	4 France	3,027
5 Republic of Ireland	1,618	5 Republic of Ireland	2,545
6 Belgium/Luxembourg	1,387	6 Belgium/Luxembourg	1,891

(b) Top 12 in 1980

	£million	% of UK exports		£million	% of UK exports
1 FR of Germany	5,071	10.7	7 Switzerland	1,953	4.1
2 USA	4,535	9.7	8 Italy	1,896	4.0
3 The Netherlands	3,843	8.1	9 Sweden	1,618	3.4
4 France	3,586	7.6	10 Nigeria	1,195	2.5
5 Republic of Ireland	2,637	5.6	11 Denmark	1,030	2.2
6 Belgium/Luxembourg	2,259	4.8	12 South Africa	996	2.1

Table 19. Top UK Exporters 1981

	£million		£million
1 British Petroleum	2,280	11 Courtaulds	493
2 ICI (Imperial Chemical Industries)	1,173	12 Unilever	455
3 British Leyland	880	13 IBM	452
4 Ford	852	14 Massey-Ferguson	428
5 General Electric Co. (GEC)	805	15 Distillers	387
6 British Aerospace	789	16 Conoco	343
7 Shell	787	17 Hawker-Siddeley	289
8 Esso Petroleum	650	18 Johnson-Matthey	251
9 British Steel	650	19 British Shipbuilders	251
10 Rolls Royce	554	20 BISCC	244

Further Reading

Drew, J., *Doing Business in the European Community*, Butterworth, London, 1979.
Morris, B., *et al.*, *The European Community: a practical guide for business and government*, Macmillan, London, 1980.
British Business in Europe, Department of Trade and Industry, HMSO, 1981.

Questions

(1) Analyse the importance of the Community market for British exporters.

(2) Describe the chief sources of information which may be of aid to British exporters.

(3) Explain the necessary steps that a firm should take in establishing a new market in Europe.

(4) What are the means by which a firm may influence the Community decision-making process?

(5) How may an awareness of Community issues be instilled in a firm's staff?

15
Enlargement and the Community's Mediterranean Perspective

On 1st January, 1981, Greece formally became a member of the European Community and the Nine became the Ten. Spain and Portugal seem certain to become members later in the decade, perhaps as early as 1984. This second enlargement may well not be the final one. Before the military coup in September 1980, Turkey's last civilian prime minister, Mr Demirel, had stated his intention to apply for membership of the Community. Perhaps in the future Cyprus, Malta and even Yugoslavia might follow suit. Although each of the new countries is less developed in terms of the Nine, their cumulative weight could affect the working of the Community in a number of important ways.

The Motives Behind Enlargement

Under Article 237 of the Rome Treaty, 'any European state may apply to become a member of the Community'. The conditions of admission have to be negotiated between the Commission and the applicant state and the agreement reached must then be ratified by all contracting states. Since the Community was established, every non-Communist country in Europe, with the exception of Finland and Iceland, has applied for membership or association and therefore the Community has been faced with the need for careful decisions over these issues. Although there were no guidelines in the Treaty as to how the founders of the Community imagined its membership would expand, in practice no enlargement has taken place without lengthy negotiations with each applicant state.

In general an applicant state must measure up to the test of three crucial principles. It must be a European state; it must be democratic to conform with the Summit declaration of October 1972 and the joint declaration by the European Parliament, the Council and the Commission of April 1977, a declaration endorsed in April 1978 by the European Council; it must be ready and able to accept not only the political and economic obligations of membership but also the major Community objectives as set out in Articles 2 and 3 of the Rome Treaty.

Given the problems over the accession of new members, the question must be asked why the Community should be enlarged and a number of general arguments have been made. The Community is committed by the Rome Treaty to remain open to new members. In the preamble to the

Treaty, the signatories declared themselves 'resolved to preserve and strengthen liberty, calling upon the other peoples of Europe who share their ideal to join in their efforts'. A second argument is that enlargement would serve to consolidate democracy in the applicant countries. Recent applicants such as Greece, Portugal and Spain have all emerged from shorter or longer periods of dictatorship and membership of the Community could help to nurture their young democracies. Strategic arguments have also been adduced. The strategic importance of Greece and Turkey is threefold. Together they constitute the southern flank of NATO, have influence on the important oil route from the Middle East to Western Europe and control the straits between the Black Sea and the Mediterranean which is the only route giving the Soviet Union direct naval access to the Mediterranean and the Atlantic throughout the year.

Enlargement would prove that the Community was not just 'a rich man's club' and would in any case strengthen the Community's political, economic and commercial weight in the world. Spain is already the tenth industrial power in the world and the Greek merchant shipping represents 13 per cent of the world merchant fleet. The historical, cultural and commercial links between Portugal and Spain on the one hand and the countries of Latin America on the other could help improve the deteriorating relations between the Community and South America.

The Commission has also pointed to specific economic advantages of enlargement. Though the level of development in these countries is lower than that in the Community, the growth rate is higher: 6.1 per cent per year on average for Greece between 1966 and 1976, 5.5 per cent in Portugal and 5.3 per cent in Spain compared to 3.7 per cent for the Nine. A larger market would be opened up for the Community's industrial goods and also some farm produce (cereals, beef and pork, milk products) in a Community expanded from 270 to 320 million consumers. Community industries in crisis might be helped if membership brought discipline and restricted production to the same industries in the applicant states.

Finally it is argued that the difficulties which enlargement poses might be an advantage in that they could provide a stimulus for reforming important aspects of Community activity—the decision-making process and improved regional, social, industrial and agricultural policies.

The chief motives of the applicant states should also be considered. Broadly their governments have seen Community membership as offering the best opportunity to secure their somewhat fragile democracies. They have assumed that any renaissance of anti-democratic forces within their societies may be deterred by the fact that a return to authoritarianism would put at risk all of the political and economic ties which flow from Community membership. Secondly they have hoped that membership would help economic development and modernisation through exposure to a large and competitive market. Already by 1979 they had substantial relations with the Community. By then the Community took 48 per cent of the exports from Greece and supplied 42 per cent of its imports; took 48 per cent of Portugal's exports and supplied 44 per cent of its imports and took 46 per cent of Spain's exports and provided 34 per cent of its imports.

The governments of these three countries by 1979 were already using the prospect of membership as the vehicle for pushing through reforms of taxation, employment policies and agriculture which would otherwise have been difficult to secure. Thirdly, the governments of the applicant states believed that Community membership offered the best means of safeguarding and promoting national interests at a time of growing difficulty in the world economic and political environment. As one Spanish official put it, 'To be outside the Community at times of crisis is very bad'.

The New and Prospective Members

Greece

The Process of Entry

There were always strong psychological factors behind the Greek accession to the Community. Greece gave Europe its name and was one of the roots of civilisation. In the myths of ancient Greece, Europa—the sister of the Phoenician Cadmos, the founder of the town of Thebes—was loved by Zeus, the most powerful of the Gods. She gave birth to Minos, who was to become king of Crete. On this island around Knossos and later on the mainland around Athens are to be found some of the origins of Western civilisation. In the period between the second millenium and the second century before Christ, Greece gave Europe its first poets, its first dramatists, its first historians, its first philosophers and scientists. It developed European ideas on reasoning, democracy and even the first concept of a universe composed of atoms. Through the centuries, Greek thought continued to flow throughout Europe, directly or indirectly, by way of the Romans, Renaissance Italy and the neo-classical revival of the eighteenth century. The re-emergence in the nineteenth century of an independent Greece won much European sympathy and formed part of the rise of nationalism in Europe.

Being the first European country to be associated with the Community, Greece has always had a preferential relationship with the Six and subsequently with the Nine. The Greek government first applied for an Association Agreement with the Community under Article 238 of the Rome Treaty in June 1959. The Agreement (the Treaty of Athens) was signed in July 1961 and came into force in 1962. It was always envisaged that this Agreement would be one step on the road towards a closer relationship; the preamble of the Treaty of Athens recognised that the support given by the Community to raise the standard of living in Greece 'will facilitate the Accession of Greece to the Community at a later date'.

The Association Agreement did not produce all that was expected of it. It had been hoped that it would lead to a customs union, to the harmonisation of policies, to the creation of common institutions and to considerable resources being given to Greece to accelerate its economic growth. However, in 1967 the parliamentary regime was overthrown by a military junta and the 'Colonels' regime, as it was called, controlled Greece from 1967 to 1974. During this period the Association Agreement was 'frozen'. Current transactions were respected but further development was shelved for better days.

By 1975 parliamentary government had been restored and in June Mr Constantine Karamanlis formally requested that Greece should become a member of the Community. He said: 'I wish to stress that Greece does not desire to become a member of the EEC solely for economic reasons. She mainly desires so for reasons which are political and concern the stabilisation of democracy and the future of the nation. The Greeks believe in the destiny of Europe; they wish to be present to make a contribution towards what will surely be the greatest event of the century.' Karamanlis also had two other considerations; he wished to reduce his country's dependence on the United States and to reinforce its strength against its most immediate enemy, Turkey.

In January 1976 the Commission adopted the 'Opinion on Greek Application for Membership' in which it was recommended that 'a clear affirmative reply be given to the Greek request and that negotiations for Greek accession be opened'. However, it also pointed out that 'structural changes of a considerable magnitude are needed and it would seem desirable to envisage a period of time before the obligations of membership, even subject to transitional arrangements, are undertaken'. Not surprisingly, this provoked much anger in Greece but the Council of Ministers in February 1976 took a more favourable view of Greek membership.

Negotiations formally began in July 1976 and finally resulted in a Treaty of Accession signed in Athens in May 1979. The negotiations were at times quite tough as the Greeks were determined not to be treated as junior partners. The Greek Minister for Agriculture, Mr Kanellopoulos was particularly combative, on occasions battering the other agricultural ministers with offensive quotations from Aristophanes to Wilde! As one British official in Brussels remarked, 'They are a very clever people.'

From 1st January, 1981 Greece became a full member of the European Community. In the Accession Treaty, the Greeks committed themselves to accepting the Community 'acquis', the body of Community rules. To ensure that accession did not constitute too harsh a shock for Greece, certain transitional arrangements were allowed. In general the harmonisation period was five years. Thus, for example, Greece was to remove all remaining tariffs and quantitative controls on industrial imports from the Community by 1st January, 1986. In some areas more time was to be given to help gradual Greek adjustment. It was to be 1988 before certain agricultural produce could move free of customs duty between Greece and the Nine and before there was completely free movement of workers.

The Greek Economy

In some respects the progress of the Greek economy has been quite impressive. The Occupation by the Axis powers during the Second World War had resulted in the death of 8 per cent of the population with 10 per cent being made homeless. Half the roads and two-thirds of the country's livestock and vehicles had been destroyed. Since then the Greek economy has achieved an annual average growth rate of 6.5 per cent and even in the 1970s it remained at over 3.5 per cent. Its unemployment has remained remarkably low and was only 2.3 per cent in January 1982. The standard of living has risen considerably and compares well with countries such as Ireland and Italy. Some sectors of industry have proved dynamic, in particular metallurgy, petrochemicals and textiles. It is these sectors which boast the largest firms—the Larco nickel plant, the Pechiney Aluminium de Greece and Heracles General Cement, Europe's largest cement exporter.

Nevertheless, there must be considerable question concerning the underlying strength of the Greek economy. Agriculture has lagged behind the growth of industrial production. Despite the rapid growth of the working population employed in farming (31 per cent), the latter only makes a small contribution to the Greek national product. Greek agriculture is plagued by too many small farm units which suffer from poor location, poor quality of soil and lack of modern techniques. As a result, output per person employed is only 40 per cent of the Community average. Industrial growth has tended to be overconcentrated in the areas of Athens–Piraeus and Thessalonika to the detriment of most of the peripheral islands and mainland areas which aggravates the regional problems with which Greece is faced. Though the overall level of industrial growth has been satisfactory, not all sectors have been dynamic. There are too many small firms with 95 per cent of all enterprises employing less than ten workers.

The economic development of Greece has been accompanied by a constant and growing trade deficit. This trade deficit is caused by the country's dependence on imported capital goods and oil products because Greece lacks indigenous energy sources. The deficit is partially compensated for by foreign currency earned through tourism and shipping but nevertheless it has reached huge proportions. In 1979 it had reached $6.2 billion (a sum equal to one sixth of Greece's Gross National Product). Fortunately tourism, shipping and remittances sent home by Greek migrant workers offset this by $4.4 billion. Finally, inflation is higher in Greece than in any other Western country. Prices rose by more than 15 per cent between 1973 and 1978, by 18 per cent in 1979 and by January 1982 the annual rate of inflation was over 25 per cent.

In the short-run Community membership seemed likely to compound these weaknesses, especially Greece's trade gap. All tariffs on Greek exports to the EEC had already been abolished under the Association Agreement but Greece after 1981 had to remove its own still considerable barriers against Community goods. Community exporters by 1986 were no longer to face the heavy tariffs and non-tariff barriers that they had hitherto had to tolerate. Many Greek industrialists were worried that the chief impact of membership would be to open the Greek market to highly competitive imports which would destroy some Greek industry.

The first year of membership soon demonstrated that the problems of adjustment would not be easy. Before it joined, the small Greek steel industry had been expanding quickly, encouraged by a buoyant construction industry and protected by heavy tariffs. But as soon as Greece joined the Community, it also joined the ECSC. Since October, 1980, all Community steel production has been subject to compulsory controls by the Commission. When Greece asked for special treatment to allow expansion of its infant steel industry, it was refused permission because of the Community steel glut. Greek steel firms also faced the prospect of an even harder position when Greece's tariffs against imported steel were phased out in 1984.

The Greek textile industry had its share of worries. Low labour costs gave the industry a competitive advantage against Greece's European competitors. However, Greece had joined the Multifibre Arrangement (see chapter 8) which meant that it had to open its market to low-cost producers like Taiwan and Hong Kong.

There were other disadvantages. Greek housewives faced higher food prices under the CAP. The Commission estimated that entry would raise food prices by 14 per cent during the transition period to full membership. Greek farmers would gain relatively little because their main products were Mediterranean fruit and vegetables, tobacco and cotton. Community prices for these goods were only slightly higher than world prices. But Greece was a big net importer of products like meat, milk and cereals for which Community prices were well above world levels.

Professor John Marsh of Aberdeen University calculated that the overall resource flow (including the cost of importing high-price Community food) would be negative. The only bright spot was that Greece's gains from the Community budget were greater than expected. In 1981 the net profit was only 124 million ECU (£68 million) and the Commission had originally estimated a similar figure for 1982. By 1982 the estimate had risen to a minimum of 500 million ECU (£290 million) and the Greeks were happily anticipating a net gain of 700 million ECU (£400 million).

The Political Perspective

Greece was steered towards Community membership by Mr Karamanlis who was then the head of the ruling conservative New Democracy Party. In 1980 he became President of Greece and New Democracy was then led by Mr George Rallis. However, in October 1981 New Democracy was defeated in the general elections by the Panhellenic Socialist Movement (Pasok) led by Mr Andreas Papandreou. His father George Papandreou had won the 1964 elections soon after which Greece was plunged into three years of instability which led to the Colonels' coup of 1967.

When Pasok was formed in 1974, Andreas Papandreou preached a re-volutionary socialism and one of his chief ideas was that Greece should be a non-aligned nation. Until 1980 he was adamant that if Greece joined the Community he would take her out again. By 1981 he had shifted his posi-tion somewhat, saying that the issue of Greek membership should be the subject of a referendum. In fact the decision whether or not to hold a referendum rests with the President and Karamanlis is strongly in favour of continued membership. He would be likely either to refuse a referendum completely or at least postpone it for a year or so.

Since he became prime minister Papandreou has proved to be a prickly and unpredictable member of the Council of Ministers. He peremptorily dismissed his Deputy Foreign Minister for signing a Community com-muniqué condemning Soviet collusion in the Polish repression and he refused to associate Greece with the mild sanctions against Poland and Russia that the other nine countries accepted. He also held up agreement for several weeks on a Community contribution to the Sinai peacekeeping force. Yet the main fear that he would wrench Greece out of the Community has evaporated somewhat. He has not spoken recently of holding a referendum and perhaps he has been influenced by the unexpectedly fast growth of Greek receipts from the Community budget. *The Economist* in March 1982 suggested that Papandreou could settle for something comparable to that achieved by Harold Wilson in 1974–75—a slight improvement in the terms of entry secured by his conservative predecessor after a bout of face-saving bargaining. The main change that the Greeks would want would be a lengthening of the five-year transition period particularly for industry, where the country's many small businesses are frightened of Community competition. They would like to retain tariff protection on sensitive industries such as those producing electrical goods, machinery, paper and furniture. They also wish for accelerated benefits from CAP (particularly for olive oil, hard wheat and fruit and vegetables) and earlier introduction of the freedom for Greek workers to emigrate to the Community. They also hope to continue paying subsidies to industry and agriculture and for more aid from the Regional, Social and Agricultural Guidance Funds.

The Community is unlikely to be sympathetic on any revision of the terms of entry. As one official phrased it, 'If they come looking for a renegotiation of entry terms in 1982 or 1983, they are liable to be told to go and stuff their olives!' Unfortunately for Greece, it is not arguing in a vacuum. The shadow of the Community negotiations with Spain and Portugal have fallen across the Greek position. The Community cannot make concessions to Greece over, for example, olive oil cultivation which would cost a billion ECU if similar arrangements had to be made with Spain. It would be difficult for the Council of Ministers to make concessions to Greece and then refuse similar concessions to Spain. Greece would be better advised to press for new forms of agricultural support for Mediterranean products which would also benefit Italian and French farmers and consequently win powerful allies for Greece.

Spain

The Background

Loukas Tsoukalis describes Spain as finding itself in a state of quarantine at the end of the Second World War because the ruthless Franco regime was generally detested. With the onset of the Cold War, however, Spain gradually returned to the comity of nations. An important element in Franco's government, the Opus Dei technocrats, sought from 1957 to implement modernisation of the Spanish economy by building closer links with Western Europe. When it was seen that Britain was attempting to move closer to the Community in 1961, the Spanish followed suit because Spanish agricultural exports depended heavily on the British market. Therefore in 1962 Spain requested negotiations with the aim of signing an Association Agreement, a move that met with complete silence from the Community for two years. Only in 1970 was such an agreement signed. It aimed at creating freer trade between Spain and the Community and indeed useful reductions in the level of tariffs were achieved between 1970 and 1976 though they were smaller reductions than were offered to other Mediterranean countries. The Community conceded a 60 per cent tariff reduction on all Spanish industrial exports in return for a 25 per cent cut on most Community industrial exports to Spain.

Only with the death of Franco in November 1975 did the objective of full Spanish membership of the Community become a real possibility though the Spanish application submitted in July 1977 met with only a cautious welcome. The Belgian President-in-Office, Henri Simonet, said, 'We must not deceive ourselves that the negotiations will be easy. The path ahead is strewn with pitfalls.' In November 1978 the Commission's 'Opinion on the Spanish Submission' reflected this caution and stressed the need for adjustment on both sides. The Council of Ministers agreed to the formal opening of the negotiations in February 1979 but took the unusual decision at the insistence of the French government that there should be no substantive talks before the two sides agreed on 'a common basis' for negotiations. Only after the European Parliamentary elections of June 1979 did real negotiations begin.

The Major Obstacles to Spanish Membership

The negotiations for Spanish entry to the Community have been difficult because of Spain's size and strength. It has a population of 36 million people, is ranked eighth in the West in terms of Gross National Product and is potentially a serious rival both industrially and agriculturally to the member states of the Community. Four issues have created particular difficulties.

It was always clear that agriculture would be the most difficult issue. Two separate but related problems will arise once Spain is admitted to the Community. Firstly, French, Italian and Greek producers of Mediterranean agricultural products will face being savagely undercut by Spanish competition. Secondly, the cost of CAP will rise steeply to accommodate surplus Spanish production.

The hard bargaining on agriculture has revolved round three main groups of products—vegetable fats (particularly olive oil), wine, and fruit and vegetables. Spanish production of olive oil is almost as great as that of the existing Community which already produces more olive oil than it can consume. The olive oil market in Spain has been protected by huge tariffs on other imported edible oils. These tariffs will be phased out when Spain joins the Community. The consumption of other oils in Spain will then increase and that of olive oil will fall. Spanish olive oil growers will then be forced to divert their production to the rest of the Community, undercutting French, Italian and Greek producers. The Community will then have two choices; it could intervene and buy up the surplus olive oil, creating a huge olive oil 'lake' which would cost a billion ECU (£560 million) a year according to Commission estimates. Alternatively, a tax could be imposed on cheaper substitutes (like soya-bean imports from the United States) to increase the consumption of olive oil by making it relatively cheaper and using it in the manufacture of margarine. This idea is unpopular in Britain, Holland and Germany where margarine is made and where the public would not be happy to pay more for it. Nor would it be popular in the United States which exports some four billion dollars worth of soya oil to the Community.

On wine, the problem is caused by the Spanish custom of strengthening the alcoholic content of their red wine by mixing it with white wine. This is against Community regulations but if the practice of mixing were forbidden it would release a vast quantity of white wine on to the market, thus increasing the Community wine lake. With fruit and vegetables, the Spanish should be able to expand their sales to the rest of the Community once tariff barriers are removed. This would not only hurt French, Italian and Greek producers but also those of the Maghreb countries, Israel and Cyprus which currently enjoy privileged access to Community markets. The apparent choice seems to be between pauperising Mediterranean farmers or raising the cost of CAP even more. The Spanish have argued that Community entry will not trigger off any expansion of Spanish farm produce because of the lack of new land and water. This argument seems spurious; higher prices under CAP will almost certainly stimulate more output of Mediterranean products like fruit and wine.

Another issue likely to cause difficulty is fishing. Spanish fishermen will crew the largest fishing fleet in a Community of 12 and will expect to haul more fish out of Community waters than other Community fishermen will haul from Spanish waters. As the Community of Ten have found agreement over fishing difficult to reach, an accommodation with Spain on this issue will not be easy.

The Spaniards' main concern about joining the Community is the effect of tariff-free competition on their own industry. To brace weak Spanish firms for the chill blast of this competition, the government has set aside some 200 billion pesetas (over £1 billion) to subsidise the necessary investment. But the most intractable and potentially explosive issue in the industrial negotiations has been steel. Since 1975 the steel industry in Community countries has faced sluggish demand and has been subject to severe reduction. From 1978 the Community brought in more protection; a minimum price was established for steel imports into the Community and any imports below this price were subject to a duty. The Spanish steel industry is ominously competitive and exported 28 per cent of all its exports to the Community in 1979. As a result the Community imposed an anti-dumping duty on some Spanish steel exports, an action which soured relations. The Spanish steel industry was in basically the same position as its Community rivals—a situation of excess capacity—yet its 1979 plans provided for an increase in steel-making capacity of 34 per cent by 1985. Such plans did not fit in with Community planning which continued to aim at a reduction in capacity, not an increase (see chapter 8).

The Progress of Negotiations to 1982

As a result of such problems, negotiations over Spanish entry have been stormy. So vociferous was France's agricultural lobby against Spanish entry that in June 1980 President Giscard d'Estaing changed his former strong advocacy of Spanish entry to a much less welcoming attitude, possibly because he had his eye on the French presidential elections of Spring 1981. 'It does not seem possible to cope at the same time with problems and uncertainties derived from the first enlargement of the Community and those which would come when new members join,' he told a meeting of French farmers. He called for a pause in enlargement negotiations until existing budgetary and agricultural problems had been solved.

The Spanish reacted sharply to the French President's speech. The Spanish Minister for European Affairs, Mr Calvo Sotelo said: 'The problems to which M. Giscard refers are absolutely unreal. Our country does not have any budgetary problems as does the United Kingdom.' He was quite right. Spain would probably be a net beneficiary from the Community budget but it was precisely this factor which concerned the French and other members. The West Germans and the French were also worried about the Community rules on free movement of labour leading to a flood of Spanish workers to West Germany and France at a time of rising unemployment. The West German Chancellor, Helmut Schmidt, made it clear that the applicant countries should not be allowed to 'export' unemployment.

Overall there was little sympathy with the Spanish among Community members, with the exception of the British. To Spanish disappointment the target date for Spain's entry of 1st January, 1983 was quietly abandoned and for a time negotiations proceeded at such a snail's pace that a revised target date of 1st January, 1984 began to look unrealistic. The Spanish public, educated to see entry into Europe as a great step forward, were surprised that the application had faced so many obstacles, particularly in the French attitudes, since it had been made to believe that the only barrier to Spanish membership had been Franco's dictatorship. Giscard's comments of June 1980 provoked resentment across the political spectrum in Spain. On the Community side, the attempted military coup of February 1981 raised doubts about Spain's democratic credentials.

In March 1982 the position appeared to improve. Spanish democracy had begun to look more solid and the first six chapters of the draft accession agreement were signed in Brussels. These covered capital movements, transport, regional policy, legal harmonisation and financial questions. Five more chapters covering Euratom, coal and steel, external relations, taxation and customs union issues were expected to be sealed in June.

However, the final third of the accession agreement included difficult issues like agriculture and fishing with the summer of 1982 seeing a hardening of French attitudes. In a visit to Spain in June President Mitterrand made his opposition to Spanish entry so clear that the 1984 target date for entry appeared less feasible.

In addition, the Falklands War, with its implications for the Gibraltar question, soured Anglo-Spanish relations. The Spanish public rather sided with Argentina and the Spanish government was the only member of the UN Security Council apart from the Soviet Union to abstain on the motion calling for the withdrawal of Argentine troops from the Falklands. The British, confident after their Falklands victory, hardened their attitude over Gibraltar, stressing that there was no possibility of Spanish accession to the Community if the border between Spain and Gibraltar remained closed. The Spanish retaliated by declaring that they had no intention of opening the border until Britain was prepared to enter into serious discussions over Gibraltar's future, though in fact the border was opened in January 1983.

Despite such knotty problems there could be benefits for both parties once Spain has finally acceded to the Community. Spain has been a heavily protected market and when its tariffs are dismantled Community countries should be able to expand their industrial exports there, particularly consumer durables which have been particularly protected. The Spaniards have experienced rising living standards since the early 1960s so the Spanish market is growing. Northern dairy farmers could expect a growing outlet in Spain as Spaniards are now consuming more milk and meat, a shift in tastes which Spanish agriculture has not fully met. Similarly Spanish producers of textiles, shoes, steel and refined petroleum products have the stimulus of a huge Community market. It is, however the Spanish agricultural interest which stands to gain most by its increased sales of Mediterranean farm produce.

Table 20. The Nine, Greece, Spain and Portugal 1980

	Greece	Spain	Portugal	EC (The Nine)
GDP per capita ($)	4,800	5,700	2,400	10,500
% in agriculture, forestry, fishing	30.80	19.5	31.3	8.4
% in industry	30.00	37.3	34.8	33.0
% in services	39.20	42.5	33.9	59.0
Population (m)	9.36	36.7	9.8	260.0
Inflation (%)	20.00	14.5	17.6	9.0
% exports to EEC	48.00	49.0	54.6	53.1
Annual real GDP growth	3.60	3.9	5.1	3.1

Portugal

Background to the Negotiations

The authoritarian regime of Antonio Salazar (1932–68) and his successor Marcello Caetano (1968–74) kept Portugal isolated from most West European political and economic developments after 1945 except membership of EFTA. Until 1973 Portuguese offical attitudes towards the Community were determined by the British position and it was after the first British application to join the Community in 1961 that Portugal first asked for the opening of negotiations with the Six. Eventually this led to a free trade agreement with the Community in July 1972. The agreement improved Portuguese access to Community markets for agricultural products while maintaining a high level of protection for industrial products. In 1974 Portugal sought improvements to this agreement which were granted, together with 180 million UA of emergency aid, in a 1976 agreement.

However, after the long Salazar–Caetano dictatorship, Portugal experienced a period of acute political instability including an abortive Communist coup in November 1975. The economy suffered severely as in addition it had been adversely affected by the recession following the energy crisis and by the loss of Portugal's African colonies (principally Angola and Mozambique). The loss of the colonies came only after protracted fighting and led to a large influx of refugees from Angola. In 1977 inflation had reached 27 per cent, unemployment was running at over 15 per cent and exports were covering less than 50 per cent of imports.

Only gradually was political stability restored and democratic procedures implemented. Then the Prime Minister Dr Soares made a large initiative towards joining the Community when he undertook a tour of the Community capitals in February and March 1977. The Portuguese then formally applied for membership stressing that they hoped negotiations would be completed by 1981 with a transitional period of at least five years with more for agricultural products. Dr Soares rather like Mr Karamanlis felt that the Community had an obligation to help the newly-established democracy by granting full membership as soon as possible.

The Commission's 'Opinion on the Portuguese Application for Membership' was published in May 1978 and pointed to major problems. The state of the Portuguese economy was such that it would face severe difficulties from the full blast of Community competition. The per capita GNP of Portugal was only about one fifth that of West Germany and this implied that the country would need massive Community assistance. Until the early 1970s Portugal's balance of payments had been sustained by earnings from tourism and from the remittances of migrant workers. But the tourist industry had been hit by the recent political disturbances and the world recession cast doubt on the future prospects of migrant workers. In addition Portugal was now cut off from cheap raw materials previously supplied by her African colonies. The country urgently needed to increase exports but agriculture which could have played a role here remained backward.

The Progress of the Negotiations

Despite such grave worries the Community welcomed the Portuguese application. It did of course wish to do what it could to nurture the new democracy. In addition Portugal could make a contribution to the Community of a strategic and political nature. Its position at the western extremity of Europe's Atlantic coast made her important in NATO security while her long association with the countries of South America (particularly the richest of them, Brazil) meant that she could bring into the Community valuable contacts and experience.

Other factors made the negotiations go relatively smoothly. The Portuguese negotiators tended to be more pragmatic and accommodating than the Spaniards but of more importance was that Portugal's tiny economy was no threat to the other European countries and was not producing the large volume of cheap wine, fruit and vegetables which had made French and Italian farmers so apprehensive of Spain. Unlike Spain, too, Portugal did not present the Community with a problem over fishing. The Portuguese were contributing waters with a fishing capacity well in excess of the needs of their own fishermen. Finally it seemed likely that Portugal's gains from the Community budget would be outweighed by the extra cost of importing high price Community temperate foods like meat and milk.

Nevertheless the negotiations did not proceed rapidly and in 1981 several difficulties emerged. The impact of Portuguese low-cost textiles on the depressed Community textile industry held up progress. The French and the British wanted to hold off Portuguese competition in textiles as long as possible and the Commission was forced to offer a compromise plan which offered some protection to textile companies in the present Community in the first few years of Portuguese membership. The Portuguese felt that this was unfair and the Portuguese Finance Minister, Mr Joao Salgueiro rejected the proposal in October 1981. The Portuguese employers' organisation had already issued a bitter comment to the effect that it would have no interest in acceding 'to a community of rich countries if the few competitive national sectors are not allowed to compete according to the most elementary rules of a customs union'.

Another Portuguese complaint was over the issue of freedom of movement for Portuguese workers within the Community. Portugal had assumed that full free movement would be available from the date of accession for Portuguese workers already in other Community states. The Community now began to suggest that Portugal would be treated no better than Greece; in other words there would be a seven-year period before full free movement for Portuguese workers was permitted. The Portuguese also complained that it had received none of the aid promised by the Community in 1980 (275 million ECU). They had proposed various projects to which the French and the Italians had raised objections.

Fortunately negotiations with Portugal recovered their momentum somewhat in 1982. In February four chapters—transport, Euratom, regional policy and capital movements—were signed. Such developments were assisted by the fact that Portugal was not looking for a lengthy transition period. The Portuguese felt that the cold shower of Community competition would make the country's industry fitter and felt that too long a transition would dilute the incentive for Portuguese industry and agriculture to modernise. They seemed perhaps too optimistic that modernisation could be implemented.

There was another danger in the approaching membership. A recent transnational poll recorded a high level of apathy or ignorance in Portugal on the subject of Community membership.

Table 21. Opinion on Community Membership (%)

	Good	Bad	Neither	Don't know
Portugal	19	6	13	62
Spain	52	6	18	24
EEC average	53	14	26	7

Source: Eurobarometer

Obviously the Portuguese government has to educate its public opinion or as *The Economist* (17th April, 1982) pointed out, 'it will risk a political heart-attack when the day of the cold shower finally arrives'.

Distant Prospects: Cyprus and Turkey

Though Cyprus is the latest country to seek close relations with the Community, an Association Agreement was signed between the Community and Cyprus as long ago as 1973. It provided for a full customs union in two stages but the full implementation of the agreement was stalled by the Turkish occupation of the northern part of the island in 1974. In 1981 the Cypriot Foreign Minister, Mr Nicos Rolandis, urged that it be completed and indeed extended by 1984.

Cypriot attitudes had been affected by the Greek entry into the Community at the beginning of 1981 and the full customs union provided for has brought Cyprus closer to the Community than any other country which is not a full member. Had it not been for the Turkish invasion, Cyprus might well have applied for full membership at the same time as Greece did (1976) and it might yet become the thirteenth member state after Spain and Portugal. However, the existing member states might not welcome a new mini-member with a population only twice that of Luxembourg's, and even if they did the political problems of Cyprus would have to be solved first.

Although Turkey has not applied for full membership of the Community, her Association Agreement of 1963 contained a clause in the preamble identical with the one relating to Greece. In other words, Turkish accession to the Community was envisaged as a long-term objective to be achieved by 1995.

Close relations have developed between Turkey and the Community in a number of ways. Over one million Turkish workers were employed in the Community in the 1970s. The Community supplied 50 per cent of all foreign investment in Turkey, supplied 40 per cent of her imports and took 35 per cent of her exports. Turkey was seen as important for European security and the country was also potentially very rich in both energy sources (coal and oil) and minerals (iron, copper, uranium, chromium and lead) although many of these have remained undeveloped.

However, relations between Turkey and the Community have been strained by a number of problems. While Turkey does nearly half its trade with the Community, it has a large trade deficit with the Ten. The Turks have been bitter at Community restrictions on Turkish agricultural exports though this position was improved in 1976 when the Community offered a measure of preference to all but a fraction (17.5 per cent) of Turkish agricultural exports to it. In 1979 the Council of Ministers agreed to phase out most tariffs on Turkish agricultural goods from 1984 over a period of six years. Another point of friction has been Community restrictions on Turkish industrial exports but the Community was itself angered in 1978 by Turkish exporters who far exceeded the quotas allocated to them in a number of textile products, notably cotton yarn.

The size and relative backwardness of the Turkish economy also pose formidable difficulties. The Turkish GNP per capita is only about one third that of Greece's. Turkey already has a population of 40 million people and owing to a high birth rate this population is expected to exceed 80 million by the end of the century. A programme of aid, therefore, which would bring Turkey up to Community levels would have to be so vast as to be unthinkable.

Enlargement in the 1980s will have an adverse effect on Turkey as the new members will gain a competitive advantage in goods like textiles, wine and Mediterranean fruit and vegetables. Turkey's substantial exports of raisins, figs, olive oil and citrus fruits will be threatened.

However, the main obstacles in Turco-Community relations have been political or psychological. On both sides there are doubts whether Turkey is in fact a European country and therefore eligible to accede to the Treaty of Rome. The aftermath of the Cyprus invasion of 1974 created a profound sense of estrangement from the West in Turkey and caused relations with Greece to deteriorate still further. The Community tried at the time to avoid becoming a party in the disputes between Turkey and Greece but the Greek entry to the Community had serious implications for Turkey. Greece now has the right to veto all decisions affecting Turkey, including a possible Turkish application for full membership.

To some extent Greek hostility is counter-balanced by Turkey's close relations with West Germany which is Turkey's largest trading partner and which has successfully pressed for more aid to Turkey in recent years. Turkey's links with West Germany have been reinforced by the presence of Turkish workers in Germany, about 600,000 in 1979, though on occasions this factor has created some strains in the relationship.

The gravest flaw in Turco-Community relations is the nature of Turkish government which hardly qualifies for the description of democratic. In September 1980 Mr Demirel's government was overthrown by a coup d'état and Turkey experienced another bout of military dictatorship similar to that of 1971–73. The military regime gave an assurance that democracy would soon be restored and was promised aid from the Community worth £324 million over five years. When no moves were made to restore democracy, the Community suspended its aid in 1981. The military, headed by General Kenan Evren, then made concessions in December 1981 by fixing general elections for 1983. However, since then the regime has imprisoned a former Prime Minister, Mr Bulent Ecevit, and a number of trade unionists, causing a further Community freezing of aid. Until Turkey establishes its democratic credentials with the Community, serious movement towards even consideration of full membership seems unlikely.

Conclusion: A General Survey of the Problems of Enlargement

Enlargement in the 1980s will clearly create further strains on the Community. The entry of Spain and Portugal will add to the costs of the Community budget, a factor particularly worrying for net contributors to the budget like Britain and West Germany. Secondly the new members compete directly with the French, Italian and Greek producers of Mediterranean agricultural goods, producers who are already among the poorest in the Community. Regional problems may therefore be exacerbated. Thirdly the entry of Spain and Portugal is likely to increase the problems of surplus capacity and growing unemployment in textiles, steel and shipbuilding, sectors often concentrated in the declining areas of the Community. Fourthly, the previously rapid growth of Greece, Spain and Portugal may be halted. Free trade may lead to the extinction of many small inefficient firms which have survived until now behind a protective wall. The balance of payments of these three countries could then worsen, forcing governments into deflationary policies which could further hamper growth. It would be difficult for the Community to compensate for this by adequate transfers of resources.

In addition to these economic problems, political difficulties may arise from enlargement. The dispute between Greece and Turkey, of which Cyprus is but one aspect, takes on an added importance in that Turkey has seen Greece's admission as an act of political discrimination at its expense and now fears that Greece will block her entry. Another Turkish fear is that Greece will endeavour to gain Community support in the Cyprus question. Between Spain and Britain, there still stands the vexed question of the status of Gibraltar.

But the main political problem arising from enlargement is its implications for decision-making within the Community. The growth of the Ten into the Twelve will add to the difficulties of decision-making which is already a cumbersome procedure with *only* ten vetoes. The enlargement process in fact highlights the need for more majority voting in the Council of Ministers. The existing need for unanimity in a club of Twelve may lead to decisions becoming virtually impossible and a split in the Community more and more likely. Loukas Tsoukalis suggests three possible scenarios for the future evolution of the Community. The Community might be diluted into a free trade area because the system of common agricultural prices would be difficult to sustain. Another possibility is that common policies would still operate but without the participation of the weaker members. This would mean, in effect, a two-tier or even a multi-tier Community, a process that has already occurred in the operation of the EMS. The third scenario is that the Community might move towards the creation of a minimum welfare state at a Community level in which regional disparities are reduced by considerable inter-regional resource transfers. The richer members of the Community would pay the necessary price for this development for the preservation of free trade on which much of their economic advantage depends.

On the positive side, it may be suggested that once Spain and Portugal have joined, the scale of the Community of Twelve will have an almost imperial dimension. Stretching from the Shetlands across to Crete in the Eastern Mediterranean, the enlarged Community will number over 313 million people as against the present 270 million. Its land area will have increased dramatically from 1.5 million square kilometres to 2.25 million square kilometres and its productive wealth in terms of combined domestic product will have outpaced that of the United States. The Community of Twelve could well gain more influence in a variety of international forums. With Greek entry, the Community owns one third of all the world's shipping and should dominate future conferences on this sector. Once Spain and Portugal join, the Community will account for half of the 24 full members of the Organisation for Economic Co-operation and Development (OECD).

Further Reading

Holland, S., *Uncommon Market*, Chapter 10, Macmillan, London, 1980.
Tsoukalis, L., *The European Community and its Mediterranean Enlargement*, Allen and Unwin, London, 1981.

Articles
'Spain and the EEC', *European Trends*, May 1979.
'Turkey and the EEC', *European Trends*, November 1979.

Questions

(1) Why should the Community wish to increase its present membership?

(2) What have been the advantages and disadvantages of Community membership for Greece?

(3) Why have the negotiations over Spanish accession to the Community been fraught with difficulties?

(4) Analyse the chief general problems raised by impending enlargement of the Community.

16
Britain, the European Community and the Way Ahead

Britain's Position in the European Community

Over ten years have passed since Britain joined the European Community but her relationship with the Community is still an uneasy one, with successive governments attempting to renegotiate the terms of entry and British contributions to the Community budget. In a sense this was only to be expected. From the outset the Community system had certain structural disadvantages for Britain, arising out of her distinctive position as a highly urbanised industrial society with a small efficient agricultural sector whose production was supplemented by substantial imports. British officials hoped to change established Community policies but found their partners unwilling to move significantly on major issues.

To some extent the timing of British entry explains this impasse. It was most unfortunate that Britain did not join the Community in 1957 when she could have influenced the ground rules of the Community to her advantage; it was equally unfortunate that she joined the Community in 1973 at the very moment when the long period of growth in the international economy was ending. The growing unemployment and high inflation that accompanied Britain's first years of membership gave member states less room for a generous approach to her demands—demands which became more insistent as Britain's fragile economy was further damaged. At the same time it may be suggested that Britain did not make sufficient efforts to exploit Community rules and institutions to further her interests, perhaps fearful of a potential loss of national sovereignty. British attitudes on Community membership still displayed a certain ambivalence; the British still thought of the Community in terms of 'them' and 'us', of British objectives clashing with those of the Community, rather than as a close group in which the members searched for mutual interests. This attitude was popular not only with the British public but also in British government circles. In the first decade of British membership only one British minister tried to promote new Community initiatives (Lord Carrington in the field of Political Co-operation). For the most part British ministers appeared intent on slowing down the progress towards European integration. On one notorious occasion Tony Benn, Secretary of State for Energy in the 1974–79 Labour government, boasted of the fact that by deliberately and unnecessarily absenting himself from Community meetings he had held up Community discussions in this vital area.

British prime ministers in the last ten years cannot escape their share of the blame for the sourness that has so often characterised Britain's relations with Europe. Only Edward Heath has seemed a genuine European and he achieved real friendship with French and German leaders. Harold Wilson, in contrast, ordered Labour members of parliament to vote against membership in 1971–72 and his renegotiation of the British terms of membership in 1974–75 (arguably a cosmetic exercise which did not cure the root causes of Britain's budgetary problem) poisoned feelings in Europe against changing the rules, when it became clear in 1979 that Britain's budget payments were indeed unfair. James Callaghan alienated Britain's Community partners in 1975 when he wanted Britain to have a separate seat at the North–South conference in Paris. He also opposed direct elections to the European Parliament and failed in 1979 to appreciate the importance of the creation of the EMS in the construction of which Britain could have played a major role. Between 1979 and 1982 Mrs Thatcher won some tangible gains in the reduction of Britain's budget contributions and in the rallying of Community support over the Falklands. She accepted the Community as the best framework within which to pursue Britain's national interest but her abrasive style was hardly calculated to win the love of Britain's European partners! Britain's reputation, in the words of William Wallace, was that of 'an awkward and ambivalent partner'.

Yet if British attitudes to the Community since 1973 seemed jaundiced and too business-like, was this surprising? To many British people it appeared that Britain was paying too high a price for membership. Membership of the Community appeared to be imposing significant extra burdens on an already sick British economy while the expected gains of entry did not materialise. Let us examine some of the crucial issues in this debate under four headings: (1) the Community budget and CAP; (2) the effects of Community membership on British trade; (3) political considerations; (4) the future.

The Community Budget and the CAP

As explained in chapter 10, gross contributions to the Community budget are based on a principle known as 'own resources' (the Community's independent revenue). Member countries in effect pay over to the Community what already belongs to it; these payments include common external tariffs and levies on agricultural imports from non-member countries. In addition the Community may levy an amount up to the yield of 1 per cent of a member country's VAT, formally part of the Community's 'own resources', though actually derived from national taxation. Anything beyond a 1 per cent levy requires further legislation which would have to be approved and ratified by all the member states.

This system of levying taxes hits Britain in a peculiarly harsh way. As levies are chargeable on imports of food from non-member countries, the gross contribution of food importers such as the United Kingdom is a larger proportion of their GDP than for countries that are self-sufficient in or net exporters of food (for example France). Also, non-agricultural imports by the United Kingdom from external sources are above average and therefore yield a relatively large amount of customs duties.

This would not have mattered unduly if the system of allocating receipts from the budget in any way compensated but this has not been the case. About three quarters of the expenditure of the Community budget is spent on agriculture, predominantly to support farm prices; the rest goes mainly to regional and social fund projects and administration. Also, whereas expenditure on agriculture is compulsory under Article 203 of the Treaty of Rome, expenditure on other fields of Community business is not. Therefore if the budget came up against a revenue ceiling, agricultural spending would be maintained and the revenues in other areas would be reduced.

The large expenditure on agricultural support has led to the United Kingdom gaining only a meagre share of Community expenditure. Britain's small farming sector can never attract more than a small share of such expenditure, normally about 5 per cent although it rose by 1982 to 10 per cent. In other areas of Community spending, Britain has gained a much bigger share but funds like the Regional and Social Fund have accounted for only about 8–10 per cent of Community expenditure. Her net contribution to the cost of agricultural support has been 25 times the amount gained from the Regional and Social Funds.

Of course it was foreseen at the time of the 1970 negotiations that this Community system of raising revenue with the great proportion spent on agriculture would result in the United Kingdom making a very large net contribution to the Community budget once the transitional period ended in the late 1970s. It was then Community opinion that such British fears were exaggerated because in time new policies would reduce the proportion of the budget taken by agriculture to 60 per cent or even 40 per cent. Thus, it was alleged, the United Kingdom net contribution would be reduced. It was also agreed that if unacceptable situations arose, the very survival of the Community would demand that equitable solutions be found.

However, from the time she joined the Community in January 1973, Britain's net contribution rose steeply. In the first year of membership Britain made a net contribution of just over £100 million. This was followed by two years, 1974 and 1975, in which the United Kingdom accounts with the Community were roughly in balance. But from then on the British contribution rose remorselessly from £178 million in 1976 to £900 million in 1979. Worse seemed likely to come in 1980; it was forecast that Britain would be a net contributor to the tune of £1,200 million, making about 60 per cent of the total net contributions to the Community budget despite the fact that the United Kingdom's GDP per head was the third lowest in the Community. Put another way, the United Kingdom would be contributing over 20 per cent to the Community funds but only receiving under 9 per cent of Community expenditure.

This seemed a patently unsatisfactory situation and the advent of a new Conservative government under Mrs Thatcher in May 1979 soon led to a long bitter dispute between the United Kingdom and her EEC partners over the question of British contributions to the Community budget. Only in May 1980 was an agreement reached at Brussels with a complicated formula being evolved to enable Mrs Thatcher to tell the British parliament that she had won considerable gains while not making it look as though the French and West German governments had succumbed too much to

Mrs Thatcher's abrasively presented demands. It was also considered necessary, if the Community was to survive as a meaningful institution, that the principle of the 'Juste retour' (a fair return) should not be openly adopted, i.e. that every member state should not expect to get back what it pays out (minus administrative costs).

The Commission had estimated that Britain would pay £1,040 million to Brussels in 1980 and £1,250 million in 1981. The agreement of May 1980 cut these 'unacceptable' figures by roughly two thirds to an estimated £335 million and £425 million respectively. But the combined effects of falling farm costs and fixed rebates reduced the amount Britain actually paid in 1980 to £200 million with a virtual break-even figure for 1981—a deficit of a mere £8 million.

Such a British gain did not make for harmonious budgetary discussions in 1982. The two years between 1980 and 1982 had not been used for any fruitful long-term restructuring of the Community budget and the agreement of May 1980 had made West Germany the chief Community paymaster; its net contribution to the Community budget in 1980 was 1,540 million EUA and 1,647 million EUA in 1981.

By the time that negotiations started in earnest on Britain's 1982 budgetary position, it was estimated by the Commission that Britain would pay a net 1,530 million ECU (£872 million) if no new agreement was reached. The British put in for annual rebates of at least 1,200 million ECU (£675 million) and thought that these should continue for five years with a built in provision for review thereafter in case the underlying problem was still unresolved. They then raised the demand to 1,400 million ECU (£795 million).

The other member states suggested rebates of only two thirds of this amount and argued that the deal should only run for three or four years. Acrimonious meetings than ensued in April and May 1982 as both sides dug in their heels. The British made clear that as a tactical move they would block agreement on farm price increases if no budget deal was agreed. It was a tactic that greatly incensed Britain's Community partners who had hoped for a more conciliatory British attitude after the Community support given over the Falklands Crisis. In the event the British tactic backfired because Community premiers like Schmidt and Mitterrand were not prepared to be bludgeoned into an agreement as they had been in 1980. Majority voting was used to force through farm price increases against the practice followed since the Luxembourg Compromise of 1966 (see chapter 3). No doubt the British were tempted to respond in some equally dramatic way, for example by refusing to attend Community meetings or by withholding VAT contributions to the EEC. However, they still needed the support of their partners in the Falklands issue and finally accepted a budget settlement which *The Economist* described as 'humiliatingly less generous than the terms which the British had been seeking'.

The rebate which Britain was to obtain amounted to only 55 per cent of its probable net contribution: 850 million ECU (£485 million) out of 1,530 million ECU (£872 million). Under the risk-sharing formula, Britain would pay the whole extra amount if the net contribution turned out to be as much as 1,580 million ECU. Between 1,580 million ECU and 1,730 million ECU, Britain and her partners would split the extra cost on a 50–50 basis.

If the sum turned out to be higher than 1,730 million ECU, Britain would pay 25 per cent and her partners 75 per cent. There was no equivalent formula if the net contributions turned out to be lower.

The overpayments received by Britain in 1980 and 1981 turned out to have undermined its negotiating position in 1982. Claude Cheysson the French foreign minister insisted on taking this into account. Another factor was the German refusal to pay more than half of the proportion of the British rebate which they had shouldered in the previous two years. Germany was to pay less than 18 per cent of the 1982 rebate compared with nearly 36 per cent previously. It was hard to find any solace for British discomfiture except for the fact that they would still retrieve about 75 per cent of net contributions during the three years 1980–82 compared with 66 per cent envisaged in 1980.

Nevertheless, the row had poisoned the whole Community atmosphere and had raised important constitutional questions. It had also further reduced British popularity in the Community and had led to some extremely harsh language. The French farm minister, Edith Cresson commented: 'British arrogance and insolence and their threats against France and Germany had become insupportable. They thought that the world would always give way to them and now they have been caught out.' The French premier, François Mitterrand, went further in raising the whole question of Britain's future in the EEC and the role which Britain saw herself playing there. On their side, the chief members of the Thatcher government were furious as a result of the forced British concessions.

Budgetary issues seem certain to bedevil British membership of the Community in a future made more uncertain by the impending enlargement. It is not clear whether enlargement of the Community will improve or worsen Britain's bargaining position on budgetary matters. Enlargement to 12 countries will bring down the general real income average to nearly the United Kingdom level and weaken Britain's case for better treatment in the EEC. However, if enlargement does eventually force through reform of CAP and the Community budget, then Britain might benefit especially if Community spending on regional, social and industrial projects were to increase in the 1980s.

Despite the disadvantages that Britain suffers under present Community regulations it would be wrong to leave this section without a reminder of the benefits that Britain enjoys under the present acquis communautaire. In a world where both political and economic conditions are volatile, secure food supplies are of great importance to Britain. We have to import about half of all our food; and of that which we produce ourselves, we depend for about half on imported foodstuffs, fertilisers and fuel. The Community with its high levels of self-sufficiency for nearly all temperate foodstuffs is now our most reliable source of supply. It is often not the cheapest food available, but world food prices can fluctuate dramatically, as they did in 1974–75, and reliance on world supplies could leave us with shortages in time of need. This occurred for example with sugar in 1975; the world price increased greatly and Commonwealth producers were no longer willing to supply sugar at the agreed price. With the price of sugar shooting up, sugar was scarce and the EEC was able to meet this scarcity at costs well below the world price.

Nor should the value of grants and loans to the United Kingdom from the EIB, the ECSC, the Regional Fund, the Social Funds and other Community funds be underestimated. The loans have to be repaid but at a favourable rate of interest. The availability of the loans has contributed to some modernisation of the coal, rail and steel industries and the exploitation of North Sea oil. The outright grants have helped worker retraining, the handicapped and farm modernisation. From the Social Fund, for example, Britain received £706 million, an average 24 per cent of commitments, over the years 1973 to 1981. Much of this money was spent on the Youth Opportunities Programme.

Table 22. The UK Net Contributions to the Community Budget 1973–82

	£million
1973	111
1974	37
1975	−45
1976	178
1977	481
1978	822
1979	900
1980	200
1981	8
1982	387 (projected)

The Effects of EEC Membership on British Trade

The importance of foreign trade to the UK economy is immense; it is a highly 'open' economy, a tendency which has increased over time. Britain is therefore more influenced by questions of international trade than many of its partners in the EEC. Since the Second World War the traditional pattern of UK trade has completely changed. In the 1950s we exported manufactures in exchange for imports of food and raw materials with the bulk of the trade being carried out with Commonwealth countries. Since then there has been a growing dependence on trade with developed areas— the EEC, Japan and North America. There has also been a change in the commodity structure of British foreign trade with a large increase in imported manufactures, a worrying development which points to the UK competitive decline.

It was hoped that entry to the EEC would greatly benefit the British economy; the UK would gain from selling in a larger market, benefiting from greater economies of scale. Certainly membership of the EEC has not arrested our relative economic decline; between 1972 and 1979 the UK per capita GNP fell from 85 to 78 per cent of the EEC average.

However, the dynamic gains of membership for trade have been difficult to quantify and the economic pundits hold a bewildering variety of views on this subject. The Cambridge Economic Policy Group took a very gloomy stance in 1979, suggesting that the net effect of EEC membership between 1973 and 1977 was to reduce UK exports by £152 million and to increase UK imports by £994 million per annum, i.e. a £1.1 billion loss per annum. Professor Metcalfe in *The United Kingdom Economy* (Prest and Coppock (eds.)) took almost as gloomy a view as the Cambridge Group. A more cheerful view is possible; Ann Morgan of the National Institute of Economic and Social Research has concluded that Britain's manufactured trade balance in 1977 would have been between £225 million and £375 million worse but for membership of the EEC. She uses figures supplied by the EEC rather than British statistics which are more gloomy. The EEC figures allow her to see benefits for Britain even in CAP, for example the increased exports won by the British food and drinks processing industry. Both the Treasury and *The Economist* have taken the view that Community membership has not had much effect on British trade either way because the tariff changes that followed our entry were relatively small and only one third of Britain's total tariff cuts since 1959.

The gains and losses for British trade, then, are difficult to quantify but certain other features of British foreign trade since 1973 are not. There has been a striking increase in the proportion of our trade with other EEC countries. In 1955 imports from the other eight countries comprised 12.6 per cent of our total imports; this percentage rose steadily to 23.6 per cent in 1965, 36.3 per cent in 1975 and 45 per cent in 1980. A similar picture emerges from an analysis of our exports. Exports to EEC countries comprised 15 per cent of our total exports in 1955; this percentage rose to 26.3 per cent in 1965, to 32.2 per cent in 1975 and 42 per cent in 1980.

Table 23. British Trade (Visibles) with the Community in £ Billion

Year	Exports	Imports	Total	Balance
1970	2.4	2.3	4.7	+0.1
1971	2.5	2.7	5.3	−0.2
1972	2.8	3.4	6.3	−0.6
1973	3.8	5.2	9.0	−1.4
1974	5.5	7.7	13.2	−2.2
1975	6.2	8.7	15.0	−2.5
1976	8.9	11.2	20.1	−2.3
1977	11.7	13.6	25.3	−1.9
1978	13.4	15.9	29.2	−2.5
1979	17.3	19.9	37.3	−2.6
1980	20.4	19.7	40.1	+0.7
1981	20.9	20.8	41.7	+0.03
1982 (to June)	11.5	12.4	23.9	−0.9

Another demonstrable development is that in most years since 1970 the UK has run a huge trade deficit with her EEC partners. D. S. Lewis explains this deficit by pointing to the rising exports of EEC food to the UK; in some years these food exports accounted for two-thirds of the deficit. Before such trends are used as evidence against the value of British membership of the EEC, it must be stressed that the trend towards a rising trade deficit with other EEC countries was already well established before we joined the Community. In 1970 there was a small visible trade balance of £91 million but by 1972 this had turned into a considerable deficit of £592 million.

The European Commission in 1980 published a report that sought to demonstrate that the tangible dynamic effects of Community membership were now working their way through into Britain's trade figures. It suggested that Britain was doing well out of the EEC with impressive rises in exports to West Germany, France and Holland. For the first time, too, since Britain joined the Community she ran a trade surplus with the other eight, a surplus of £709 million compared to a huge deficit of £2,629 million the previous year. Nor was this merely to be explained by our exports of North Sea oil, important an element though this was. Several areas of manufacturing did well in terms of high exports to Europe including organic and inorganic chemicals, dyeing and tanning materials, pharmaceutical products, leather and rubber goods, scientific instruments, power generating machinery, office machines and telecommunications and electrical equipment.

Another encouraging aspect to British trade is that since the early 1970s the trend has been for British exports to the Community to rise faster than imports from the Community. By 1979 exports had risen on average by 6 per cent annually more than imports; the 1980 figure accelerated this trend when exports to the EEC increased by 18 per cent while imports to Britain from the Community fell by 1 per cent. Before British entry, the United Kingdom's trade performance with the Community was on the decline, with a deterioration from an export–import ratio of 104 per cent in 1970 to 83 per cent in 1972. Entry was in 1973 and after this the ratio fell to an all time low of 75 per cent in 1975. Since then there has been a steady improvement with seven of Britain's EEC trading partners in the country's top twelve export markets. West Germany in 1979 replaced the United States as the largest single market for British exports.

Table 24. British Exporters' Percentage Share of Import Markets

	West Germany	France	Italy	The Netherlands	Belgium/ Luxembourg	Denmark	Ireland
1973	3.5	4.7	3.4	4.6	6.6	11.1	50.8
1980	6.7	5.4	4.4	8.2	8.1	12.1	50.8

Source: Department of Trade.

However, there have been disappointing aspects to British exploitation of trading opportunities in the Community. Some sectors have continued to perform relatively poorly, including road vehicles (which accounted for two-thirds of the deficit in manufactures in 1980), textiles, iron and steel and livestock. Nor should British penetration of particular Community markets be cause for unalloyed satisfaction. The United Kingdom share of West Germany imports in 1980 amounted to a modest 6.5 per cent, some considerable way behind the 11 per cent and 8 per cent achieved by France and Italy respectively. In fact Britain was the principal supplier to only one Community market, Ireland and after that its best position was third, in supplying 12 per cent of Denmark's total imports. In contrast, West

Germany was the most important supplier to all the Community countries, except Ireland and Britain where it came second only to the United States.

Nearly 20 per cent of all British exports to the EEC in 1980 were oil or oil products. It may also be asserted that Britain sold more to her Community partners in 1980 because their economies were relatively healthy and that they sold less to Britain because British industry was so depressed that it was busy de-stocking rather than buying new goods for expansion. In 1982 with British consumers spending more, Britain's visible trade balance with the Community again went into the red.

The key to success is in manufactures and in this section Britain is regularly let down by road vehicles, a sector where it is difficult to predict a reversal of this trend in the near future. Some areas where Britain is currently competitive, for example telecommunications and metalworking machinery, are also areas where other Community countries are making considerable progress. Thus those British industries which are still in surplus could find themselves in deficit if they fall behind in the new advanced technology now being applied by the United Kingdom's chief competitors. Oil continues to cast a shadow over the total trade results, concealing weaknesses which require remedying. If oil is excluded, the outlook for British trade in the Community is not reassuring.

Despite such pessimistic projections, the Community market of 270 million people must still be regarded as essential to Britain's economic survival in a world becoming increasingly protectionist. Many important trading countries now impose very heavy duties on imports. In 1982 a British car exported to South Korea faced a duty of 150 per cent plus a special excise tax of between 15 and 40 per cent; the same country imposed a 200 per cent duty on Scotch whisky while Brazil imposed a 185 per cent duty on British biscuits. It was in fact such newly industrialising countries like Korea and Brazil that were among the worst offenders.

The worst of all offenders remained Japan, where it had become almost impossible for foreign car exporters to succeed. When the French tried to export Renault 5 cars to Japan, they found that they had to build parking facilities at the port of Yokohama; it took two years to obtain a building permit and over another year to lay on essential services like electricity. Meanwhile the cars rusted.

Given that such practices will increase in the current world recession, it is the Community arena which still offers real opportunities to British businessmen, with comparatively few obstacles in their way (though it has to be admitted that protectionism inside the Community is increasing). The Community is also a stable trading group. Political changes within the individual member states do not disrupt trade. This is not the case elsewhere. In 1979 British exports were badly hit by political upheavals in Iran and changes in import regulations in Nigeria. Our exports to these two countries fell by £1.8 billion that year.

Finally any British failure to export more manufactures to the Community must be put in a wider perspective. Britain's export performance in manufactures deteriorated much more sharply, both to the EEC and to non-Community countries before 1973 than since. Tracing the export–import ratios for manufactures back to 1962, we find that Britain's exports in this field fell by 75 per cent between 1962 and 1973. The ratio to non-

Community countries fell by 120 per cent. Since 1973 the British export–import ratio on manufactures with Japan fell from 48 per cent in 1973 to 28 per cent in 1980 and with North America from 96 to 66 per cent. Comparable figures with the Community were 87 to 86 per cent.

The overall figures suggest that not only was Britain losing her competitive position more rapidly in the decade before 1973 than in the ten years since but that exports of manufactured goods to the rest of the Community in recent years have maintained their position against imports much better than export of manufactures to non-Community countries.

Political Considerations

Our partners in the Community have been fond of reminding the British of the political benefits of membership. They complain that the British insistence on a broad balance between budget payments and receipts is short-sighted, given the high principles which motivated the founders of the original Community. They also argue that there cannot be much wrong with a club that has so many new applicants like Spain and Portugal so keen on the idea of joining.

However, it has been argued that there are political disadvantages arising from membership. When Britain joined the EEC it had to legislate to give the force of law to those existing Community provisions intended to take direct internal effect within the member states, for example over customs duties, agriculture and the free movement of labour, capital and services. Britain also had to commit herself for the future by promising to accept future Community legislation. This was a striking constitutional innovation because it meant giving Community law precedence over national law. Well-known critics of entry like Tony Benn and Enoch Powell have stressed that this has meant a serious loss of national sovereignty.

Nevertheless, it may well be that the political advantages of membership outweigh the disadvantages. It is too easy to forget that the result of the gradual movement towards European unity since 1945 has been to make war between western European states almost impossible. By binding together the nations of western Europe in a peaceful partnership, the founding fathers of the Community made an important contribution to European and world stability. Membership of such a Community enhances our effective sovereignty by giving Britain a measure of real bargaining strength. In a dangerous world it is crucial that the nations of Europe unite in defence of their common interests and heritage. Britain is far more likely to be able to defend her interests at home and to exert influence abroad as a member of an expanding Community than she would be on her own. As William Whitelaw told the House of Commons in 1975: 'Whether we are members of the Community or not, our present partners will take decisions which are bound to affect us. If we are in the Community, we shall be able to influence these decisions. If we are outside on our own, naturally we shall have no say in them. Therefore I believe that we should actually have less power over our own affairs by attempting to remain on our own in the modern world.'

It is important here to distinguish between the substance and the symbols of sovereignty. A Britain which withdrew from the Community would certainly have the symbols of sovereignty but in practice very little freedom of action because so many vital issues are governed by external factors such as international economic trends and by the policies of other nations or blocs. To gain the substance of sovereignty, the United Kingdom needs to pool her resources with those of other member states of the Community in order to secure a more effective common sovereignty.

With the evolution of Political Co-operation (see chapter 2) the Community is slowly emerging as an organisation of considerable weight and on many issues has been taken seriously by the outside world. For example in the General Agreement on Tariffs and Trade, between 1973 and 1979, in the United Nations and the European Conference at Helsinki and Belgrade and in negotiations over fish with the Russians the Community has shown itself able to act vigorously in defence of its collective interests. The Lomé Conventions that the Community negotiated with the ACP countries (see chapter 13) represented a major gain for British interests as tariff preferences and aid were extended to all the Commonwealth countries of Africa, the Caribbean and the Pacific. These advantages would not have been obtainable for most of the Commonwealth without British membership. Since these countries tend to import more from Britain than do other developing countries, British trade benefits.

Community political involvement with the rest of the world still requires further expansion and moving in a convoy of ten (perhaps soon to rise to twelve) is clearly a more cumbersome business than moving alone. But from inside, a country can influence the direction of the whole fleet (if necessary by exercise of its veto). Many issues vital to British interests are now exercising the minds of Community officials from fishing rights to Japanese imports; Britain must be there to defend those interests.

The Future

There are no easy options for the United Kingdom in the 1980s; the roots of poor industrial performance go back a century. The slow growth of productivity compared to Britain's European partners has been caused by many factors but particularly perhaps by failures in the fields of technical innovation, education and training, labour relations and industry's relations with banking and government. As industrial change becomes ever more rapid, Britain is in danger of being left behind in the new technologies.

Mere membership of the Community in itself cannot transform this situation. As Mrs Thatcher has said, 'Europe provides us with opportunities, but only we can take them.'

In the future Britain must push for changes in Community structures which are incomplete and not in accordance with British needs. William Wallace is right to comment that a Community which revolves round a customs union and an agricultural policy is, after all, a peculiarly unbalanced enterprise. Community industrial policy needs to be vigorously developed. A National Institute of Economic and Social Research Conference in 1979 pointed to four developments here that could assist the British economy. One was the completion of the common market; the Community has insisted on free trade in manufactures but allowed barriers to invisible trade to continue. Britain with a highly competitive financial sector would gain from freer access to financial and insurance markets in other countries. It has competitive enterprises too in transport which would benefit from full implementing of the principles of Articles 74–84 of the Rome Treaty. A second line of development is to extend Community help to industrial sectors under pressure more than has occurred so far. Thirdly the operations of the European Investment Bank in providing cheap finance to help enterprises to modernise could be expanded. A fourth strategy would be to develop regional policy and press for substantial transfers to the poorer regions of the Community.

These developments would be expensive to finance and require a much larger Community budget. In fact the MacDougall Report to the Commission in 1977 suggested that a budget of twice the current size was needed, especially with the impending access of new Mediterranean members. Britain might gain from such a development if Community funds could help the necessary restructuring of the whole economy. But if Britain is to win such support, she will have to show more enthusiasm for a maximalist strategy, i.e. a more integrated Community. She would need to join the European Monetary System; press for a more powerful European Parliament and for majority voting in the Council of Ministers; urge changes in CAP that would benefit poor farmers in Southern Europe as well as British consumers, and accept the need for a Community energy policy which embraced North Sea Oil.

A bold course like this might succeed in reviving both British prestige and the British economy but it has risks and difficulties, not the least of which would be the winning of domestic support for such a strategy. In particular more British businesses would have to be won over to developing their European operations. As stressed in chapter 14, some companies have taken Europe seriously but others have simply paid lip service to the concept of a home market of 270 million people. The Community is after all the largest trading bloc in the world and industry needs to inject the necessary level of effort. The European Commission which normally tries to put the best interpretation on evidence has felt constrained to observe a need for more confidence, more aggressive marketing and a greater knowledge of European languages and Community law on the part of British business.

It has been argued that if Britain cannot go forward in the Community, then perhaps she would be better off outside instead of plodding on in the worst of all worlds. However, it is instructive to bear in mind the experience of the country which rejected membership of the Community. A senior Norwegian representative addressing a meeting of the European Parliament's Committee for External Economic Relations in 1981 observed that his country was suffering from an increasing stagnation in all sectors of its economy except oil and in consequence was suffering from high levels of unemployment. Moreover, it was extremely concerned at its exclusion from Community economic and political decision-making and anxious to establish ever closer relationships with Community institutions. It seems hard to believe that non-membership of the Community is a viable option for Britain.

A case for British withdrawal from the Community will no doubt continue to be made but it seems unlikely whether such a move would lead to a better economic future. The result might well be a siege economy with reduced foreign trade, high tariffs and poorer living standards.

Why might this well be the case? Firstly Britain would lose the gains from the increased volume of trade with the Community. This development has benefited not only manufacturers and traders but consumers who have enjoyed the cheaper imports which result from freer trade. In 1979 the British Treasury tried to estimate the overall 'welfare gain' from freer trade with the Community in a paper called 'The Economic Significance of UK Membership of the Community'. It suggested that freer trade with the Community made Britain about £120 million a year richer as a result of tariff cuts made since 1973. If Britain left the Community, the welfare loss from less free trade would probably be much higher than the £120 million figure because in the present climate Britain would face considerable protectionism from her current partners. British industry which has now become heavily dependent on the Community market would suffer severely. Nor would alternative new markets be easily found; if they existed, British industry would be selling hard to them already.

Secondly much direct investment by Japanese and American firms in the United Kingdom would be affected by Britain leaving the Community. Such investment is not entirely an unmixed blessing but it does give a country more factories, more high technology and more employment. For example in 1982 the American computer giant IBM employed 100,000 Europeans including 15,000 in the United Kingdom. With factories at Greenock and Havant and a development laboratory at Winchester, IBM (UK) exported £420 million worth of goods from, and invested £118 million in, the United Kingdom in 1981. Its plan to expand its Greenock plant, for the manufacture of its best selling personal computer, was one of the few pieces of good news for the Scottish economy in 1982.

There is an argument that high technology businesses create relatively few jobs but it is a specious one to use against foreign investment because is overlooks the spin-off employment among local contractors, shops and services and it ignores the reality that other industries in Britain which employ relatively more people need to adopt more high technology if they are to survive.

The American and Japanese multi-nationals plan their manufacturing in a European context, no matter how important the British market for their products might be. If Britain left the Community, the products of such firms could well face Community tariffs or quotas. Their reaction could often be to slim down or eliminate the plant in Britain. Typical of what many managers of foreign firms in Britain believe is the comment of Peter Polgar of General Instrument Microelectronics, based at Glenrothes in Scotland: 'We are just finishing a part of a new building to the tune of several million dollars. I doubt there would be another penny put into that place if you got out of the Common Market.'

Such a development would be serious for the British economy because one clear benefit of British membership of the Community has been the encouragement of more direct investment from abroad. Although total American investment in Europe has dropped since the prosperous 1960s the proportion of it going to Britain has sharply increased. In 1980 58.8 per cent of all direct American investment into the EEC went to Britain. This has particularly aided the depressed areas; in Scotland 70,000 jobs depend on American firms and in Northern Ireland a quarter of all manufacturing jobs are in American companies. Japanese investment in Britain has also accelerated since 1973. The Japanese understand English and see Britain as a good base for their export drives in Europe. Since 1969 Britain has therefore attracted almost 50 per cent of Japanese investment in Europe. Finally, membership has encouraged more investment in Britain by European firms. Between 1973 and 1979 there was 75 per cent more investment by EEC companies in Britain than by British companies in the EEC.

   The process of leaving the Community would create enormous political and economic problems for Britain besides which the existing difficulties of membership would pale into insignificance. As Stanley Henig asserts: 'Year by year, Britain, like other countries of Western Europe, is becoming ever more integrated with her neighbours. Finance, trade, tourism, movements of capital and persons are all factors binding us ever more closely with the rest of Western Europe. If we wish to control all these factors which affect our lives we need some shared machinery with our neighbours. We need also some means by which as a small country, not very powerful economically or politically, we can express our interests in the world. In or out of the Community, our lives will be affected by the impersonal economic factors mentioned above, by the decisions taken by that Community and by the pressures of the international polity. There is no viable option called "leaving the Community". Whatever the problems may be, Britain is now an integral part of that Community.' Only time will tell whether such a positive opinion is correct!

Conclusion: The Community's Difficult Future

In March 1982 the twenty-fifth anniversary of the signing of the Rome Treaties was celebrated in a most muted manner. Prolonged crises over budgetary disputes and a prolonged period of stagnation precluded any possibility of a joyous occasion. Public opinion in the member states added to the air of general gloom over the state of the Community in the next few months. The people of Greenland had voted to leave the Community and the Greek government was demanding a renegotiation of its terms of entry. British opinion over Community membership was still clearly ambivalent; whatever swing in opinion towards support of membership took place as a result of the Falklands Crisis was quickly dissipated by the decision in May to force through farm price increases against Britain's wishes, a decision which was ammunition for the anti-Marketeers in the Labour Party. Already in the previous February the Labour leader Michael Foot had committed the party to taking Britain out of the Community if Labour won the next general election. Labour attitudes disappointed other European socialists. One Dutch socialist Johan van Minnen said: 'It would be desertion. What has happened to socialist solidarity? We want a Labour government in Britain to help us change things here.' Worst of all, the strongest Community nation, West Germany, had become less enthusiastic about the European idea; a poll in April 1981 found that only 35 per cent of West Germans were 'very favourably disposed' towards the EEC. The West German government was patently jaundiced by Community matters; it was angry that West Germany was the Community's chief paymaster yet it had backed away from its demands for a reform of the CAP and had opposed plans to improve the EMS.

Such disillusion at both public and government levels was hardly surprising. Only in one area—the development of a common foreign policy—had much tangible progress been made while the great achievement of the 1960s, the CAP, had become a major burden. Faced with such a catalogue of gloom, the arguments of opponents of the European experiment have become more persuasive. Yet in at least three ways the Community matters—its disintegration could: (a) cut living standards throughout Western Europe; (b) weaken the Western alliance; and (c) undermine the new Mediterranean democracies. As regards living standards the Community has succeeded in removing tariffs between its members and this has contributed to a vast increase in trade between its members. According to *The Economist*, between 1958 and 1980 exports among the nine EEC countries rose by 3,000 per cent in dollar terms when their exports to the rest of the world rose only 1,300 per cent. Britain shared in this expansion; since joining the EEC, its exports to the Community have risen by 560 per cent (in dollars) while its exports to the rest of the world have risen by only 290 per cent. By 1982 two-fifths of British exports went to the EEC and 2.5 million British jobs depended on access to the Community market. Few tariff barriers now remain in place and the Community's rules on free trade have at least checked the slide towards protectionism during the worst recession for 50 years.

A second risk is that the disintegration of the Community would weaken the Atlantic Alliance. NATO is more popular than the EEC but in recent years the unpopularity of nuclear missiles has led to agitation in favour of more neutral attitudes in countries like The Netherlands and Denmark. If the Community then fell apart, member states might well return to more insular and nationalist foreign policies and NATO would lose its cohesion. The Community is an essential instrument for maintaining more European attitudes. As *The Economist* has put it: 'Nationalism has already been responsible for two world wars in Europe this century. The EEC was created to stop this sort of history repeating itself; it is a forum for fighting things out with reasoning words rather than killing arms. It is wrong to despise it because it is a place for arguing in: that is what it is for.'

The third evil consequence of a disintegration of the Community would be a decline in the progress of the Mediterranean states towards democracy. A major attraction of Community membership for Greece, Spain and Portugal has been that it would help to stabilise democracy. Not only would Community institutions extend help to these countries while they remain democracies; Community membership in theory and perhaps in practice should make it harder for military coups to occur in these countries again. Since the Community is a club of democracies, the advent of military dictatorship in one of these countries would lead to that country's expulsion.

However, if the Community is to gain new momentum in the 1980s, progress requires to be made in five crucial areas: (a) the solving of budgetary arguments; (b) the creation of stronger institutions; (c) a Community with a more human face; (d) more political co-operation; (e) closer economic integration.

The rows over Community budgets in recent years have been exacerbated by the need for all member governments to cut spending. There is, however, a deeper issue at stake. The 1957 Community was based on a simple bargain; West Germany would profit from industrial free trade while in return the CAP would enrich French farmers. When Britain joined in 1973, it was assumed that the British would derive considerable industrial benefit but the advent of recession prevented this. In the meantime, the cost of the CAP rose remorselessly.

The urgent need for a thoroughgoing reform of the budget has continued to be postponed, partly because the extent of the problem was masked by movements in world food prices in 1981–82. As a result of poor world cereal harvests, world cereal prices rose sharply, cutting considerably the cost of the Community's food export subsidies. As a result the EEC's farm spending rose by only 2.6 per cent in 1981, reduced Britain's net contribution to zero and helped Community revenue to equal expenditure. However, such a situation is unlikely to last long and when world prices fall, the EEC's farm spending will increase sharply as will Britain's net contributions to the Community budget.

There appear to be two main solutions to the budget problem. A system could be introduced similar to West Germany's own federal revenue sharing scheme which transfers cash from rich states to poor ones. Yet there should be limits to the size of profits or losses that any one country could make. This would create a fairer burden for West Germany and ensure that rich countries like France, Denmark and the Benelux countries make a net contribution to the Community budget which at present they do not. This reform would need to be accompanied by changes in the CAP either by income subsidies instead of by high fixed prices or by considerably more limited price support. The virtue of this approach would be that it would win the support of West Germany and Britain, would not be inflationary and would reduce butter mountains and wine lakes. On the other hand, there seems to be little prospect that it would be politically acceptable to France, Denmark or the Benelux countries.

The second alternative as suggested earlier when considering Britain's place in the Community is that the Community budget should be increased by the amount proposed by the MacDougall Report. This solution would provide extra resources for the Regional and Social Funds from which the poorer countries, Britain included, would benefit while allowing considerable sums to be expended on the CAP. Again the prospects of such a solution being politically acceptable appear remote. Most member states are trying to control public spending as a means of fighting inflation and it is doubtful whether any member state would wish to agree to an increase in the Community's own resources on political grounds.

If budgetary reform appears to be hedged about with difficulties, then so does the field of institutional reform. The supranational ideas of Monnet and Schuman were acceptable in the years after 1945 when national sentiment was at its weakest among most Europeans. Today all governments of the member states seem determined to preserve a narrow autonomy. As a result few see the Commission as an embryo European government and it is all too easy to pour scorn on the European Parliament as a talking shop. Fewer than 1 per cent of European electors have the slightest idea of what business is conducted there and its power is still patently limited. Nevertheless the influence of the Parliament is increasing, albeit slowly, and it may be that it is this institution that will see most development in the future. In the Council of Ministers the future of decision-making has become unclear at the time of writing owing to the way in which farm price increases were forced through in May 1982 (see chapter 3). But if, as seems likely, the principle of unanimity is again generally followed, then an increase in the powers of the Parliament may be deemed essential as a means of forcing decisions through. As the President of the Parliament Piet Dankert has claimed: 'The Commission is in decline, the governments are blocked; the Parliament is the only European body that can prevent the whole system breaking down.' Such developments will, however, surely take time.

It could be argued that the need to create a Community with a more human face is really the most basic and urgent task facing Europe in the late 1980s. Unemployment in the Ten was well over ten million by 1982. Particularly insidious in this figure was the high percentage of young unemployed. In Britain, for example, in 1982 over 900,000 out of six million young people between the ages of 18 and 25 were registered as unemployed and 250,000 had not been able to find work for a year or more. Unless the Community can be seen to be acting more positively in its attempts to alleviate this evil, then faith in the European idea will surely founder. Major instruments for an assault on unemployment are to hand in the Regional and Social Funds which have hitherto been starved of resources when they could contribute more in many important areas like housing, education and training. However, a more co-ordinated Community response is generally needed through the funding of imaginative projects in the fields of energy, high technology and transport.

Fortunately the prospects for political co-operation and more economic integration appear more promising. There have been useful advances in political co-operation with the Ten's foreign offices developing an efficient network for exchanging telegrams daily on foreign policy issues and with the regular meetings of Community ministers and officials. The improvement of the mechanism has led to some extra cohesion in policy though there is still room for improvement through the creation of a really permanent foreign policy secretariat. On major policies the Community countries have increasingly found their self-interest coinciding—over Afghanistan, the Middle East, Poland and the dangerous disagreements with the United States.

One future area of development might be the formation of a common defence policy along the lines suggested by West Germany's foreign minister, Hans-Dietrich Genscher. There are some arguments in favour of this. It might head off the tendency towards neutralism in the smaller countries and would provide a forum in which France, which has been outside NATO's command structure since the 1960s, could take part. It might even help to rationalise Western Europe's overlapping arms industries. However, the formation of a common defence policy would also face enormous problems. For example Ireland is a member of the Community but is not in the Western Alliance. Moves towards a European defence community might antagonise the United States and reduce its commitment to Europe to a point where it would pull its 300,000 troops out of Europe. Finally, as with all major Community policies, the old problem of persuading the ten member states to take a common view on defence would be a difficult one. The difficulty was symbolised by the attempts of Greece to veto the Community's idea of a Sinai peacekeeping force.

The final area of reform, closer economic integration, is perhaps the most promising—and urgent. The Community is still a long way from achieving the common market which it claims to be. As *The Economist* phrased it in November 1982, the common market is becoming less common by the day. Increasingly member states have been creating new protectionist barriers against imports from each other. Instead of reimposing tariffs, they have introduced a variety of administrative and non-tariff barriers to block imports. A good example of this is the survival of costly and time-consuming frontier formalities. Dutch lorry drivers claim that they have to get 300 rubber stamps on their documents to drive their lorryloads of Gouda cheese into France. Such red tape can add up to 10 per cent to the cost of the goods being transported. National regulations on health and safety standards have been forged into weapons of indirect protectionism. The Community competition rules have been broken in a number of ways in recent years, especially the rules on state subsidies for industry and on open tender for public contracts. By 1982 the Commission was taking action against member states for a total of 140 confirmed infringements of the rules on the free circulation of goods with the chief culprits being France (40 cases) and Italy (28 cases). Here at least the British came out well with only 9 cases!

The best way of creating a genuine common market is to forge ahead with harmonisation of health and safety rules so that prices can be cut and jobs created by the extra trade. A new drive also needs to be made against red tape and for the promotion of competition in services in the EEC in areas like banking, insurance and airlines. Freer competition is needed in many other industries. The head of Siemens' microchips division told a correspondent of *The Economist* in 1981: 'If only the EEC would stop trying to spend a few pfennigs here and there on industry and give us a real break by creating really free competition for European telecommunications contracts. Then with a huge home market, we might be able to take on the Japanese and Americans and beat them.' Free competition in telecommunications and other industries would allow the most efficient companies to enjoy economies of scale and would result in lower prices for consumers.

Such then are the chief challenges for the Community in the last two decades of the twentieth century. The difficulties are patently immense and the political leaders will need much vision and practical realism to resolve them. However, it would be fitting to end this book with the words of the greatest of the founding fathers, Jean Monnet: 'The building of Europe is a great transformation which will take a very long time. Nothing would be more dangerous than to regard difficulties as failures.'

Further Reading

Commission of the European Communities, *Britain in the Community 1973–83: The Impact of Membership*, HMSO, 1982.

Holland, S., *Uncommon Market*, Macmillan, London, 1980.

Prest, A. R. and Coppock, D. J., *The UK Economy*. 9th Edition, Weidenfeld and Nicolson, London, 1982.

Twitchett, C. and K., (eds.), *Building Europe: Britain's Partners in the EEC*, Europa Publications, 1981.

Wallace, W., (ed.) *Britain in Europe*, Heinemann, London, 1980.

Articles

Economist, 25th December, 1982.

Europe 82 (No. 12), 'Ten Years in Europe', December 1982.

Lloyds Bank Economic Review, 'The Gains of EEC Membership', January 1983.

Questions

(1) Why has Britain tended to be a net contributor to the Community budget?

(2) Has Community membership benefited Britain's overall trading position?

(3) What are the political implications of Community membership for Britain?

(4) What are the chief problems which the Community is required to tackle in the 1980s?

(5) Do we really need a European Community?

Appendix 1
A Note on European Units of Account

The idea of an accounting currency goes back 1,500 years to the Egyptians. Therefore there was nothing original about the EEC action in instituting its own unit of account. The first unit of account (UA) was equal in value to the American dollar before it was devalued in 1971 and was worth 0.888 grams of gold. It was an integral part of the operation of some Community business especially the Common Agricultural Policy (CAP).

In 1975 the Community's Monetary Committee recommended that a unit of account based on a basket of Community currencies would best suit some operations, for example the European Development Fund. It was called the European Unit of Account (EUA) and from 1978 it was employed in connection with the Community budget. A crucial question was what weight would be attached to each of the Community currencies in the basket. Three criteria were employed—a country's size, its share of total Community GNP and its share of total trade. This gave the following percentage weighting:

German mark	27.3	Dutch florin	9.0
French franc	19.5	Belgian and Luxembourg franc	8.2
Pound sterling	17.5	Danish krone	3.0
Italian lira	14.0	Irish pound	1.5

The European Currency Unit (ECU) was the third unit of account introduced by the Community. It came fully into operation in 1981 and was identical in value to the EUA (see chapter 10). In 1982 the ECU was worth 56 pence (sterling).

Appendix 2
Directorates-General

The departmental structure of the Commission is based on directorates-general which look after a particular service policy. There are 19 of these in all and they are usually identified by number, with people speaking of 'DGI', 'DGIV', and so on. The directorates-general have the following responsibilities:

    I—External Relations
   II—Economics and Financial Affairs
  III—International Market and Industrial Affairs
  IV—Competition
   V—Employment and Social Affairs
  VI—Agriculture
 VII—Transport
VIII—Development
  IX—Personnel and Administration
   X—Spokesman's Group and Information
 – —There is no DGXI
 XII—Research Science and Education
XIII—Scientific and Technical Information
XIV—Fisheries
 XV—Financial Institutions and Taxation
XVI—Regional Policy
XVII—Energy
XVIII—Credit and Investments
 XIX—Budget
 XX—Financial Control

Index